P9-DJL-014

THE BLIND SIDE

ALSO BY

MICHAEL LEWIS

Liar's Poker
The Money Culture
Pacific Rift
Losers
The New New Thing
Next
Moneyball
Coach

THE BLIND SIDE

Evolution of a Game

—

MICHAEL LEWIS

W. W. NORTON & COMPANY

New York London

Copyright © 2006 by Michael Lewis

All rights reserved
Printed in the United States of America
First Edition

For information about permission to reproduce selections from this book,
write to Permissions, W. W. Norton & Company, Inc.,
500 Fifth Avenue, New York, NY 10110

Manufacturing by R. R. Donnelley, Harrisonburg
Book design by Barbara Bachman
Production manager: Amanda Morrison

Library of Congress Cataloging-in-Publication Data

Lewis, Michael (Michael M.)
The blind side : evolution of a game / Michael Lewis. — 1st ed.
p. cm.
ISBN-13: 978-0-393-06123-9 (hardcover)
ISBN-10: 0-393-06123-X (hardcover)
1. Oher, Michael. 2. Football players—United States—Biography.
3. University of Mississippi—Football. 4. College sports—United States.
I. Title.
GV939.O44L49 2006
796.332092—dc22
[B]
2006023509

W. W. Norton & Company, Inc.
500 Fifth Avenue, New York, N.Y. 10110
www.wwnorton.com

W. W. Norton & Company Ltd.
Castle House, 75/76 Wells Street, London W1T 3QT

1 2 3 4 5 6 7 8 9 0

For Starling Lawrence

Underpaid guardian of the author's blind side.

CONTENTS

—

THE BLIND SIDE

BACK STORY

FROM THE SNAP OF THE BALL TO THE SNAP OF THE FIRST BONE IS closer to four seconds than to five. One Mississippi: The quarterback of the Washington Redskins, Joe Theismann, turns and hands the ball to running back John Riggins. He watches Riggins run two steps forward, turn, and flip the ball back to him. It's what most people know as a "flea-flicker," but the Redskins call it a "throw back special." Two Mississippi: Theismann searches for a receiver but instead sees Harry Carson coming straight at him. It's a running down—the start of the second quarter, first and 10 at mid-field, with the score tied 7–7—and the New York Giants' linebacker has been so completely suckered by the fake that he's deep in the Redskins' backfield. Carson thinks he's come to tackle Riggins but Riggins is long gone, so Carson just keeps running, toward Theismann. Three Mississippi: Carson now sees that Theismann has the ball. Theismann notices Carson coming straight at him, and so he has time to avoid him. He steps up and to the side and Carson flies right on by and out of the play. The play is now 3.5 seconds old. Until this moment it has been defined by what the quarterback can see. Now it—and he—is at the mercy of what he can't see.

You don't think of fear as a factor in professional football. You assume that the sort of people who make it to the NFL are immune to the emotion.

Perhaps they don't mind being hit, or maybe they just don't get scared; but the idea of pro football players sweating and shaking and staring at the ceiling at night worrying about the next day's violence seems preposterous. The head coach of the Giants, Bill Parcells, didn't think it preposterous, however. Parcells, whose passion is the football defense, believed that fear played a big role in the game. So did his players. They'd witnessed up close the response of opposing players to their own Lawrence Taylor.

The tackle who had just quit the Philadelphia Eagles, for instance. Jerry Sisemore had played tackle in the NFL for eight years when, in 1981, Taylor arrived. Sisemore played on the right side of the offensive line and Taylor usually came off the other end, but Sisemore still had to worry about the few times Taylor lined up across from him. Their teams were in the same NFL division and met twice each regular season. The week leading up to those games, Sisemore confessed, unnerved him. "Towards the middle of the week something would come over you and you'd just start sweating," he told the *New York Times*. "My last year in the league, opening day, he immediately got past me. . . . He just looked at me and laughed. Right there I thought I had to get out of this game." And after that season, 1984, he did.

The feelings of those assigned to prevent Taylor from hurting quarterbacks were trivial compared to those of the quarterbacks he wanted to hurt. In Taylor's first season in the NFL, no official records were kept of quarterback sacks. In 1982, after Taylor had transformed the quarterback sack into the turning point of a football game, a new official NFL statistic was born. The record books defined the sack as tackling the quarterback behind the line of scrimmage as he attempts to pass. Taylor offered his own definition: "A sack is when you run up behind somebody who's not watching, he doesn't see you, and you really put your helmet into him. The ball goes fluttering everywhere and the coach comes out and asks the quarterback, 'Are you all right?' That's a sack." After his first NFL season Taylor became the only rookie ever named the league's most valuable defensive player, and he published a treatise on his art. "I don't like to just wrap the quarterback," he explained. "I really try to make him see seven fingers when they hold up three. I'll drive my helmet into him, or, if I can, I'll bring my arm up over my head and try to axe the sonuvabitch in two. So long as the guy is holding the ball, I intend to hurt him. . . . If I hit the guy right, I'll hit a nerve and he'll feel electrocuted, he'll forget for a few seconds that he's on a football field."

The game of football evolved and here was one cause of its evolution, a new kind of athlete doing a new kind of thing. All by himself, Lawrence Taylor altered the environment and forced opposing coaches and players to adapt. After Taylor joined the team, the Giants went from the second worst defense in the NFL to the third best. The year before his debut they gave up 425 points; his first year they gave up 257 points. They had been one of the weakest teams in the NFL and were now, overnight, a contender. Of course, Taylor wasn't the only change in the New York Giants between 1980 and 1981. There was one other important newcomer, Bill Parcells, hired first to coach the Giants' defense and then the entire team. Parcells became a connoisseur of the central nervous system of opposing quarterbacks. The symptoms induced by his sack-happy linebacker included, but were not restricted to: "intimidation, lack of confidence, quick throws, nervous feet, concentration lapses, wanting to know where Lawrence is all the time." The players on the Giants' defense picked up the same signals. As defensive back Beasley Reece told the *New York Times*, "I've seen quarterbacks look at Lawrence and forget the snap count." One opposing quarterback, finding himself under the center before the snap and unable to locate Taylor, called a time-out rather than run the play—only to find Taylor standing on the sidelines. "I think I saw it more with the quarterbacks in our division," says Giants linebacker Harry Carson. "They knew enough to be afraid. But every quarterback had a certain amount of fear when he played us."

By his fourth pro season Taylor was not just feeding these fears but feeding off them. "They come to the line of scrimmage and the first thing they do is start looking for me," he said. "I know, and they know. When they'd find me they'd start screaming: *56 left! 56 left!* [Taylor wore No. 56.] So there's this thing I did. After the play was over I'd come up behind them and whisper: *don't worry where I am. I'll tell you when I get there.*"

A new force in pro football, Taylor demanded not just a tactical response but an explanation. Many people pointed to his unusual combination of size and speed. As one of the Redskins' linemen put it, "No human being should be six four, two forty-five, and run a four-five forty." Bill Parcells thought Taylor's size and speed were closer to the beginning than to the end of the explanation. New York Giants' scouts were scouring the country for young men six three or taller, 240 pounds or heavier, with speed. They could be found. In that pool of physical specimens what was precious—far more precious than an inch, or ten pounds, or one tenth of a second—was Taylor's peculiar energy and mind: relentless, manic, with grandiose ambitions and private standards of performance. Parcells believed that even in the NFL a lot of players were more concerned with seeming to want to win than with actually winning, and that many of them did not know the difference. What they wanted, deep down, was to keep their jobs, make their money, and go home. Lawrence Taylor wanted to win. He expected more of himself on the field than a coach would dare to ask of any player.

Parcells accumulated lots of anecdotal evidence in support of his view of Taylor's football character. One of his favorites involved these very same Washington Redskins. "Joe Gibbs in a game in Giants Stadium basically decided that Taylor wasn't going to make any plays," said Parcells. "He put two tight ends on Taylor's side—along with the left tackle—and two wide receivers in the slot away from Taylor." This was extreme. An NFL football field is a tightly strung economy. Everything on it comes at a price. Take away from one place and you give to another. Three men blocking Taylor meant two Giants with no one to block them. Taylor's effect on the game, which the Giants won, was not obvious but it was nonetheless great. "But after the game," Parcells continued:

> The press sees that Lawrence doesn't have a sack and hasn't made a tackle and they're all asking me "what's the matter with Taylor?" The next week we go out to San Diego to play the Chargers. Dan Henning is the coach. He sees the strategy. They do the same thing. Two tight ends on Lawrence, two wide receivers in the slot. Lawrence doesn't get a sack. We win again. But after the game everyone is asking me all over again: "what's the matter with Taylor?" I grab Lawrence in the

locker room and say to him, "I'm going to change your first name from Lawrence to What's The Matter With?" At practice that next week he was What's The Matter With? "What you doin' over there What's The Matter With?" "Hey, What's The Matter With?, how come you aren't making plays?" By Thursday it's not funny to him. And I mean it is really *not* funny.

The next game we have is against the Vikings on Monday Night Football. Tommy Kramer is the quarterback. They don't employ the strategy. He knocks Kramer out of the game, causes two fumbles and recovers one of them. I'm leaving the field, walking down the tunnel towards the locker room for the press conference. And out of nowhere this . . . *thing* comes and jumps on my back. I didn't know he was coming. He basically knocks me over. He's still got his helmet on. Sweat's still pouring down his face. He comes right up into my face and hollers, "I tell you what Coachy, they aren't going to ask you What's The Matter With?!!"

Parcells believed Taylor's greatness was an act of will, a refusal to allow the world to understand him as anything less than great. "That's why I loved him so much," he said. "He responded to *anything* that threatened his status." When in the middle of his career Taylor became addicted to cocaine, Parcells interpreted the problem as a simple extension of the man's character. Lawrence Taylor trusted in one thing, the power of his own will. He assumed that his will could control NFL football games, and that it could also control his own chemical desires.

He was right about the NFL games. By November 18, 1985, when the Giants went into Robert F. Kennedy Stadium in Washington, DC, to play the Redskins, opposing teams have taken to lining up their players in new and creative ways simply to deal with him. The Redskins are a case in point. Early in the very first game in which his Redskins had faced this new force, back in 1981, Joe Gibbs had watched Taylor sprint past the blocker as if he wasn't there and clobber Joe Theismann from behind. "I was standing there," said Gibbs, "and I said, 'What? Did you see that? Oh Lord.' " Gibbs had flopped about looking for a solution to this new problem, and had come up with the "one back offense"—a formation, widely imitated in the NFL, that uses one running back instead of two. Until that moment, football offenses had typically used running backs to block linebackers who came charging after quarterbacks. But running backs were smaller, weaker, and, surprisingly often, given their job description, slower than Lawrence Taylor. Lynn Cain, a running back for the Atlanta Falcons, was the first to dramatize the problem. The first time Cain went to block Taylor he went in very low, got up underneath him, and sent Taylor flying head over heels. The next play Cain tried it again—and was carried off the field on a stretcher. "People figured out *very* quickly that they couldn't block Lawrence with a running back," Parcells said. "Then the question became: who do you block him with?" Hence Joe Gibbs's first solution: to remove the running back from the game and insert, across the line from Lawrence Taylor, a bigger, stronger tight end. The one back offense.

That will be the strategy tonight, but Joe Theismann knows too well its imperfections. Having that extra blocker to help the tackle addressed the problem, Theismann thought, without solving it. Too often Taylor came free. The week of practice leading up to the game had been a seminar on Lawrence Taylor. "If you looked at our overhead projector or our chalkboard," said Theismann, "all the other Giants players were X's or O's. Lawrence was the only one who had a number: fifty-six. He was a little red fifty-six and the number was always highlighted and circled. The goal was: let's identify where Lawrence is on every play." Taylor moved around a lot, to confuse the defense, but he and his coach were happiest when he came from his own right side and the quarterback's left. "The big reason I put him over there," said Bill Parcells, "is the right side is the quarterback's blind side, since most quarterbacks are right-handed. And no one wants to get his ass knocked off from the back side." Lawrence Taylor was more succinct: "Why the hell would I want to come from where he can see me?" But then he added: "It wasn't really called the blind side when I came into the league. It was called the right side. It *became* the blind side after I started knocking people's heads off."

Where Taylor is at the start of the play, of course, isn't the problem. It's where he ends up. "When I dropped back," says Theismann, "the first thing I still did was to glance over my shoulder to see if he was coming. If he was dropping back in coverage, a sense of calm came over me. If he was coming, I had a sense of urgency."

Four Mississippi: Taylor is coming. From the snap of the ball Theismann has lost sight of him. He doesn't see Taylor carving a wide circle behind his back; he doesn't see Taylor outrun his blocker upfield and then turn back down; and he doesn't see the blocker diving, frantically, at Taylor's ankles. He doesn't see Taylor leap, both arms over his head, and fill the sky behind him. Theismann prides himself on his ability to stand in the pocket and disregard his fear. He thinks this quality is a prerequisite in a successful NFL quarterback. "When a quarterback looks at the rush," he says, "his career is over." Theismann has played in 163 straight games, a record for the Washington Redskins. He's led his team to two Super Bowls, and won one. He's thirty-six years old. He's certain he still has a few good years left in him. He's wrong. He has less than half a second.

The game is on ABC's *Monday Night Football,* and 17.6 million people have tuned in. Frank Gifford is in the booth, flanked by O. J. Simpson and Joe Namath. "Theismann's in a lot of trouble," the audience hears Gifford say, just before Taylor's arms jackknife Theismann's head to his knees and Taylor's torso pins Theismann's right leg to the ground. Four other players, including, oddly, the Redskins' John Riggins, pile on. They're good for dramatic effect but practically irrelevant. The damage is done by Taylor alone. One hundred and ninety-six pounds of quarterback come to rest beneath a thousand or so pounds of other things. Then Lawrence Taylor pops to his feet and begins to scream and wave and clutch his helmet with both hands, as if in agony.

His reaction is a mystery until ABC Sports clarifies the event, by replaying it over and again, in slow motion. "Again, we'll look at it with the reverse angle one more time," says Frank Gifford. "And I suggest if your stomach is weak, you just don't watch." People watched; the replay was almost surely better attended than the original play. Doug Flutie was probably a representative viewer. Flutie had just finished a glorious college quarterbacking career at Boston College and started a professional one in the USFL. On the evening of November 18, 1985, he was at home with his mother. She had the football game on; he had other things to do. "I heard my mother scream," he told a reporter. "And then I saw the replay. It puts fear in your heart and makes you wonder what the heck you're doing playing football."

THERE'S AN INSTANT before it collapses into some generally agreed-upon fact when a football play, like a traffic accident, is all conjecture and fragments and partial views. Everyone wants to know the whole truth but no one possesses it. Not the coach on the sidelines, not the coach in the press box, and certainly not the quarterback—no one can see the whole field and take in the movement of twenty-two bodies, each with his own job assignment. In baseball or basketball all the players see, more or less, the same events. Points of view vary, but slightly. In football many of the players on the field have no idea what happened—much less why it happened—until after the play is done. Even then, most of them will need to watch a videotape to be sure. The fans, naturally more interested in effect than cause, follow the ball, and come away thinking they know perfectly well what just happened. But what happened to the ball, and to the person holding the ball, was just the final link in a chain of events that began well before the ball was snapped. At the beginning of the chain that ended Joe Theismann's career was an obvious question: who was meant to block Lawrence Taylor?

Two players will be treated above all others as the authorities on the play: Joe Theismann and Lawrence Taylor. The victim didn't have a view of the action; the perpetrator was so intent on what he was doing that he didn't stop to look. "The play was a blur," said Taylor. "I had taken the outside. I was thinking: keep him in the pocket and squeeze him. Then I broke free." Why he broke free he couldn't say, as he didn't actually notice who was trying to block him. Theismann, when asked who was blocking Taylor on that play, will reply, "Joe Jacoby, our left tackle." He won't *blame* Jacoby, as the guy was one of the two or three finest left tackles of his era, and was obviously just doing his best. That's why it made no sense, in Joe Theismann's opinion, for an NFL team to blow big bucks on an offensive lineman: there was only so much a lineman could do. Even when his name was Joe Jacoby.

That was one point of view. Another was Jacoby's who, on that night, was standing on the sidelines, in street clothes. He'd strained ligaments in his knee and was forced to sit out. When Joe Jacoby played, he was indeed a splendid left tackle. Six seven and 315 pounds, he was shaped differently from most left tackles of his time, and more like the left tackle of the future. "A freak of nature ahead of his time," his position coach, Joe Bugel, called him, two decades later. Jacoby wasn't some lump of cement; he was an athlete. In high school he'd been a star basketball player. He could run, he could jump, he had big, quick hands. "We put him at left tackle for one reason," said Bugel, "to match up against Lawrence Taylor." The first time they'd met, Jacoby had given Lawrence Taylor fits—he was a 300-pounder before the era of 300-pounders, with hands so big they felt like hooks. Taylor had been forced to create a move just for Jacoby. "Geritol," Taylor called it, "because after the snap I tried to look like an old man running up to him." Unable to overwhelm him physically, Taylor sought to lull Jacoby into a tactical mistake. He'd come off the ball at a trot to lure Jacoby into putting his hands up before he reached him. The moment he did—*Wham!*—he'd try to knock away Jacoby's hands before he latched on. A burst of violence and he was off to the races.

Still, Jacoby was one of the linemen that always gave Taylor trouble, because he was so big and so quick and so long. "The hardest thing for me to deal with," said Taylor, "was that big, agile left tackle."

Offensive linemen were the stay-at-home mothers of the NFL: everyone paid lip service to the importance of their contribution yet hardly anyone could tell you exactly what that was. In 1985 the left tackle had no real distinction. He was still expected to believe himself more or less interchangeable with the other linemen. The Washington Redskins' offensive line was perhaps the most famous in NFL history. It had its own nickname: the Hogs. Fans dressed as pigs in their honor. And yet they weren't understood, even by their own teammates, in the way running backs or quarterbacks were understood, as individual players with particular skills. "Even people who said they were fans of the Hogs had no idea who we were," said Jacoby. "They couldn't even tell the black ones from the white ones. I had people see me and scream, 'Hey May!' " (Right tackle Mark May was black; Jacoby was not.)

That night, with Jacoby out, the Redskins moved Russ Grimm from his position at left guard to left tackle. Grimm was four inches shorter, 30 pounds lighter, and far less agile than Jacoby. "Little Porky Grimm," line coach Joe Bugel called him. As a result, he needed help, and got it, in the form of the extra tight end, a fellow named Don Warren. If Taylor made his move to the inside, Grimm was expected to deal with him; if Taylor went on a wide loop outside, Grimm was meant, at most, to punch him, to slow him down, and give Warren the time to stay with him. From his spot on the sidelines, Jacoby watched as Taylor went outside. Grimm couldn't lay a hand on him and so Warren was left alone with Taylor. "They weren't used to his speed," said Jacoby. He watched Taylor race upfield and leave Warren in the dust, then double back on the quarterback.

Jacoby then heard what sounded like a gunshot—the tibia and fibula in Joe Theismann's right leg snapping beneath Taylor. He watched as Grimm and Warren removed their helmets and walked quickly toward the sidelines, like men fleeing the scene of a crime. He listened as Grimm told him that Theismann's bone lay exposed, and his blood was spurting straight up in the air. "Russ was a hunter," said Jacoby. "He'd gutted deer. And he said, 'That's the most disgusting thing I've ever seen.' " And Jacoby thought: *It happened because I'm standing over here.* Years later he wouldn't be surprised that Theismann did not realize his great left tackle was standing on the sidelines. "But that's why his leg got broken," he said.

A few minutes later, six men bore Theismann on a stretcher to an ambulance. In ABC's booth, Joe Namath said, "I just hope it's not his last play in football." But it was. Nearly a year later Joe Theismann would be wandering around the Redskins locker room unable to feel his big toe, or to push off his right leg. He'd become a statistic: the *American Journal of Sports Medicine* article on the injuries to NFL quarterbacks between 1980 and 2001 would count Theismann's two broken bones as just one of a sample of 1,534—77.4 percent of which occur, just as this one had, during games, on passing plays. The game continued and the Redskins, surprisingly, won, 28–23. And most people who did not earn their living in the NFL trying to figure out how to protect their increasingly expensive quarterbacks shoved the incident to the back of their minds. Not ten minutes after Theismann was hauled off the field, Lawrence Taylor himself pounced on a fumble and ran to the bench, jubilant. Frank Gifford sought to persuade his audience that Taylor was still obviously feeling upset about what he had done to Joe Theismann. But the truth is that he didn't look at all upset. He looked as if he'd already gotten over it.

What didn't make sense on that night was Taylor's initial reaction. He leapt out of the pile like a man on fire. Those who had watched Taylor's career closely might have expected a bit more sangfroid in the presence of an injured quarterback. The destruction of Joe Theismann may have been classified an accident, but it wasn't an aberration. It was an extension of what Lawrence Taylor had been doing to NFL quarterbacks for four and a half years. It wasn't even the first time Taylor had broken a quarterback's leg, or ended a quarterback's career. In college, in the Gator Bowl, he had taken out the University of Michigan's quarterback, John Wangler. Before Taylor hit him, Wangler had been a legitimate NFL prospect. ("I was invited to try out for the Lions and the Cowboys," Wangler said later. "But everyone was kind of afraid of the severity of my injury.")

As it turned out, there was a simple explanation: Taylor was claustrophobic. His claustrophobia revealed itself in the way he played the game: standing up looking for the best view, refusing to bend over and get down in the dirt with the other players, preferring the long and open outside route to the quarterback over the short, tight inside one. It revealed itself, also, in the specific fear of being trapped at the bottom of a pile and not being able to escape. "That's what made me so frantic," he said. "I've already dreamed it— if I get on the bottom of a pile and I'm really hurt. And I can't get out." Now he lay at, or near, the bottom of a pile, on top of a man whose leg he'd broken so violently that the sound was heard by Joe Jacoby on the sidelines. And he just had to get out. He leapt to his feet screaming, hands clutching the sides of his helmet, and—the TV cameras didn't pick this up—lifting one foot unconsciously and rubbing his leg with it. It was the only known instance of Lawrence Taylor imagining himself into the skin of a quarterback he had knocked from a game. "We all have fears," he said. "We all have fears."

CHAPTER TWO

THE MARKET FOR
FOOTBALL PLAYERS

S OMEONE HAD SENT TOM LEMMING A TAPE, BUT THEN TOM
Lemming received thousands of tapes from thousands of football coaches
and parents who wanted their kids to make the various high school All-
American teams he selected. He at least glanced at all of them—usually
quickly. This tape was different; this tape he watched in wonder. He knew
right away that this boy was a special case. He lived and played in Memphis,
Tennessee, and Memphis was always rich in raw high school football talent—
so that wasn't it. "The tape was grainy and you couldn't see very well," said
Lemming. "But when he came off the line, it looked like one whole wall was
moving. And it was just one player! You had to look at it twice to believe it:
he was that big. And yet he would get out and go chase down, and catch,
these fast little linebackers. When I saw the tape I guess I didn't really believe
it. I saw how he moved and I wondered how big he really was—because no
one who is that big should be able to move that fast. It just wasn't possible."

As he drove into Memphis in March of 2004, Lemming thought: everything about Michael Oher, including his surname, was odd. He played for a
small private school, the Briarcrest Christian School, with no history of generating Division I college football talent. The Briarcrest Christian School

team didn't typically have black players, either, and Michael Oher was black. But what made Michael Oher especially peculiar was that no one in Memphis had anything to say about him. Lemming had plenty of experience "discovering" great players. Each year he drove 50,000 to 60,000 miles and met, and grilled, between 1,500 and 2,000 high school juniors. He got inside their heads months before the college recruiters were allowed to shake their hands. It didn't happen as much as it used to, but he still found future NFL stars to whom the recruiters were oblivious. For instance, no one outside of Newport News, Virginia, had ever heard of Michael Vick—future number one pick in the entire NFL draft and quarterback of the Atlanta Falcons—before Lemming stumbled upon him and wrote him up in his newsletter. But even in the case of Michael Vick, the people closest to him knew he had talent. Michael Vick was no secret in Newport News, Virginia. Michael Oher was as good as invisible, even in Memphis, Tennessee. Lemming asked around, and the local high school coaches either didn't know who he was or didn't think he was any good. He hadn't made so much as the third string all-city team. He hadn't had his name or picture in any newspaper. An Internet search for "Oher" yielded nothing on him. The only proof of his existence was this grainy videotape.

From the tape alone, Lemming couldn't say how much Michael Oher had helped his team, just that he was big, fast, and fantastically explosive. "To make my lists they almost always have to have production," said Lemming. By "production" he meant honors and achievements—not mere potential. "He was different from just about every other kid I picked to be a high school All-American in that he didn't have any." But if Michael Oher in the flesh was anything like Michael Oher on the videotape, Lemming was afraid *not* to make an exception of him. He had his reputation to protect. Nothing was as embarrassing to him as leaving a kid off his lists who, four years later, was a first-round NFL draft pick. And the last time he had seen a player with this awesome array of physical gifts was back in 1993, when he went to the Sizzler Steakhouse in Sandusky, Ohio, and interviewed a high school junior working behind the counter named Orlando Pace.

"Michael Oher's athletic ability and his body—the only thing you could compare it to was Orlando Pace," said Lemming. "He kind of even looked like Orlando Pace. He wasn't as polished as Orlando. But Orlando wasn't Orlando in high school." Pace had gone from Lemming's All-American team to Ohio State, where he'd played left tackle and won the Outland Award given to the nation's finest college offensive lineman. In 1997, he'd signed the largest rookie contract in NFL history, to play left tackle for the St. Louis Rams, and he was about to sign an even bigger one (seven years, $52.8 million). Pace became, and would remain, the team's highest paid player—more highly paid than the star quarterback, Mark Bulger, the star running back, Marshall Faulk, and the star wide receiver, Isaac Bruce. He was an offensive lineman but not just any offensive lineman. He protected the quarterback's blind side.

When Tom Lemming walked into the football meeting room at the University of Memphis, looking for Michael Oher, the ghost of Lawrence Taylor was waiting. Taylor's legacy had led to a queasy tilting of the finances on the NFL's line of scrimmage. The players on the blind side of a right-handed quarterback—both offensive and defensive—became, on average, far more highly paid than the players on the visible side. This was strange. There was no financial distinction between left and right guards. Right-side linebackers who (unlike Taylor) routinely played off the line of scrimmage continued to be paid the same, on average, as left-side linebackers.* Right-side cornerbacks, even further from the line of scrimmage, were paid the same as left-

---

* Most NFL teams line up in what is called a 4-3 defense. In the 4-3, the seven defenders closest to the line of scrimmage are arranged like this:

X X X

X' X X X

In this formation the right defensive end, X', becomes the leading blind side pass rusher. Bill Parcells—and a few other NFL coaches—prefer to line up their defense in a 3-4, which looks like this:

X' X X X

X X X

In the 3-4, the outside right-side linebacker (X') plays the role of lead blind side rusher.

side cornerbacks. Only the two players engaged in the battle for control of the turf between the line of scrimmage and the right-handed quarterback's back were paid more than their counterparts on the side that the typical, right-handed quarterback faced. A lot more. By 2004, the five most highly paid NFL left tackles were earning nearly $3 million a year more than the five most highly paid right tackles, and more than the five most highly paid running backs and wide receivers.

The fantastic general rise in overall NFL salaries since 1994, when players were granted the right of free agency, obscured a more striking shift in relative pay. The players all made so much more money each year than they had the year before that few paid much attention to the trends within the trend. But there were several, and this was the most revelatory. In the early 1980s, the notion that a single lineman should be paid much more than any other—and more than star running backs, wide receivers, and, in several cases, quarterbacks—would have been considered heretical had it not been so absurd. The offensive line never abandoned, at least in public, its old, vaguely socialistic ideology. All for one, one for all, as to do our jobs well we must work together, and thus no one of us is especially important. But by the mid-1990s the market disagreed: it had declared this one member of the offensive line a superstar. Not some interchangeable homunculus, not low-skilled labor, but a rare talent. This judgment was not rendered overnight; it was the end of a long story, of football coaches and general managers sifting and judging and scrambling to determine the relative importance of the positions on a football field, and to find the people best suited to play them. And at the beginning of the story was Tom Lemming.

BACK IN 1978, at the age of twenty-three, Lemming had an idea: he'd travel America and meet the top high school football players in the country, and decide which ones were the best. There was no videotape, so he had to visit high schools and ask to see the 16mm film of their players. While there he'd interview the players, get a sense of their characters, and extract from them everything from their college preference to their grade point averages. Then he'd publish a book ranking them. "I had such excitement knowing I was doing something no one else was doing," he said later. "No one had ever gone to see everyone in the country." When he drove away from his home in Chicago he had to wonder who was going to pay for his bizarre enterprise. No one, at first: In the early days he spent every other night sleeping in his car at an Oasis truck stop. ("But then people started shooting people in Oasises, so I had to find different places to park.") The first year his budget allowed him to meet and interview every notable high school football player east of the Mississippi. The next year he crossed the Mississippi and went right to the base of the Rockies. "I would go as far as my cash would take me," he said. "I was sort of like Lewis and Clark, except instead of waiting for resupply I was waiting for enough radio shows to promote my books." In 1983 he crossed the Rockies and never looked back.

It took him seven years to turn a profit, but by then he had a frantic following in college football. What must have seemed at first a mad notion— why would anyone care what some twenty-three-year-old guy with no experience thought about high school football players? Why would any high school football star waste his time answering the questions of a stranger and filling out intrusive forms?—became a thriving business. Bear Bryant, Dan Devine, Bo Schembechler—all these big-time football coaches took an interest in Lemming's work. He was, in effect, the only national football scout in America. Baseball had hundreds of scouts—guys who spent 365 days a year traveling the country to evaluate teenagers. Strictly speaking, of course, a sixteen-year-old football player wasn't a commodity in the way a sixteen-year-old baseball player was. A high school baseball player could be drafted to play in the pros; a high school football player could not. Less strictly speaking, high school football players were far more highly prized, in part because colleges could usurp a great deal of their (skyrocketing) market value. Eight times a year Lemming published a newsletter to which all but seven of the 117 Division I college football programs subscribed. After they'd read it, all these college football coaches would call Lemming for the kids' addresses, phone numbers, and anything else he might know about them. High school football players across the country, with the help of their fathers and their coaches, inundated Lemming's little office in Chicago with tapes of their performances, press clippings, and letters of recommendation. All they wanted was for him to make them famous.

There simply was no one else doing what Lemming was doing. Overnight he became, by default, the leading independent authority on the subject of U.S. high school football players. It was a booming market with an obvious gap: colleges on one side of the country had no information about players on the other. Even in the lawless days of football recruiting—before the NCAA began seriously to crack down, in the late 1980s—recruiters from big-time football schools hunted for talent mostly in their own backyards. Coach Bear Bryant's machine at the University of Alabama spent its time and energies on southern players; Bo Schembechler's machine at the University of Michigan spent its time and energy on players in the Midwest. In the late 1980s, when the NCAA began to pass, and enforce, elaborate rules governing the interaction between college football coaches and high school football players, the hole in the market widened. College football coaches were forbidden to so much as wink at a prospect until he began his senior year. By then Lemming had studied the prospect's play, his character, and his grade point average. Plus he'd have a pretty good idea of where the kid might like to go to college.

The flow of information improved—videotape, cell phones, the Internet all made his life a lot easier—and Lemming's ability to make sense of it improved as well. When he started out, he felt, he had been too impressed by sheer physical talent and insufficiently respectful of actual on-field achievement. He'd thought future great NFL running back Barry Sanders was too small, for instance, even though he'd run for a zillion yards in high school. He still made mistakes, but fewer. By the 1990s he had a vast, informal network of informants whom he trusted—high school coaches and fans, mainly—who allowed him to shrink the pool of 3 million high school football players down to a few thousand. He watched tapes of those players and winnowed the pool to about 1,500, whom he interviewed in person. From those he selected 400 for his annual book of the nation's top prospects, and from the book he culled his list of the Top 100 players in the nation. And finally, he selected his most rarified group, the 25 or so high school players he pronounced "All-Americans." His hit rate was very high. Of the twenty-five players he picked in 1995, for instance, fourteen wound up becoming number one draft choices in the NFL. In the mid-1990s, ESPN began to publish an All-American team, selected by Lemming. *USA Today* published another one, also mainly selected by Lemming. In 2000, the U.S. Army High School All-American football game was born, and broadcast on national television. Lemming selected the eighty players for the game. Reggie Bush, Vince Young, Adrian Petersen, Dwayne Jarrett, Chris Leak, LenDale White, Brady Quinn: the game became a turnstile for future Heisman Trophy candidates and top NFL draft picks.

As the noise grew louder, and the money got bigger, the politics became worse: coaches and players pestered Lemming to be included in his books, and on his lists, and in the Game. At some point he basically ceased to believe what anyone told him about a high school football player. "There's a reason I'm on the road six months a year," he said. "I would never rely on what people tell me. I have to see 'em." By the spring of 2004, he found himself interviewing the sons of players he had interviewed twenty-five years earlier. His business, and his influence, grew, but Lemming kept on doing what he'd always done. He still drove 50,000 to 60,000 miles each year and interviewed, in the flesh, between 1,500 and 2,000 high school football players. He was a one-man sifting machine.

One of the perks of Lemming's role in the market was a worm's-eye view of its trends. When he opened for business, he assumed he was simply identifying future college football stars. He didn't give much thought to their professional futures. College football was mainly a running game, for instance, and the NFL, increasingly, was a passing game. College football had an appetite for all sorts of players the pros had no use for: option quarterbacks, slow fullbacks, midget linebackers. That changed as the big-time football programs came to function as training schools for the NFL. To attract the best high school players they had to persuade them that they offered the smoothest path to the NFL. It helped, then, if they ran NFL-style offenses and defenses. Because of this—and because of the steady flow of NFL coaches into college football—college football became more homogenous, and less distinguishable from the game played in the NFL. In the late 1980s, Lemming began to notice the erosion in the differences between college and pro football. By the mid-1990s he saw that, in identifying the best future college football players, he was identifying the best future professional ones, too.

The other, related trend was a trickle-down of NFL prototypes into America's high schools. The NFL would discover a passion for athletic (read: black) quarterbacks, or speedy pass rushers, and first the colleges and then the high schools would begin to supply them. There was a lag, of course. If Lawrence Taylor created a new vogue in the NFL for exceptionally violent and speedy pass rushers with his dimensions in 1981, it might be 1986 before Lemming encountered a big new wave of similarly shaped violent and speedy high school pass rushers. But the wave always came. What the NFL prized, America's high schools supplied, and America's colleges processed. "It goes from Sunday to Saturday to Friday, five years later," said Lemming. The types came and went—one decade there would be a vogue for speedy little receivers, the next decade the demand would be for tall, lanky receivers. And there were anti-types; Lord help the white running back or wide receiver or, until the early 1990s, the black quarterback. The Lawrence Taylor type, however, came and never left. When Lemming hit the road in 2004, he knew he would find big linebackers, and small defensive ends, whose chief future use would be to wreak havoc with the minds and bodies of quarterbacks. He also knew that he'd find the type that had arisen across the line of scrimmage in response. The guy who could stop the Lawrence Taylor type. The left tackle type.

When Tom Lemming looked at left tackles, he thought in terms of others he had selected for his All-American teams who went on to be stars in the NFL: Jonathan Ogden, Orlando Pace, Walter Jones, Willie Roaf. These people looked nothing like most human beings, or even the players Lemming interviewed in the late 1970s and 1980s. "Two hundred and fifty pounds used to be huge for a high school lineman," he said. "Now you've got to be three hundred pounds or no one will look at you." Even in this land of giants, the left tackle type stood out. *Freak of nature*: when he found one of these rare beasts, that's the phrase that popped into Lemming's mind to describe him. When Lemming put high school junior Jonathan Ogden on the cover of his *Annual Prep Report*, Ogden was six foot nine inches tall and weighed 320 pounds. (He'd fill out in college.) When he did the same with Orlando Pace, Pace stood six six and weighed 310 pounds. (And hadn't stopped growing.) The ideal left tackle was big, but a lot of people were big. What set him apart were his more subtle specifications. He was wide in the ass and massive in the thighs: the girth of his lower body lessened the likelihood that Lawrence Taylor, or his successors, would run right over him. He had long arms: pass rushers tried to get in tight to the blocker's body, then spin off of it, and long arms helped to keep them at bay. He had giant hands, so that when he grabbed ahold of you, it meant something.

But size alone couldn't cope with the threat to the quarterback's blind side, because that threat was also fast. The ideal left tackle also had great feet. Incredibly nimble and quick feet. Quick enough feet, ideally, that the idea of racing him in a five-yard dash made the team's running backs uneasy. He had the body control of a ballerina and the agility of a basketball player. The combination was just incredibly rare. And so, ultimately, very expensive.

The price of protecting quarterbacks was driven by the same forces that drove the price of other kinds of insurance: it rose with the value of the asset insured, with the risk posed to that asset. Quarterbacks had become wildly expensive. Even the rookie quarterback contracts now included huge guarantees. The San Francisco 49ers had agreed to pay Alex Smith $56 million over seven years; and if his career ended tomorrow, they'd still owe him $24 million. The New York Giants were paying their young quarterback, Eli Manning, $54 million for his first seven years of service; if an injury ended his career, they were still on the line for $20 million. The highest paid NFL quarterback, Eli's brother, Peyton Manning of the Indianapolis Colts, had a seven-year contract worth $99.2 million. Several others made nearly $10 million a year. The money wasn't all guaranteed, but a career-ending injury still cost an NFL franchise millions of dollars—if Peyton Manning suffered a career-ending injury, the Colts were out of pocket about half of their entire 2005 payroll. And those lost dollars would be but a fraction of the Colts' misery; there would also be the cost of playing without their star quarterback. When a star running back or wide receiver is injured, the coaches worry about their game plans. When a star quarterback gets hurt, the coaches worry about their jobs.

Their anxiety came to be reflected in the pay of left tackles. By the 2004 NFL season, the *average* NFL left tackle salary was $5.5 million a year, and the left tackle had become the second highest paid position on the field, after the quarterback. In Super Bowl XL, played on February 5, 2006, the highest paid player on the field was Seattle quarterback Matt Hasselbeck—who had just signed a new six-year deal worth $8.2 million a year. The second highest paid player on the field was the man who protected Hasselbeck's blind side, left tackle Walter Jones, who made $7.5 million a year. (The closest Steeler trailed by $1.9 million.)

The other force that drove the price of quarterback insurance was the supply of human beings who could plausibly provide it. There weren't many people on the planet, and only a few in the NFL, with Walter Jones's combination of size, speed, agility, hands, feet, and arms. Jonathan Ogden, Orlando Pace, maybe Chris Samuels of the Redskins. They were the prototypes. And it was these men—Walter Jones, and the few NFL left tackles of his caliber—that Tom Lemming had in mind when he arrived in Memphis in March of 2004 and went looking for Michael Oher.

EVEN MORE THAN USUAL, Lemming needed to see this kid. It just smelled fishy: there was no way an American high school player in 2004 with this kind of talent could be such a mystery. Film occasionally deceived: maybe he wasn't as big as he looked. Maybe there was something seriously defective about his character. Football was a team game; there was a limit to the pathological behavior it would tolerate, especially in a high school player. "Baseball can tolerate a Barry Bonds," said Lemming. "In football you never do anything alone. Even though you're Joe Montana you still need Jerry Rice, and the nine other guys on offense, if you're going to be any good. That's why [NFL receiver] Terrell Owens got himself in so much trouble. He thought he was bigger than the game. And no one player is bigger than the game."

Lemming had seen hundreds of NFL-caliber players with social problems come to inglorious ends. In 1995, Lemming picked as a first team high school All-American a sensational defensive end from Louisiana named Eric Jefferson. Jefferson signed to play football for the University of Illinois, and Lemming and a lot of other people couldn't see him as anything but a future NFL star. Before he played a down of college ball he pled guilty to armed robbery and is now serving a five-year sentence in California state prison. In 1996, a Chicago kid named Michael Burden had been easily the nation's most promising defensive back ("a future NFL star without a doubt") when he was charged with rape. Ohio State still took him, and he even played a year—then got into trouble at school and vanished without a trace. In 1997, a defensive lineman named Boo Boo Williams had been the most likely future NFL player in the nation. "He was the next Reggie White," said Lemming, referring to the Hall of Fame pass rusher for the Green Bay Packers. As a junior in high school, Boo Boo was six five, 265 pounds, ran a 4.7 40, and bench-pressed 375 pounds, despite never lifting weights. He'd not merely won the heavyweight state wrestling champion; he had picked up the runner-up, a 220-pound star running back, and lifted him straight over his head, then tossed him to the ground. Boo Boo Williams was the most promising player in a graduating class that included all kinds of future NFL stars. But Boo Boo's grades were so bad that he was required to sit out of college ball not just one but two years. And then Boo Boo, too, vanished: poof.

And so it went in football. The game attracted the very people most likely to get in trouble outside the game: aggressive people. Lemming was wary of kids with bad grades, criminal records, or anything else that suggested they'd never get to college, much less through it. To play in the NFL for money it was practically necessary to play three years in college for free. It was true, as Lemming put it, that "there are some colleges that would take Charles Manson if he could run a four-four forty and get his work release."

Their existence didn't prevent the premature end of a shocking number of potentially lucrative careers.

After he'd seen Michael Oher's tape, Lemming tried to reach the kid by phone. He found out that his surname was pronounced "Oar," but that's about all he learned. He was accustomed to the social lives of high school football stars: the handlers, the harems, the informal advisers, the coaches. The kids Lemming sought to meet were not, typically, hard to find. This kid not only had no handlers, he didn't appear to exist outside of school. He had no home; he didn't even have a *phone number.* Or so said the Briarcrest Christian School when Lemming called looking for Michael Oher. They had been mystified by Lemming's interest in their student, but they were also polite, and finally agreed to have someone drive Michael Oher over to the University of Memphis football facility for a face-to-face interview. "I'll never forget when he walked into the room," says Lemming. "He looked like a house walking into a bigger house. He walked in the door and he barely fit through the door." He wasn't just huge, he was huge in exactly the right ways. "There's the big blob three-hundred-pounder, and there's the solid kind," said Lemming. "He was the solid kind. You also see big guys, tall guys who weigh a lot, but they have thin legs. They're fine in high school, but in college they'll get pushed around. He was just massive everywhere."

What happened next was the strangest encounter of Lemming's twenty-seven-year football scouting career. Michael Oher sat down at the table across from him . . . and refused to speak. "He shook my hand and then didn't say a word," said Lemming. ("His hands: they were huge!") Lemming asked him the usual questions.

"What colleges are you interested in?"

"What do you want to major in?"

"Where do you think you'll be in ten years?"

They were met with total silence. Not knowing what else to do, Lemming handed the kid his questionnaire. Michael Oher looked at it and put it to one side. Lemming then handed him the ultimate prize: the form to play in the U.S. Army high school all-star football game. Michael Oher looked at it and put it, too, to one side. ("I noticed his arms were really long.")

"You want to fill it out or not?" asked Lemming, finally.

Michael Oher just shrugged.

In hopes of generating some kind of response, Lemming asked what he assumed was a simple question: "So, you want to play in the Army game or not?" It was the equivalent of asking a four-year-old if he'd like a lifetime supply of ice cream. But Michael Oher didn't say yes or no. "He made some sound of total indifference," said Lemming. "First guy ever to say that. First and last."

Lemming decided further interaction was pointless. Michael Oher left, and left behind blank forms and unanswered questions. In the past twenty-six years Lemming had interviewed between forty and fifty *thousand* high school football players. Never—not once—had a player simply refused to talk to him, or declined to fill in his forms. They *begged* to answer his questions and fill in his forms. Once, a player had had the audacity to delegate the form-filling to a coach and it had left a bad taste in Lemming's mouth. That incident had occurred in this very room, in Memphis, Tennessee. The player was named Albert Means. Albert Means's sure-thing career had gone up in smoke after the NCAA discovered a University of Alabama booster had paid his high school coaches one hundred fifty grand to guide him to Alabama. (And the Crimson Tide spent the next two seasons on probation.)

Lemming didn't exactly write off Michael Oher, but he put him to one side with a mental asterisk beside his name. "I thought he was trouble," he said. "It's not only size and strength and speed and athletic ability in football. Football's an emotional game. It's about aggression, tenacity, and heart. I didn't have any idea what was in his heart. I got no sense of anything about him." If Lemming picked twenty high school All-Americans, he expected ten of them to fulfill their potential. The other ten would be lost to injury or crime or bad grades or drugs. The sponsors of the U.S. Army All-American game worried a great deal about their good name. Every year there was a player or two they declined to invite because they didn't want dope in their rooms, or criminal records on their rosters, or even boorish behavior. Michael Oher fell into that category, Lemming decided, a character risk. Still, he couldn't deny his talent. "I didn't hold a grudge," said Lemming. "He wasn't rude to me. And I try to go with the best players. I thought he could be the best offensive lineman to come out of the South in the last five years. He was an instant All-American. I saw him as a number one NFL draft choice. Playing left tackle." But there was no way he'd invite Michael Oher to play in the U.S. Army All-American game.

What never crossed Tom Lemming's mind was that the player he would rank the number one offensive lineman in the nation, and perhaps the finest left tackle prospect since Orlando Pace, hadn't the faintest idea who Lemming was or why he was asking him all these questions. For that matter, he didn't even think of himself as football player. And he'd never played left tackle in his life.

CHAPTER THREE

CROSSING THE LINE

WHEN BIG TONY PUT THE TWO BOYS IN HIS CAR ON THE WEST side of Memphis and drove them out, he was taking the longest journey he could imagine, and yet he only had to travel about fifteen miles. Driving east, he left the third poorest zip code in the United States and headed toward some of the richest people on earth. He left a neighborhood in which he could drive all day without laying eyes on a white person for one where a black person was a bit of a curiosity. Memphis could make you wonder why anyone ever bothered to create laws segregating the races. More than a million people making many millions of individual choices generated an outcome not so different from a law forbidding black people and white people from mingling.

As Big Tony puttered along in his ancient Ford Taurus, he passed what was left of Hurt Village, a barracks-style housing project built for white working-class families in the mid-1950s, reoccupied by blacks, and, in the end, controlled by gangs: Hurt Village was where Big Tony had grown up. He passed schools that had once been all white and were now all black. He passed people, like himself, in old clothes driving old cars. He passed Second Presbyterian Church, from which Martin Luther King Jr. staged his last march before he was shot and killed—now abandoned and boarded shut.

Further east, he passed the relatively prosperous black church, Mississippi Boulevard, housed in a building abandoned by the white Baptists when they fled further east to a new church so huge and sprawling that it had been dubbed Six Flags Over Jesus. Even God, in the west end of Memphis, felt like a hand-me-down. As Big Tony drove east he left what was, in effect, a secondhand city occupied by black people and entered the place for which it had been exchanged: a brand-new city, created by Born Again white people. And now here came Big Tony, chugging along in his beat-to-hell Taurus, chasing after them.

Everyone called him Big Tony—his actual name was Tony Henderson—because he stood six three and weighed nearly 400 pounds. It was in Big Tony's nature to cross lines, if for no other reason than when he looked down he couldn't see them. But today he had a motive: his mother had died. And her dying wish had been for him to go east. Big Tony's mother's name was Betty, but she went by "Betty Boo." Right up until Big Tony reached the sixth grade, Betty Boo had been the party girl of Hurt Village. She smoked, she drank, she ran around; then suddenly, in 1973, she gave up alcohol, then her three-pack-a-day cigarette habit, then sin itself. She announced she had been saved, and accepted Jesus Christ as her Lord and Savior—and spent most of the next twenty-five years mailing pamphlets and pressing Christian literature and videos into people's hands. She wasn't tedious about it, though, and all the kids in Hurt Village called her "Grandma." Her first real grandson was Tony's son, Steven. As Betty Boo lay dying, in the early summer of 2002, she asked Tony for one thing: that he take Steven out of public school and get him a Christian education. She wanted her grandson to become a preacher.

Big Tony would have preferred Steven to become an NBA point guard. Still, he didn't consider Betty Boo's request unreasonable. Steven was one of the best students in his class, and always had been. There wasn't any difficulty in Memphis finding a school that offered a Christian education: the nation's largest private school system had sprung up in the mid-1970s, in East Memphis, to do just that. The problem was that Steven wasn't the only child living in Tony's small house. Occasionally, one of the boys from Hurt Village would crash on his floor; but a few months before, a boy came to stay the night and never left. His name was Michael Oher, but everyone just called him "Big Mike." Tony liked Big Mike, but he also could see that Big Mike was heading at warp speed toward a bad end. He'd just finished the ninth grade at a public school, but Tony very much doubted he'd be returning for the tenth. He seldom attended classes, and showed no talent or interest in school. "Big Mike was going to drop out," said Big Tony. "And if he dropped out, he'd be like all his friends who dropped out: dead, in jail, or on the street selling drugs, just waiting to be dead or in jail."

Tony decided that as long as he was taking Steven out on this search for a Christian education, he should take Big Mike, too. Just a few days after he buried his mother, he put Steven and Big Mike in his car, and drove east. White Memphis had use for a great variety of Christian schools: Harding Christian Academy, which had been around forever; Christian Brothers, which was Catholic and all male; and the Evangelical Christian School, known as ECS. ECS was as close to a church as a school could get. ECS wouldn't accept kids unless both parents gave testimony of their experience of being Born Again—and the stories better be good. Finally, and furthest east, was the Briarcrest Christian School. Briarcrest, also evangelical, was as far east as you could get and still be in Memphis. Briarcrest, more than the others, had been created to get away from Big Tony.

From the point of view of its creators, Briarcrest was a miracle. Its founder, Wayne Allen, had long been distressed by the absence of the Bible from public schools; the white outrage over busing was a chance to do something about it. In the year after the court decision—on January 24, 1973—that forced the city to deploy 1,000 buses to integrate the public schools, the parents of white children yanked more than 7,000 children out of those schools. From the ashes arose an entire, spanking new private school system. The Briarcrest Christian School—originally named the Briarcrest Baptist School—was by far the biggest. It was a system unto itself: fifteen different campuses, inside fifteen different Baptist churches. Its initial enrollment was just shy of 3,000 children, and every last one of them was white. By the summer of 2002 Briarcrest had a handful of black students, but these tended to be, like the black families in the fancy white neighborhoods, imports from elsewhere. The school had existed in East Memphis for nearly thirty years and yet no one who worked there could recall a poor black person from the west side of Memphis marching through its front door to enroll his child. Big Tony was the first.

All Tony knew about Briarcrest was that John Harrington was the basketball coach who had coached in the public schools, where Tony had met him. But any doubt that the Briarcrest Christian School served up the sort of education Betty Boo had in mind was allayed by the sight of the passage from the Book of Matthew inscribed on the outside of the main building: *With men this is impossible; with God all things are possible.* Two very lost-looking boys at his heels, Big Tony marched beneath it and inside the building and went hunting for the basketball coach.

JOHN HARRINGTON HAD SPENT two decades coaching in the public schools and was about to begin his first year at Briarcrest. When Big Tony walked into his office, unannounced, Harrington knew he couldn't do anything for him. The problem presented by Big Tony was too large for the new guy. They chatted for a few minutes and then Harrington sent him over to see the senior coach at Briarcrest, Hugh Freeze. Freeze was only thirty-three, and with his white-blond hair and unlined face might have passed for even younger than he was—if he weren't so shrewd. His shrewdness was right on the surface, so it had an innocent quality to it, but it was there just the same. Slow to speak and quick to notice, Hugh Freeze had the gifts of a machine politician. He was a man of God—if he hadn't been a football coach, he said, he'd have liked to have been a preacher—but he was also, very obviously, adept at getting his way on earth without any help from the Almighty. He'd coached at Briarcrest for eight years, taken the boys' football team to the Tennessee State Championship game five years in a row, and the girls' basketball team to the last seven state championship games, where they had won four of them. This year his girls were ranked ninth in the nation. Freeze was at his desk preparing for the first day of the new school year when his secretary alerted him to the presence of someone who insisted on calling himself "Big Tony."

In walks this 400-pound black man in a mechanic's shirt with a little white name tag that says: *Big Tony*. This huge man introduces himself as Big Tony—again, no last name—and proceeds to tell Hugh about Steven. "He told me about his son, and how he wanted more for him than the school he was at," said Freeze. "I told him how admirable that was but he had to understand that it cost a lot of money to go to Briarcrest, and not everyone got in. You had to have good grades. Big Tony said he knew about the cost and the grades; but Steven was an honor student and he was able to pay whatever the financial aid didn't cover." Freeze gave him the financial aid forms and thought: *Good luck*. That's when Tony said, "And Coach, I've also got one of Steven's friends." He told him about Big Mike, a basketball player who, in Big Tony's modest opinion, might also be of use to the Briarcrest football team.

"Where are his parents?" asked Freeze. He felt a twinge of interest. If a man who weighed 400 pounds was referring to someone else as "Big Mike," he'd like to see the size of that someone else.

"It's a bad deal, Coach," said Tony. "No Dad, Mom's in rehab. I'm pretty much all he has."

"Who is the guardian?" asked Freeze. "Who has legal authority over him?"

"The mom."

Big Tony said he could get Big Mike's mom to fill in the forms, then just sat there, a bit uneasily. Finally, he asked, "You want to meet them?"

"The boys are *here*?"

"Right outside."

"Sure," said Freeze, "bring 'em on in." Tony went out and came back with Steven. Hugh sized him up: almost six feet, and maybe as much as 180 pounds. Plenty big enough for the Briarcrest Christian School Saints football team. "But where's the other one?" he asked.

"Big Mike! Come on in here!"

Hugh Freeze will never forget the next few seconds. "He just peeks around the corner, with his head down." Hugh didn't get a good first look—it was just a sliver of him but it suggested an improbably large whole. Then Michael Oher stepped around the corner and into his office.

Good God! He's a monster!

The phrase shrieked inside Hugh's brain. He'd never seen anything remotely like this kid—and he'd coached against players who had gone to the NFL. When football coaches describe their bigger players, they can sound like ranchers discussing a steer. They use words like "girth" and "mass" and "trunk size." Hugh wasn't exactly sure of the exact dimensions of Big Mike—six five, 330 pounds? Maybe. Whatever the dimensions, they couldn't do justice to the effect they created. That mass! That . . . girth! The kid's shoulders and ass were as wide as his doorway. And he'd only just turned *sixteen*.

"How can I get their transcripts?" asked Hugh.

Big Tony said he'd go get them and bring them in person.

Then Hugh tried to make conversation with this man-child. "I couldn't get him to talk to me," he said. "Not a word. He was in a shell."

A few days later, Big Tony delivered the transcripts to Hugh Freeze. Steven, as advertised, was a model student and Briarcrest could see no reason not to supply him with a Christian education. Big Mike was another story. Hugh was a football coach and so he tended to take an indulgent view of bad grades, but he had no pleasant category in his mind for Big Mike's. "I knew it was too good to be true," he said. He sat on the transcript for two days, but he knew that eventually he'd have to hand it over to Mr. Simpson, the principal, to pass judgment. But his wheels already were spinning.

Steve Simpson, like John Harrington, was new to Briarcrest. He'd spent thirty of his fifty-six years working in the Memphis Public School system. When you first met him, you thought that whatever happened next it wasn't likely to be pleasant. His social manner was, like his salt-and-pepper hair, clipped short. He had the habit of frowning when another would have smiled, and of taking a joke seriously. But after about twenty minutes you realized that though the hard surface was both thin and brittle, beneath was a pudding of sentiment and emotion. He teared up easily, and was quick to empathize. When you mentioned his name to people who knew him well, they often said things like, "Steve Simpson has a heart that barely fits in this building." When teachers came to Briarcrest from the public schools, they often felt liberated, and took great pleasure in advertising their Christian faith. When Simpson arrived in this new place, he placed front and center on his desk a framed passage from the Bible that he never would have placed on his public school desk. But it was special to him:

> And God is able to provide you with every blessing in abundance, so that by always having enough of everything, you may share abundantly in His good works.

> —II CORINTHIANS 9:8

Still, when the file on Michael Oher from the Memphis City School system hit his desk, Simpson was frankly incredulous. The boy had a measured IQ of 80, which put him in mankind's 9th percentile. An aptitude test he had taken in the eighth grade had measured his "ability to learn" and ranked him in the 6th percentile. The numbers looked like misprints: in a rich white private school, under the column marked "percentile," you never saw single-digit numbers. Of course, logically, you knew such people must exist; for someone to be in the 99th percentile, someone else had to be in the 1st. But you didn't expect to meet them at the Briarcrest Christian School. Academically, Briarcrest might not be the most ambitious school. It spent more time and energy directing its students to Jesus Christ than to Harvard. But the students all went on to college. And they all had at least an average IQ.

In his first nine years of school Michael Oher had been enrolled in eleven different institutions, and that included a hole of eighteen months, around the age of ten, when he apparently did not attend school at all. Either that or the public schools were so indifferent to his presence that they had neglected to register it formally. But it was worse than that. There were schools Big Tony mentioned that did not even appear on the transcripts. Their absence might be explained by another shocking fact: the boy seldom showed up at the schools where he was enrolled. Even when he received credit for attending, he was sensationally absent: forty-six days of a single term of his first-grade year, for instance. His *first* first-grade year, that is—Michael Oher had repeated first grade. He'd repeated second grade, too. And yet Memphis City Schools described these early years as the most accomplished of his academic career. They claimed that right through the fourth grade he was performing at "grade level." How could they *know* when, according to these transcripts, he hadn't even attended the third grade?

Simpson knew what everyone who had even a brief brush with the Memphis public schools knew: they passed kids up to the next grade because they found it too much trouble to flunk them. They functioned as an assembly line churning out products never meant to be market-tested. At several schools Michael Oher had been given F's in reading his first term, and C's the second term, which allowed him to finish the school year with what was clearly an ignoramus's D. They were giving him grades just to get rid of him, to keep the assembly line moving. And get rid of him they did: seldom had the boy returned to the school that had passed him the year before. His previous year, in the ninth grade, he'd spent at a high school called Westwood. According to his transcripts, he'd missed fifty days of school. Fifty days! Briarcrest had a rule that if a student missed fifteen days of any class he had to repeat the class no matter what his grade. And yet Westwood had given Michael Oher just enough D's to move him along. Even when you threw in the B in world geography, clearly a gift from the Westwood basketball coach who taught the class, the grade point average the boy would bring with him to Briarcrest began with a zero: 0.6.

If there was a less promising academic record, Mr. Simpson hadn't seen it—not in three decades of working with public school students. Mr. Simpson guessed, rightly, that the Briarcrest Christian School hadn't seen anything like Michael Oher, either. And yet here he was, courtesy of the football coach, seated across the desk staring hard at the floor. The boy seemed as lost as a Martian stumbling out of a crash landing. Simpson had tried to shake his hand. "He didn't know how to do it," he said. "I had to show him how to shake hands." Every question Simpson asked elicited a barely audible mumble. "I don't know if 'docile' is the right word," Simpson said later. "He seemed completely intimidated by authority. Almost nonverbal." That, in itself, Simpson found curious. Even though Michael Oher had no business applying to Briarcrest, he showed courage just being here. "It was really unusual to see a kid with those kinds of deficits that wanted an education," he said. "To *want* to be in this environment. A lot of kids with his background wouldn't come within two hundred miles of this place."

The disposition of Michael Oher's application to Briarcrest was Steve Simpson's decision, and normally he would have had no trouble making it: an emphatic, gusty rejection. Beneath the crest of the Briarcrest Christian School was the motto: *Decidedly Academic, Distinctly Christian.* Michael Oher was, it seemed to Simpson, neither. But Mr. Simpson was new to the school, and this great football coach, Hugh Freeze, had phoned Simpson's boss, the school president, a football fan, and made his pitch: *This wasn't a thing you did for the Briarcrest football team,* Freeze had said, *this was a thing you did because it was right!* Briarcrest was this kid's last chance! The president in turn had phoned Simpson and told him that if he felt right with it, he could admit the boy.

Simpson thought it over and said: sorry. There was just no chance Michael Oher could cut it in the tenth grade; the fourth grade might be a stretch for him. But the pressure from the football coach, coupled with a little twinge inside his own heart, led Simpson to reject the applicant gently. "There was just something about the boy's desire to be here," he said. "I couldn't justify sending him away without any hope." He granted a single concession: if Michael Oher enrolled in a home study program based in Memphis called the Gateway Christian School, and performed at a high level for a semester, Briarcrest would admit him the following semester. Simpson knew there wasn't much chance Gateway would pass him, and suspected he'd never hear from the football coach, or Michael Oher, again.

He was wrong. Two months later—six weeks into the school year—his phone rang. It was Big Tony. It was a sad sight, said Big Tony, watching Big Mike stare at these books sent to him by the Gateway Christian School, without any ability to make heads or tails of them. Big Tony didn't have the time or the energy to work with him. Big Mike was trying so hard but getting nowhere, and it was too late for him to enroll in a public school. What should they do now?

That's when Mr. Simpson realized he'd made a mistake. In effect, he had removed a boy from the public school system. He'd tried to handle this problem the easy way, for him, and it had backfired. "It was one of those things," Simpson said. "I should have said, 'You don't qualify and there's no chance you will ever qualify.' When Big Tony called back, I thought, 'Man, look what I've done to these people. I sent them out of here with false hope.' " He went to the Briarcrest president, Tim Hilen, and told him that he had made a big mess for these people. Then he called Michael Oher—who appeared still to be living with Big Tony—and said, "We're gonna take a chance on you but you're not going to play ball." The message was delivered simultaneously to Hugh Freeze: no football, no basketball—the kid couldn't even sing in the choir until he proved to the school that he could handle the schoolwork. Michael didn't say much at all in response, but that didn't matter to Mr. Simpson. "My conscience would be clear if we gave him a chance," he said. His thoughts turned to the teachers: how would he explain this mess to them?

JENNIFER GRAVES HAD RUN Briarcrest's program for students with special needs for nine years. "I decided early on in my life," she said, "that Christ was calling me to work with the kids who did not have it so easy." But her mission took on a different and less hopeful tone when, six weeks into the school year, this huge black kid was dumped in her lap. She, too, had seen the file on Big Mike that had come over from the Memphis City School system. After the transcript came the boy himself, accompanied by Mr. Simpson. "He said this is Michael Oher and you'll be working with him," recalled Graves. "And Michael didn't say a thing. His head was always down. He kept his head down and his mouth shut." And she thought: *Oh Lord what have we gotten ourselves into?* She knew the coaches thought that he might help their sports teams, but even that surprised her. "He was *fat,*" she said. "I didn't see how he could move it around. We weren't real sure what we're going to do with him, and I'll bet they weren't either." After Michael left her office, she went right back to Mr. Simpson to ask what good he imagined would come from letting this child into the Briarcrest Christian School. "He said, 'Jennifer, let's give him until Christmas.' "

She took him around and placed him in the middle of every classroom. "By sixth period of the first day everyone knew who he was," she said. "And he hadn't said a word." It was a matter of days before the reports poured in from the teachers, every last one of them asking the same question of her that she asked of Mr. Simpson: why had they let this kid in? "Big Mike had no conception of what real school was about," she said. "He'd never have his books with him, didn't speak in class, nothing. He had no academic background, no foundation at all. His transcript said he'd had algebra but he'd obviously never laid eyes on it." Another shocking discovery: "I don't know that he'd ever even held a Bible."

At length, in response to an especially loud complaint from the English teacher, Graves brought Big Mike into her office. She pulled out a remedial English test, and gave it to him. "The first thing he was supposed to do," she recalled, "was to identify parts of speech. He says, 'What do I do?' And I say, 'You mark all the parts of speech.' He says, 'I don't know 'em.' So I say, 'Let's start out with nouns.' He says, 'I don't know 'em.' I tell him that 'a noun names a person, place, or thing.' He says, 'It does?' For him English was almost like a second language."

She noticed things about him. She noticed, for instance, that he wore the same pair of cutoff jeans every day, and that he hadn't the first idea how to interact with other people. Everyone in the school knew who he was—he was the biggest human being anyone had ever seen—and they tried to engage him, but he refused to comply. One day while she was sitting with Michael, sorting out some mess or other, her own little girls, aged six and nine, came into her office. "And they just stood there with their mouths open. They'd never seen anyone who looked like that. But then Big Mike left and my six-year-old asked, 'Mama, who was *that*?' And I told her it was Big Mike." The next few days the little girl went out of her way to find Big Mike in the school halls, just to say, "Hi, Big Mike!" And Big Mike just stared at her. The little girl came back to her mother, obviously frightened, and said, "Mama, he doesn't speak to me!" Graves called Big Mike into her office and explained that if he wanted to stare at the ground mutely in her presence, that was fine. "But when a little child tells you hello and you don't respond, you scare that little child." A few days later Graves caught sight of Big Mike in the hallways, smiling and shaking hands with a crowd of small, awed children.

Still, Michael Oher was only a few weeks into his tenure at the Briarcrest Christian School before several teachers suggested he should be on his way out. He wasn't merely failing tests, he wasn't even starting them. The only honest grade to give him in his academic subjects was zero. And it wasn't just the academic subjects. Briarcrest offered a class in weightlifting, and Jennifer Graves had gotten him into it on the assumption it might offer him some relief from relentless failure. If there was one class Big Mike should have been able to ace, this was it. But the weightlifting teacher, Coach Mark Boggess, said that the boy was neglecting even to change into gym clothes. He just sat around, lifting not even his eyes. Boggess doubled as the Briarcrest track coach, and already had made vague plans for Big Mike to put the shot for his team, once he became academically eligible. The third time he watched Michael sit through class in street clothes—not even bothering to change into his sweats—he doubted that would ever happen, and he jumped on him. "Michael, there are a lot of people in this school waiting to see you fail," he said. "Every little step that you make, people are watching. This is the one class in this whole school that can help you with your grades. All you have to do is show up. And right now, you're flunking *weightlifting*."

The situation appeared hopeless, and humiliating for all concerned. Word of the new boy's various failures inevitably reached Mr. Simpson, who also began to sense the dimensions of the void in the boy's life experiences. Michael Oher didn't know what an ocean was, or a bird's nest, or the tooth fairy. He couldn't very well be taught tenth-grade biology if he had no clue what was meant by the word "cell," and he couldn't very well get through tenth-grade English if he'd never heard of a verb or a noun. It was as if he had materialized on the planet as an overgrown sixteen-year-old. Jennifer Graves had the same misgivings: the boy reminded her of a story she had read in a psychology journal, about a child who had been locked away inside a closet for years. "That child didn't even have tactile sense," she said, "but it felt like the same sort of thing. Big Mike was a blank slate." The obvious problem, that he suffered from some learning disability, had been ruled out. Graves had called the Memphis school system and been told that Michael Oher had been tested for learning disabilities, and he had none. In short, they said, he was just stupid. "By their standards," she said, "he was achieving what was expected."

It was then that the Briarcrest biology teacher, Marilyn Beasley, came to Graves in despair. She said that giving Michael yet another weekly biology test was pointless: nothing came back. "We've got to find out what he does and doesn't know," she said. She proposed that Graves replace her in the biology class, and proctor the exam while she, Beasley, took Michael into a separate room and gave him the test verbally. The next day, Ms. Beasley took him into a room and sat down beside him, test in hand. By now she, like the other teachers, knew about his academic record. She had taught at Briarcrest for twenty-one years—and had entire classrooms of children with learning disabilities—and had never experienced a student so seemingly hopeless. "I had never encountered anybody at Michael's reading and comprehension level," she said. His brain did not appear to contain any sort of intellect.

As they sat down together she noticed, once again, how enormous his hands seemed when set beside hers. She had a son who was six one, but compared to Big Mike, his hands were the hands of a child. She picked up the test and read aloud the first question from the multiple choice exam:

Protozoans are classified based on:

a. How they get their food

b. How they reproduce

c. How they move

d. Both *a* and *c*

She waited for his answer and received nothing but a blank look. She knew the problem: many of the words, words every tenth-grader should know, were foreign to him. "Classified" overwhelmed him. "Science has its own vocabulary," she said. "He didn't know it. He didn't know what a cell was, or an atom. He didn't have the foundation to figure out meanings through prefixes and suffixes. He didn't know what the prefixes and suffixes were—they might as well have been Greek." The vast quantity of things he didn't know paralyzed his mind. A word at a time, she talked him through the problem.

"Michael, do you remember what a protozoan is?"

Just down the hall Jennifer Graves waited for what she assumed would be bad news. She was already wondering about the best way to ease Big Mike out of the school. An hour later Marilyn Beasley emerged with wonder on her face and a simple observation:

"He knows it."

"What?"

"Jennifer, he knows the material!"

Or, at any rate, he knew something. As he had given no sign of picking up anything, Beasley was shocked at how much he had absorbed. His brain wasn't dead; he simply had no idea how to learn in a classroom. Even so, he knew enough biology to get himself a C on the test, and a high D for the semester instead of an F. He wasn't yet eligible to play any sports, but Graves could see that he longed to. He'd missed the football season, but it was basketball he was most eager to play. She hinted that if the biology test was any indication of the contents of his mind, he might well be eligible to play ball after Christmas, and catch the last part of the season. "The first thing he did," she said, "was start hanging around the basketball court."

WHEN SEAN TUOHY first spotted Michael Oher sitting in the stands in the Briarcrest gym, staring at basketball practice, he saw a boy with nowhere to go but up. The question was how to take him there.

Sean was an American success story: he had come from nothing and made himself rich. He was forty-three years old. His hairline had receded but not quite to the point where you could call him bald and his stomach had expanded but not quite to the point where you could call him fat. He was keenly interested in social status—his own, and other people's—but not in the Old Southern kind. Not long after he'd become a figure in Memphis—a rich businessman who had his own jet and was the radio voice of the Memphis Grizzlies—he'd had feelers from the Memphis Country Club. He didn't encourage them because, as he put it, "I don't hang with the blues. I'd rather go to a high school football game on Friday night than go to a country club and drink four scotches and complain about my wife." Sean Tuohy loved success. He delighted in the sight of people moving up in the world. Country clubs were all about staying in one place.

When he introduced himself to Big Mike, Sean was already knee-deep in the various problems and crises of the few black students at Briarcrest. Sean's daughter, Collins, a junior at Briarcrest and Tennessee State champion in the pole vault, had guaranteed him almost constant exposure to them. She ran track, they ran track. The first time Sean decided to play a role in their social education had been a couple of years earlier, when the track team traveled to Chattanooga for a meet. Coincidentally, also in Chattanooga, a Briarcrest tennis player was playing a tournament at the fancy local country club. Sean thought the black kids at Briarcrest might benefit from some exposure to tennis and golf and other white country club sports; and he thought the Briarcrest tennis player would enjoy a cheering section. Gathering up all two of the black kids on the track team—which amounted to two thirds of the blacks at Briarcrest—he drove them to the Chattanooga Country Club. Sure enough, it was, for them, an entirely new experience. Neither had ever seen a tennis match in person. And while they had no idea how to keep score, they quickly worked out that the Briarcrest kid was making mincemeat of his opponent. After each point they'd stand and holler and raise their fists:

Woo!
Woo!
Woo!

Rather than explain tennis club etiquette, of which he vaguely disapproved anyway, Sean let them have their fun. Between sets they ran over to the concession stand where a little old lady sniffed at them, "I just think y'all are in bad taste." To which one of the kids replied, "You must be rootin' for that other little white guy." The lady went off in a huff and the kids returned to the match, where the Briarcrest player kept on winning. The breaking point came when one of the kids stood up and screamed: "Keep on! You beatin' him like a two dollar whore!" Sean tried to drag the boy by his oversized jersey back into his seat, but before he could get him down, the boy spotted the little old lady in the stands, glaring at him, and screamed: "It's got to be killing ya, ma'am! It's got to be killing ya!"

Afterward, Sean realized that it had been awhile since he had had so much fun. And by the time he met Big Mike, he had a new unofficial title: Life Guidance Counselor to whatever black athlete stumbled into the Briarcrest Christian School. The black kids reminded him, in a funny way, of himself.

Sean knew what it meant to be the poor kid in a private school, because he'd been one himself. First off, none of the rich kids realized that one big difference between public schools and private schools is that, in the public schools, lunch was free. Every day for several years in high school Sean arrived without lunch, or money to buy it, and bummed what he could from friends. "When food is finite," he said, "you'd be surprised how much time you spend thinking about it."

He also knew what it was like to think of sports as a meal ticket. His sense that his future depended on his athletic ability was driven home during his freshman year in high school, when his father, a legendary but ill-paid basketball coach, suffered a stroke and ceased to function. Sean had adored his father. From the age of three, when he had grabbed a basketball and followed him to work in the morning, he had spent the better part of his life on his father's heels, soaking in everything he could about basketball and life. Twenty-five years later he would say, "Everything I do is still all about my daddy." And yet when he lost his father, he, and everyone around him, went on about their lives as if the earth had not just opened and swallowed the most important person in his life. The fancy New Orleans private school was still, for him, free; lunch was not.

He'd left New Orleans for the University of Mississippi on a basketball scholarship. When he set out for Ole Miss he was a six one, 147-pound exception; he wasn't even sure he could cut it as a college basketball player. When he walked off the court after his final game, he'd set the NCAA record for career assists; and, twenty-five years later, he still holds all meaningful SEC assist records. After he'd led Ole Miss to its first (and still only) SEC Championship, in 1981, a photograph of him, perched on top of the rim and bleeding from a cut on his chin as he cut down the nets, appeared in the *New York Times*. At a college still trying to figure out why their white boys were being whipped so routinely by the other team's black boys, he was an instant legend.

That was the joy; the misery was his essential powerlessness. He was at the mercy of a single man who specialized in tearing his players apart and leaving them in pieces. From the moment he had arrived at the Ole Miss gym, Sean realized that his coach had him trapped: he could only afford to stay in school so long as he played basketball, and he played at his coach's pleasure. His entire identity hung in the balance. "From the age of five I had been trained to do this one thing, play basketball. And if I couldn't do that, where did it leave me?" And this coach, who had him by the short hairs, loved nothing more than to give them a yank: threatening to bench him, pull his scholarship, humiliate him in front of his hometown crowd when the Ole Miss team played in New Orleans. Early in his freshman year, for instance, the team had traveled to Bloomington-Normal, Illinois, to play in a tournament. In the first game they beat Loyola Chicago; in the finals they got beaten badly by a nationally ranked Illinois State team. The game ended just before midnight, and they were supposed to drive the four hours to the St. Louis airport, then catch an early morning commercial flight back to Memphis. Sean had played every minute of both games with a torn cartilage in his knee, and afterwards had to be treated by trainers. When he emerged from the locker room, he found a fleet of cars and only one spot left in them, right beside his coach. No one else on the team wanted to sit next to the coach.

"For the next four and a half hours," he said, "not one word was spoken. Not one word. I got a cramp in my leg and I remember holding back a scream because I was afraid of getting in trouble."

They caught their plane, and returned to Memphis, where a bus picked them up and carried them the rest of the way to Oxford, Mississippi. "We drove onto campus. There isn't anyone there. It's Christmas Day. It's now eleven in the morning and we still haven't slept. Coach gets up in the front of the bus and says, 'Dressed, stretched, and taped. Thirty minutes.' And I just remember going: 'I don't know about y'all but I haven't slept.' "

Still, the players all trudged to the locker room, donned practice uniforms, and set out for the film room. That's how practice always started: by watching films of their most recent performance and being humiliated by Coach. The players found their seats, the lights went down, and Coach entered the room. He always took a wide circle on his way to his lounge chair in the back: the players felt watched. "I had played forty minutes of both games," Sean said. "My knee was swelled up as big as Dallas. We hadn't slept. It's my first Christmas away from home. Coach walked around so he was right behind me and stopped. Never once in four years did he call me 'Sean.' It was either 'Buddy' or 'Twelve.' Now he comes right up behind me and says,

" *'Hey Twelve. Merry Fucking Christmas.'*

"The lights went out and I cried for the next forty-five minutes. The assistant coach literally sat there rubbing my back and patting me."

For four years he'd played what he called "survival ball." He had to play, or he couldn't afford school. The New Jersey Nets drafted him in a late round to play in the NBA, but the desire had gone out of him. He left Ole Miss with a fiancée and a new religion. But he left without a penny.

Now, by the fall of 2002, he'd become, by just about every way they measured it in Memphis, a success. He'd been Born Again, and helped to create one of the fastest growing evangelical churches in Memphis, the Grace Evangelical Church. He'd married the Ole Miss cheerleader who, twenty-five years later, could still pass for an Ole Miss cheerleader. He owned a chain of eighty-five Taco Bells, KFCs, and Long John Silver restaurants, along with a mountain of debt. His financial life remained risky. If everything broke right, he might soon be worth as much as $50 million. If everything did not break right, he could always call games for the Memphis Grizzlies. What Atlanta was to the American South, Sean Tuohy was to the white southern male. Prosperous. Forever upgrading the trappings of his existence. Happy to exchange his past at a deep discount for a piece of the future.

It wasn't enough. The restaurants ran themselves, the Grizzlies gig was a night job, church was on Sundays. He needed overt drama in his life. He was a person for whom the clock was always running out, the game was always tied, and the ball was always in his hands. He'd played the role for so long that he'd become the role. And he now had all the time in the world for what he still loved more than anything: hanging around school gyms and acting as a kind of consultant to the coaches at Briarcrest in their dealings with their players. Sean was interested in poor jocks in the same way that a former diva might be interested in opera singers or a Jesuit scholar in debaters. What he liked about them was that he knew how to help them. "What I learned playing basketball at Ole Miss," he said, "was what not to do: beat up a kid. It's easy to beat up a kid. The hard thing is to build him up."

Collins had mentioned Big Mike to him. When she tried to pass him on the stairwell, she said, she had to back up to the top, because she couldn't fit past him. Without uttering a peep, the kid had become the talk of the school. Everyone was frightened of him, she said, until they realized that he was far more terrified of them. Sean had seen Big Mike around the halls three or four times. He'd noticed that he wore the same clothes every day: cutoff blue jeans and an oversized T-shirt. Now he saw him in the stands and thought: *I'll bet he's hungry.* Sean walked over and said, "You don't know me, but we have more in common than you might think."

Michael Oher stared intently at his feet.

"What did you have to eat for lunch today?" Sean asked.

"In the cafeteria," said the kid.

"I didn't ask where you ate," said Sean. "I asked what you ate."

"Had a few things," said the kid.

Sure you did, thought Sean. He asked if he needed money for lunch, and Mike said, "I don't need any money."

The next day, Sean went to the Briarcrest accounting department and arranged for Michael Oher to have a standing charge card at the lunch checkout counter. He'd done the same for several of the poorer black kids who had come to Briarcrest. In a couple of cases he had, in effect, paid their tuition, by giving money to a school fund earmarked for scholarships for those who couldn't afford tuition. "That was my only connection with Michael," he said later. "Lunch."

Sean left it at lunch, and at lunch it might have ended. But a few weeks later, the Briarcrest Christian School took its Thanksgiving Break. One cold and blustery morning Sean and his wife, Leigh Anne, were driving down one of the main boulevards of East Memphis when, off a bus just ahead of them, steps this huge black kid. He was dressed in the same pair of cutoff jeans and T-shirt he always wore. Sean pointed him out to his wife and said, "That kid I was telling you about—that's him. Big Mike."

"But he's wearing shorts," she said.

"Uh-huh. He always wears those."

"Sean, it's snowing!"

And so it was. At Leigh Anne's insistence, they pulled over. Sean reintroduced himself to Michael, and then introduced Michael to Leigh Anne.

"Where are you going?" he asked.

"To basketball practice," says Big Mike.

"Michael, you don't have basketball practice," says Sean.

"I know," says the boy. "But they got heat there."

Sean didn't understand that one.

"It's nice and warm in that gym," said the boy.

As they drove off, Sean looked over and saw tears streaming down Leigh Anne's face. And he thought: *Uh-oh, my wife's about to take over.*

The next day afternoon, Leigh Anne left her business—she had her own interior decorating outfit—turned up at Briarcrest, picked up the kid, and took off with him. A few hours later, Sean's cell phone rang. He picked up and heard his wife's voice on the other end of the line:

"Do you know how big a fifty-eight long jacket is?" she asked.

"How big?"

"Not big enough."

Leigh Anne Tuohy had grown up with a firm set of beliefs about black people but had shed them for another—and could not tell you exactly how it happened, other than to say that "I married a man who doesn't know his own color." Her father, a United States Marshal based in Memphis, raised her to fear and loathe blacks as much as he did. (Friends who saw Tommy Lee Jones in the movie *U.S. Marshal* would say to her, "Oh my God, that's your father!") The moment the courts ordered the Memphis Public School system integrated, in 1973, he pulled her out of public school and put her into the newly founded Briarcrest Christian School, where she'd become a member of the first graduating class. "I was raised in a very racist household," she said. As her father walked her up the aisle so that she might wed Sean, he looked around the church, filled with Sean's black ex-teammates, and asked, "Why are all these niggers here?" Even as an adult, when she mentioned in passing that she was on her way into a black neighborhood on the west side of Memphis for some piece of business, he insisted on escorting her. "And when he comes to get me, he shows up with this magnum strapped to his chest."

Yet by the time Michael Oher arrived at Briarcrest, Leigh Anne Tuohy didn't see anything odd or even awkward in taking him in hand. This boy was new; he had no clothes; he had no warm place to stay over Thanksgiving Break. For Lord's sake, he was walking to school in the snow *in shorts*, when school was *out of session*, on the off chance he could get into the gym and keep warm. Of course she took him out and bought him some clothes. It struck others as perhaps a bit aggressively philanthropic; for Leigh Anne, clothing a child was just what you did if you had the resources. She had done this sort of thing before, and would do it again. "God gives people money to see how you're going to handle it," she said. And she intended to prove she knew how to handle it.

For Leigh Anne, the mystery began once Michael climbed into her gray minivan. "He got in the car and didn't say anything," she said. "Not one word."

"Tell me everything I need to know about you," she said.

She noticed his sneakers—all beat-up and raggedy.

"Who takes care of you?"

He didn't answer.

"I've noticed in the African American community the grandmother often helps to raise the kids. Do you have a grandmother?"

He didn't, but he didn't explain.

This wouldn't do. Leigh Anne Tuohy was an extreme, and seemingly combustible, mixture of tenderness and willfulness. She cried when a goldfish died. On her daily walks, when she spotted an earthworm sizzling on the sidewalk, she picked it up and put it back on the grass. On the other hand, when a large drunk man pushed and cut his way in front of her in a line outside a football game, she grabbed him by the arm and screamed, "You just get your fat ass right back where it belongs. *Now!*" When she did things like this, her husband would shrug and say, "You have to understand that my wife has a heart the size of a *pea*. If you cross her, she will step on your throat and take you out and she won't *feel a thing*." Sean had decided, no matter what the potential gains, it was never worth provoking his wife.

And this child's reluctance to answer her questions had provoked her. "We're gonna keep talking about this," she said. "We can do this the easy way. Or we can do it the hard way. Take your pick."

That worked, sort of. She learned that he'd not laid eyes on his father in many years. He never had much to do with his grandmother, who was now gone. He had a sister but didn't know where she was. His mother was, Leigh Anne surmised, an alcoholic. "But he never actually used the word 'alcoholic.' He let me say it and never corrected me. I didn't know then, but Michael will let you believe what you want to believe." After torturing him for a bit, she decided to leave him be. She'd had too much success getting what she wanted to pay much attention to temporary setbacks: it was only a matter of time before he'd tell her everything. "I knew that 103.5 FM was kind of a black station so I had that playing," she said. "I didn't want him thinking this was some charity thing and 'oh poor, pitiful me.' So I said that the Briarcrest basketball team needed its players looking spiffy and we were just going out to make sure that happened."

If it were up to her, she would have driven him straight to Brooks Brothers or Ralph Lauren, but she realized it might make him feel uncomfortable.

"No offense, but where do you go to buy clothes?" she asked.

He mentioned a place—it was in a less affluent section of Memphis. Not the safest neighborhood. She set off in that direction, heading west.

"You okay going there?" he asked.

"I'm okay going there with you. You're going to take care of me, right?"

"Right," he said. She sensed a little shift in him. Sooner or later she'd break him. "I can talk to a wall," she liked to say.

For the next couple of hours that's just what she did. She was facing a new problem: trying to guess, from his body language, what a sixteen-year-old black child of the ghetto might wear to his new white Christian school. They arrived at the first of many Big and Tall shops and ran smack into another problem: nothing fit him! He wasn't big *or* tall. He was big *and* tall. The selection of clothing into which he could painlessly squeeze himself was limited, and he reduced it by refusing to wear anything that wasn't loose-fitting. For twenty minutes or so she pulled the biggest articles of clothing she could find off shelves and racks, without a comment from the boy.

"Michael!" she finally said. "You got to tell me if you like it or not. I cannot read your mind. Or we'll be here till Christmas, with me trying to guess what you like."

She pulled down the absolute biggest shirt she could find.

"I think that's okay," he said, at length. For him it counted as a soliloquy.

"No! Not okay! You need to love it! If you don't love it in the store, you'll never wear it once you get it home. The store is where you like it best."

She pulled down a gargantuan brown and yellow Rugby shirt.

"I like that one," he said.

She was five one, 115 pounds of blond hair, straight white teeth, and the most perfect pink dress. He was black, poor, and three times her size. Everyone—*everyone*—stared at them. And as they moved from shop to shop, the surroundings, and the attention, became more discomforting. At the final Big and Tall Shop on the border of what had just been pronounced, by the 2000

United States Census, the third poorest zip code in the country, Leigh Anne said, "I've lived here my whole life and I've never been to this neighborhood." And Big Mike finally spoke up. "Don't worry," he said. "I got your back."

Along the way she asked him more questions. "But of course they were the wrong questions," she said later. She noticed little things about him, however, and in these were tiny clues. "I could tell he wasn't used to being touched," she said. "The first time I tried to touch him—he just freezes up."

When they were finished shopping, he was heaped with packages and yet he insisted he wanted to take the bus home. ("I am *not* letting him ride the bus with all these bags!") She drove him back—into what she assumed must be the worst neighborhood in Memphis. They stopped in at McDonald's. He ordered for himself two quarter pounders with cheese. On a hunch she bought six extra burgers for him to take home with him. At length, they reached what he said was his mother's house. It was an ominous dark red-brick building behind a tall metal gate. Across the street was an abandoned house. The scrub grass, the dead plants in pots, the flaking paint on the houses: everything, including the small children in the streets, looked uncared for. She parked and stepped out of the car, to help him with all the bags. That's when he sprang into action:

"Don't get out!" he said.

"I'll just help you with the bags."

"You don't need to get out of the car," he said.

He was so insistent that she stepped back inside the car and promised to stay put, with the doors locked, while he went in and found someone to help him with his packages. A few minutes later a line of small children streamed out of the front gates of the depressing apartment building and, antlike, lifted the sacks and carried them inside. When the last child had moved the last package, the gate closed behind him.

He hadn't given her the first clue of what he thought of her, or of their strange afternoon together. "Probably," she figured, "that I'm some nice lady who wanted something from him." So when he thanked her, she made a point of saying, "Michael, it was my pleasure. You don't owe me anything." And that, she thought, was that.

It wasn't, of course. He was different from the other children that she and Sean had helped out. For a start, he was obviously more destitute. And she couldn't explain why just then, but she was drawn to him and felt the urge to do things for him. He was just this big ol' kid who could have been mean and scary and thuggy, but everything about him was soft and gentle and sweet-natured. With him she felt completely safe; even if he wasn't saying anything, she sensed he was watching out for her.

She went home and thought about the problem still at hand: how to clothe the biggest sixteen-year-old boy she had ever laid eyes on. She flipped through her Rolodex. Several of her interior decorating clients were professional athletes. All but one were basketball players, and all of them were tall and *thin*. The other was Patrick Ramsay, the Washington Redskins' new starting quarterback. "I know how these athletes are about their clothes," she said. "They're very particular and they're tossing them out and getting new ones all the time." What more fertile source of extra-large hand-me-downs than the NFL? She called Ramsay, who said he was more than happy to dun his teammates for their old clothing. She gave him Michael's measurements, and Patrick Ramsay took them down.

A few days later, he called back. "You've got these measurements wrong," he said, matter-of-factly. She explained that she had taken the measurements herself, and written them down on a piece of paper. It must be Patrick who had them wrong. He read them back to her—20-inch neck, 40-inch sleeve, 50-inch waist, 58-inch chest, etc.—nope, he had them right.

"There's no one on our team as big as he is," Ramsay said.

She thought he was kidding.

"Leigh Anne," said the Redskins quarterback, "we only have one player on this team who is even close, and he wears Wrangler blue jeans and flannel shirts and no black kid is going to be caught dead wearing that stuff." That would be Jon Jansen, the Redskins' starting right tackle.

There was a moment of silence on the other end of the line.

"Who *is* this kid?"

CHAPTER FOUR

THE BLANK SLATE

EVERY ONE OF THE COACHES AT BRIARCREST CAN RECALL THE MOMENT they realized that Big Mike was not any ordinary giant. For Hugh Freeze the moment was a football practice at which this new boy, who had just been admitted on academic probation, had no business. He just wandered onto the field, picked up a huge tackling dummy—the thing weighed maybe fifty pounds—and took off with it, at high speed. *"Did you see that!!!? Did you see the way that kid moved?"* Hugh asked another coach. "He ran with that dummy like it weighed nothing." Hugh's next thought was that he had mis-judged the boy's mass. No human being who moved that quickly could pos-sibly weigh as much as 300 pounds. "That's when I had them weigh him," said Hugh. "One of the coaches took him into the gym and put him on the scale, but he overloaded the scale." The team doctor drove him away and put him on what the Briarcrest coaches were later informed was a cattle scale: 344 pounds, it read. On the light side, for a cow, delightfully beefy for a high school sophomore football player. Especially one who could *run*. "I didn't know whether he could play," said Freeze. "But I knew this: we didn't have anyone like him on campus."

The basketball coach, John Harrington, had a similarly incidental encounter with Big Mike in action, inside the Briarcrest gym. Whenever a new kid he thought might play on his team showed up, Harrington tossed him a ball, unexpectedly, just to test his reactions and instincts. The first time Big Mike walked onto the Briarcrest court he was wearing his cutoff blue jeans and grubby sneakers. Harrington tossed him a ball anyway, just to see. Instead of taking it to the rim, or kicking it into the stands, as you might expect a boy his size to do, he caught it and swirled. He dribbled three times between his legs, spun, and, from the dead corner of the floor, nailed a three-point shot. "Walking into the gym he sort of became a different person," said Harrington. "He was doing things a guard would do. Here's this kid—what, six five and three hundred-something pounds, and he's moving like he's a hundred sixty-five pounds. My head's spinning."

Coach Boggess, the track coach, who doubled as the weightlifting instructor and tripled as an assistant football coach, had his own shocking encounter with the boy's freakish physical gifts. It came on the Briarcrest football field. Big Mike wasn't allowed to play, but every now and then he came out onto the field and played, in effect, by himself. One afternoon he took a sack of footballs out to midfield. Standing on the fifty-yard line he threw them, one by one, through the goalposts at the back of the end zone. As a rule, a good college quarterback's range was 60 yards—from midfield to the line along the back of the end zone. Here was this kid, a sophomore in high school, shaped nothing like a quarterback, chucking the ball 70–75 yards. And making it look *easy*.

From the moment he'd laid eyes on Michael Oher, Coach Boggess thought he might invite him onto the track team as a shot putter. He was shaped like a shot putter, and also like the shot itself, round and heavy. It hadn't occurred to Boggess to ask Big Mike to throw anything else until he saw him chucking these footballs and realized he was not merely huge and strong, but flexible and long-armed. There was elegance about him. High school track didn't have the javelin. That was a pity, Boggess thought, as he watched the footballs rocket through the goalposts. Still, there was the discus. "I hadn't thought of him throwing the discus," said Boggess, "because with the discus it's not how big you are, it's the technique you use. The discus is not physiologically suited to the football lineman-type body, in the way the shot put is. Those bodies don't have the grace to do it."

Throwing a discus is more complicated than it appears. The discus thrower needs to separate his lower half from his upper half so that the lower half rotates faster than the upper and creates a torque effect. To achieve the proper spin on the discus requires the body control of an ice skater. None of the Briarcrest coaches was able to teach "spinning" by example, as none of them could do it themselves. When they had a kid who was ambitious enough to try it, they showed him instructional videos.

In Michael Oher's case, the coaches' ignorance hardly mattered. When the first track meet rolled around that first spring, he hadn't spent a minute with the coaches. He was earning straight D's in the classroom and spending five hours a day with tutors, in exchange for being allowed to finish up the basketball season on the Briarcrest team. When Coach Boggess led him out Briarcrest's back door and onto the old grass field for that first meet, he sensed, rightly, that Michael Oher was witnessing track and field for the first time in his life. "He didn't know what a discus was," said Boggess. "He'd never seen one." The track coach inserted Michael at the back of the queue of discus throwers from the other schools, and left him to give it a whirl. Michael, for his part, never said a word, or asked a question. "I just watched them a couple of times," he said, much later, "and then I threw it."

Across the field Collins Tuohy, daughter of Sean and Leigh Anne, future Tennessee State champion in the pole vault, watched the discus competition as she waited herself to compete. When Big Mike's first throw landed, she picked up her cell phone and called her father. "Daddy," she said, "I think you better come over here and see Michael throw the discus. It looks like a *Frisbee*."

Boggess watched, too. "I think I just laughed," he said. "It wasn't spinning or doing anything fancy. But, man, it *flew*."

Michael's first throw won him first place in that meet. But it was a crude victory, the track and field equivalent of bludgeoning when a sword was at hand. Big Mike wasn't spinning, and neither was the discus. "That first time he did it he didn't really have anyone to watch, because the other kids at that meet weren't really able to spin either," said Boggess. Still, he was amazed, even then, how much the kid looked like he knew what he was doing. Even on the first throw, after watching the kids in front of him, he acquired the basic snap release. Boggess had had kids on his team who never even got that far. At the bigger meets, Boggess knew, some of the discus throwers had serious technique, and would offer Michael a more sophisticated model to imitate. To Boggess, the striking thing was how quickly Michael Oher learned. He wasn't just big and strong and agile; he had a kind of physical intelligence. "He basically taught himself," said Boggess. "Because we couldn't teach him. I remember going out on the field one day and saying: *Oh my God, he's spinning. He's figured it out.* Evidently he just figured it out by watching."

That was the point: Big Mike was able to learn with his body, when he could see other people in action. It wasn't long before Boggess was watching, with glee, as his professional-looking high school discus thrower hit 166 feet—the longest throw in Tennessee in six years. He never had time to practice, as he had to be tutored after school. He just wandered out to the meets and threw whatever needed to be thrown. By the time he finished his quixotic track career, Michael Oher would break the West Tennessee sectional record in the discus, and threaten it in the shot put. In his spare time! It came so easily to him, said Boggess, that if his talent for throwing the discus did not wind up seeming so trivial when set beside his other talents, "they'd have taken him away and trained him up and he'd have been big time."

For his first year and a quarter, until the spring of his junior year, there was some question as to the highest use of Michael Oher. Once the teachers figured out he needed to be tested orally, he proved to them that he deserved high D's instead of low F's. It wasn't clear he was going to acquire enough credits to graduate with his class, but Mr. Simpson and Ms. Graves stopped thinking they were going to send him back out on the streets, and they let him play sports. He joined the basketball team at the end of his sophomore year, and soon afterwards the track and field team. In his junior year he finally got onto the football field.

The problem there, at first, resembled his problems in the classroom. He was a blank slate. He had no foundation, no idea what he was meant to do as a member of a team. He said he had played football his freshman year, at Westwood, but there was no sign of it in his performance. When Coach Hugh Freeze saw how fast he could move, he pegged him as a defensive tackle. And so, for the first five games of the 2003 season, he played defense. He wasn't any worse than his replacement, but he wasn't much better either. One of his more talented teammates, Joseph Crone, thought Big Mike's main contribution came before the game, when the opposing team stumbled out of their locker room or their bus, and took the measure of the Briarcrest Christian School. "They'd see all of us," said Crone, "and then they'd see Mike and say, *oh crap.*"

That, at first, was his highest use: to intimidate the opposition before the game. During the games he seemed confused. When he wasn't confused, he was reluctant. Passive, almost. This was the last thing Coach Hugh Freeze expected. Freeze didn't know much about Michael Oher's past but he knew enough to assume that he'd had some kind of miserable childhood in the worst part of Memphis. A miserable childhood in the worst part of Memphis was typically excellent emotional preparation for what was required on a football defense: it made you angry, it made you aggressive, it made you want to tear someone's head off. The NFL was loaded with players who had mined a loveless, dysfunctional childhood for sensational acts of violence.

The trouble with Michael Oher as a football player was the trouble with Ferdinand as a bull: he didn't exhibit the anger of his breed. He was just a sweet kid who didn't particularly care to hit anybody, or, as Hugh put it, "He just wasn't aggressive. His mentality was not a defensive player's mentality." The depth of the problem became clear during Briarcrest's fourth game, when the team took buses up into Kentucky to play a pretty tough Calloway County team. Early in the game Michael caught his hand on an opponent's face mask and gashed the webbing between his fingers. "You'd a thought he was going to die," said Hugh. "Screaming and moaning and carrying on. I thought we were going to have to go and get a stretcher." His defensive tackle ran to the bench, clenched his hand, and refused to allow anyone to look at it.

In the stands Leigh Anne Tuohy watched as two, then three, then four grown men tried to subdue Michael Oher, and then coax him into allowing them to examine his hand. "He was in a fetal position," she said. Men were next to useless in getting Michael to do things, because he didn't trust men: she knew this about him, and more. After their shopping trip, when she turned up at Briarcrest, Michael had sought her out. He had mentioned that he hated to be called "Big Mike" and so from then on he was, to her and her family, Michael. "I don't know what happened," Leigh Anne said. "Whether it was attrition of other people, or whatever. But I became the person Michael came to. At his basketball games he'd just walk over and start talking to me. When I was at school, he'd find me and talk to me. I think everyone kind of noticed that he'd gotten close to me. Maybe before I noticed."

She walked down from the stands, crossed the track, walked onto the football field, and went straight to the bench.

"Michael, you need to open your hand," she said, crossly.

"It hurts," he said.

"I realize it hurts. But your head is going to hurt a lot worse when I hit you upside it."

He unclenched his hand, one giant finger at a time. The gash went to the bottom of the webbing and down the finger, where the bone was visible. "I wanted to throw up," said Leigh Anne. "It was gross." She pretended it wasn't and told him he needed to be taken to the hospital.

"The hospital!!" he wailed. She thought he was going to faint.

They were a good two and a half hours from home, so Carly Powers, the Briarcrest athletic director, took him to a Kentucky emergency room. "The first question he asked when we got in the car," said Powers, "and he kept asking it, 'Is it going to hurt? Is it going to hurt?' He was a nervous wreck. You could see it in his eyes. When we walked into that hospital, he was scared to death." Powers sensed that Big Mike had perhaps never seen the inside of a hospital.

A nurse checked them in, told Powers to wait in the lobby, and escorted Big Mike to the back. A few minutes later, Powers heard "this blood-curdling scream. And you can tell it's Big Mike." The nurse comes running out and says, "Mr. Powers, I think we're going to need you back here. We need your help to hold him down." Powers followed her back to see what the problem was. A needle, as it turned out. The doctors were trying to give Big Mike a simple shot to numb his hand, and Big Mike had taken one look at the needle and leapt off the table. A staff of three had tried to put him back on it, without success. "He'd never seen a needle," said Powers.

Even a rich private school was ill-equipped to deal with a parentless child. Like all schools, it was hard-wired to call, at the first sign of conflict, a grown-up. In the eight months since she had taken him shopping for clothes, Leigh Anne Tuohy had become that grown-up. Briarcrest teachers knew that, increasingly, Big Mike was spending time with Sean and Leigh Anne. Sean was becoming something like a private basketball coach to him, and Leigh Anne was grappling with the rest of his life. The Tuohys were now covering not only his school lunches but also, indirectly, his tuition. For this reason and one other, when Carly Powers, as athletic director, asked himself which adult he might call to talk reason to Big Mike, he settled on Leigh Anne. The other reason was that he'd never seen Leigh Anne fail to get her way. "She is going to get it done," said Powers, "or she is going to drive you nuts."

He called Leigh Anne's cell phone. She was on the bus with the Briarcrest cheerleaders, riding back to the school. After she had sorted Michael out on the bench, Leigh Anne sensed she had glimpsed another little sliver of his childhood. "I just thought: this kid has never been injured before," she said. "Or if he has been injured, he said, 'I'm not gonna tell anyone about it.' " She suspected this might be the first time he had no choice but to allow someone else to do something for him. "When he was sitting on the bench refusing to let those men look at him," she said, "it was as if he thought: 'If I just keep my hand clenched tightly to my chest, it'll go away.' "

Now Carly Powers was in her ear, saying, "Leigh Anne, you got to talk to him because he's being completely irrational." Carly handed his cell phone to Mike.

"Michael, you have to let them take care of you," she said.

"But it really hurts," he said.

"Michael, you're being a baby! You're acting like Sean Junior!" Sean Junior was nine.

"They trying to stick me with a needle!"

"It's better than getting your *hand cut off* when *gangrene* sets in."

He didn't say anything to that.

"Michael," she said, "people lose *limbs* because of things like this. You want to lose your arm?"

No, he didn't want to lose his arm.

"Okay," she said. "And please don't make it hard on Coach Powers because he's just trying to help. And if I have to drive down there, it's going to be *bad news*."

"All right."

Powers came on and asked Leigh Anne if she thought Big Mike had medical insurance, and Leigh Anne said there was no chance he had medical insurance or any other kind, and he should just put Sean's name on all the forms.

To food, clothing, and tuition add medical care. It was an odd situation. A boy without a nickel in his pocket, no private mode of transportation, no change of clothes, no history of medical care, had stumbled into one of the more expensive private schools in Memphis. Lunch materialized, courtesy of Sean Tuohy, though Michael never asked, and so never learned, where it had come from. Clothes materialized, courtesy of Leigh Anne. He still exhibited an odd tendency to show up at school in the same clothes every day, but now they were different clothes: long pants and the brown and yellow Rugby shirt Leigh Anne had bought for him. That shirt became so worn that Leigh Anne, the fiftieth time she saw him in it, threatened to rip it off his back. She noticed all the details. One of these was that the Rugby shirt was fitting him more snugly. "I'm not sure he's stopped growing," she told Sean.

Michael's biggest need—a place to sleep at night—wasn't, at first, an issue. He spent most nights on Big Tony's floor. But because Big Tony lived such a long way from school, Michael had bivouacked some nights here and there in East Memphis, several of them on the Tuohys' sofa. There were also nights when he took the express bus back to the poorest neighborhoods on the west side of town. There he stayed, Leigh Anne assumed, with his mother.

Transportation was the big issue: Michael had no money and no reliable way to get around. He was totally dependent on whoever might give him a lift, and he had no idea, when he arrived at school in the morning, where he might spend the night. He sort of shopped around every day for the best deal he could find. If he had no place else to stay, he went home with Big Tony. But then his safety net vanished, suddenly. It happened the night the team returned from Myrtle Beach.

The Briarcrest basketball team had flown to Myrtle Beach, South Carolina, in the winter of 2003 to play two games. It had been Michael's first trip on an airplane, and also his first trip outside of Memphis. The first game had been traumatic, and both he and his coach, John Harrington, came to think of it as the moment Michael began to accept who he was, and fit himself into the team. The back end of his sophomore year and the front end of his junior year he had been an obviously physically gifted but disappointing basketball player. "He had no concept of his role," said Harrington. "Basketball's all about players accepting their roles. You want to know why the Lithuanians beat the Americans? It's because the Lithuanians know and accept their roles." Michael, now six five and a half and 350 pounds, was built to control the area under a high school basket. (To put his width into perspective, Shaquille O'Neal, the Miami Heat center who is seven one and seemingly wide as a truck, weighs 330 pounds.) But he insisted to everyone that he was a shooting guard, and if they put him at center, he stepped out, dribbled around, shot threes, and generally pissed off his coach, as well as the parents of his teammates. Plus, he didn't play defense. "He was a liability on the defensive end," said Harrington. "That's why he didn't play but about half of most games."

That changed at Myrtle Beach. At Myrtle Beach, something happened. "At Myrtle Beach," said Harrington, "Big Mike got angry." The minute he walked onto the court for their first game, the crowd was on him. They called him names. *Black Bear. Nigger.* They called him names that neither he nor his coach cared to repeat. Harrington wasn't shocked by more subtle forms of racism away from the basketball court, but it had been a long time since he'd seen the overt version on it. "I don't think there's a white coach with a black kid on his team, or a black coach with a white kid, who could have any racism in him," he said. Big Mike responded badly; Harrington hadn't seen this side of him. He began to throw elbows. Then he stopped on the court, turned on the fans, and gave them the finger.

One of the handicaps of coaching at an evangelical Christian school is that a technical foul isn't regarded by your own fans as a rallying cry but a spiritual transgression: you really didn't want Briarcrest people to think that you didn't have your passions well under control. "At Myrtle Beach," said Harrington, "that was the closest I've ever come in my career to a technical foul." He yelled at the refs for a bit and then called them, and the opposing coach, over. Pointing to the fans causing the trouble, he said, "You can take care of this problem or Big Mike can take care of this problem. And I think it'll be a lot better for them and for you if you take care of it. Because he's gonna clean house." Big Mike overheard this exchange and apparently liked the sound of it. He stayed in the paint for the rest of the game, grabbed 15 rebounds and scored 27 points, and helped his team thrash a team to whom they'd been expected to lose. "I think he realized then that this kind of thing didn't just happen in Memphis," said Harrington. "It happened everywhere. And we were on his side."

Then they flew home. It was when they landed at the Memphis airport that Big Mike's chronic housing problem became a crisis. The other players all had parents to meet them. Big Tony's girlfriend had come to pick up Steven—who was also on the team—but Mike refused to get in her car. "I'm not spending another night in that lady's house," he told his basketball coach. Pressed, he explained that he had overheard her talking about him on the telephone and that she had said many rude things: that he was a free-loader, that she didn't like him in their house, that he was stupid, that he was never going to amount to anything. When the players had all gone home, Michael Oher and his basketball coach were left together in the Memphis airport. Harrington asked Big Mike where he wanted to go, and Big Mike gave him an address, and Harrington drove his emerging star into the worst neighborhood in Memphis. "Every hundred yards he said, 'You can just let me off here, Coach. You can just let me off here.' It was the middle of the night and I said, 'Mike, I'm driving you to your front door.' "

After he had let Big Mike off in front of a dark and seemingly empty building, Harrington telephoned his volunteer assistant coach, Sean Tuohy. He told him the problem. "And Sean said, 'Maybe it's time I looked into this.' "

The next few months there was a lot to look into. Michael stayed nights in East Memphis with at least five different Briarcrest families: the Franklins, the Freezes, the Saunders, the Sparkses, the Tuohys. He somehow persuaded another black kid on the Briarcrest basketball team, Quinterio Franklin, to let him use his house as a kind of base camp. One night after a track meet, Michael was left without a ride home and Leigh Anne offered to take him wherever he wanted to go. "Terio's," he said, and off they went . . . thirty miles into Mississippi. "It was a *trailer*," she said. From the outside she couldn't believe there was room enough inside the place for him. She insisted on following him in, to see where he slept. There she found an old air mattress on the floor, flat as a leaf. "I blow it up every night," he said. "But it runs out of air around midnight."

"That's it," she said. "Get all your crap. You're moving in with me."

Crossing a new line, Michael picked up a single Glad trash bag and followed her back into the car. Right up until that moment Leigh Anne had hoped that what they and other Briarcrest families had done for Michael added up to something like a decent life. Now that she knew it didn't, she took over the management of that life. Completely. "The first thing we did," she said, "was have a cleansing of the clothes."

Together they drove to every house in Memphis where Michael had stashed his clothing. *Seven* houses and four giant trash bags later she was staring at "this pile of crap. It was stuff people had given him. Most of it still had the tags on it. Stuff he would never wear. I mean there were polo shirts with little penguins on them." For the next couple of weeks Michael slept on the Tuohys' sofa, and no one in the family stated the obvious: this was Michael Oher's new home, and probably would be for a long time. He was, in effect, a third child. "When I first saw him, I was like, 'Who the heck is this big black guy?' " said Sean Junior, aged nine at the time. "But Dad just said this was a kid we were trying to help out and so I just said all right." Sean Junior had his own uses for Michael: the two would vanish for hours on end into his bedroom and play video games. Just a few months after his arrival, Leigh Anne would point to Michael and say, "That is Sean Junior's best friend." "He got comfortable quickly," said Collins Tuohy, then sixteen. "When he kept staying and staying, Mom asked him if he wanted to move in. He said, 'I don't think I want to leave.' That's when Mom went out and bought the dresser and the bed."

After she organized his clothing, Leigh Anne stewed on where to put this huge human being. The sofa clearly would not do—"it was *ruining* my ten-thousand-dollar couch"—but she was worried that no ordinary bed would hold him, or, if it did, it might collapse in the middle of the night and he and it would come hurtling through the ceiling. Sean had mentioned that he recalled some of the larger football players at Ole Miss sleeping on futons. That day Leigh Anne went out and bought a futon and a dresser. The day the futon arrived, she showed it to Michael and said, "That's your bed." And he said, "That's *my* bed?" And she said, "That's your bed." And he just stared at it a bit and said, "This is the first time I ever had my own bed."

That was late February 2004. Leigh Anne sat Michael down and established some rules. She didn't care if she ever saw his mother, and didn't need to know her problems, but he would be required to visit her. "I'm not going to have you say that I took you away from your mother. I don't care if you don't want to go, you're going." She didn't know who his friends were from back on the west side of Memphis but they were welcome in the house and he should bring them home. Didn't he have anyone he grew up with who he might like to bring over? He didn't offer up any names. "Anything you wanted to know you had to pry out of him," she said. And so she pried. "He finally mentioned someone named Craig but this Craig never materialized."

Sean, for his part, had long since given up interest in probing into

Michael's past, or anything else. The boy had a gift for telling people as little as possible, and also for telling them what they wanted to hear. "The right answer for Michael is the answer that puts an end to the questions," said Sean. He finally decided that Michael had not "the slightest interest in the future or the past. He's just trying to forget about yesterday and get to tomorrow. He's in survival mode: completely focused on the next two minutes." He persuaded his wife to take a more detached view of the question, who is Michael Oher? and Leigh Anne agreed, at least in principle. "What does it matter if he doesn't know the names of his brothers and sisters," she said, unconvincingly. "Or where he went to school. Or if he went to school."

They decided to move forward with Michael on a need-to-know basis: if they needed to know some detail about his past, she harassed Michael until he gave her an answer. If they didn't—and mostly they didn't—she'd leave him alone. "It is what it is," she said. "The past is the past." In her big talk with Michael she told him, "We're just going to go forward. There is nothing I can do about whatever might have happened to you before now. If it's going to cause you problems, and you're not going to be able to go forward without dealing with it, maybe we need to get help from someone smarter than I am."

He just looked at her and asked, "What does that mean?"

She tried to explain about psychiatrists, but it was obvious he didn't know what therapy meant. So she said to herself: *Oh, what the hell. There's no way he's ever going to lie on some couch and talk about himself.*

And, she half thought, his past actually didn't matter all that much to him. "Like the way a woman blocks out childbirth," she said, "I think he just blocked out a lot of his childhood."

Sean had a different take: Michael's mind was finely calibrated to get from one day to the next. Whatever had happened to him in the past he couldn't afford to dwell on it. He couldn't afford to be angry, or bitter. "Michael's gift," Sean said, "is that the Good Lord gave him the ability to forget. He's mad at no one and doesn't really care what happened. His story might be sad, but *he's* not sad."

But even if they had decided not to interrogate him, there was nothing that said she couldn't *notice* the little tics and quirks about him. Information took many forms and both Leigh Anne and Sean had a talent for acquiring it. When they stopped in at the Taco Bell just around the corner, for instance, Michael would order more food than he wanted. The next morning Sean would open the refrigerator and find the coagulated, extra Mexican pizza. "He was in the habit of guaranteeing himself an extra meal," said Sean. "I had to explain that he didn't need to do that. That he could get it whenever he wanted it. He said, 'Really?' I said, 'Michael, I *own* the restaurant. You can go over there any time you want and eat for free.'" But the habit was hard to break. Sean would see him come into the house, extra free Mexican pizza in hand, and "it was like he would catch himself. He'd come in with the extra pizza and see me and go, 'Oh, man, I forgot.'" Collins noticed, "He hoarded *everything*: food, clothes, money. He'd get stuff and he'd hide it away." It was as if he didn't actually believe that this free stuff would remain free.

There were tiny revelations that had Leigh Anne upset for days, for what they implied about his childhood. She took Michael with her and Sean Junior to a Barnes & Noble. As they walked through the store, Sean Junior spotted *Where the Wild Things Are* and said, "Look, Mom, you used to read that to me when I was little." To which Michael replied, in the most detached tone, "I've never had anyone read me a book."

There were also things about him that caused Leigh Anne and Sean to think of him as an even deeper mystery. He refused to wear clothes that, in his opinion, didn't match. He refused to wear clothes that had even a spot on them. He *ironed* his T-shirt; and if he wore the same T-shirt every day, he ironed it every morning. "That ain't a socioeconomic issue," said Sean. "That's a where-the-hell-did-that-come-from? issue." Sean had him out one day, buying basketball sneakers for himself. He asked Michael if he'd like a pair and Michael said, sniffily, he didn't like the colors on display. "I said, 'Michael you have *none*. How can you turn down shoes when you don't have shoes?' And he said, 'Well, I don't want those unless they have it with the blue stripe.' 'For someone who has no shoes you're pretty damn picky about what shoes you get.'" When they finally found the sneaker shoe color that Michael liked, they had another argument about his shoe size. Michael refused to wear the size 15 shoes that the salesman proved he needed. He insisted that he wore a size 14, and so it was size 14 shoes Sean bought for him, even though it meant a bit of pain when he walked.

Around the house he was a neat freak. Leigh Anne ran a tight ship and within weeks it was clear that Michael was the only member of the crew who passed muster. "You might drop your underwear on the floor," said Sean, "but one minute later they'd be gone. They might have wound up in the silverware drawer but they were not on the floor." Michael's were the only underwear never dropped. Collins, who was the same age as Michael, had never made her bed in her life and, no matter how often her mother hollered at her, never would. Michael not only made his bed, he removed the sheets from the futon, folded them, and returned the thing to its couchlike state. Every day, without exception. "It was like God made a child just for us," said Sean. "Sports for me, neat for Leigh Anne."

From the moment Michael moved in with them, Sean began to stew on his future. ("Because I figured I was going to have to pay for it.") Michael was approaching the end of his junior year in high school, and while they hadn't seen his transcripts, they knew his grades were poor. Since Myrtle Beach he'd been good enough on the basketball team that Sean thought he might be able to play at a small college. "And I figured if he wasn't, I could *make* him good enough," said Sean. At six five he wasn't tall enough to be a post player in major college basketball but he might make it in Division II. Sean had contacts in college basketball all over the South. He began to write letters on Michael's behalf to coaches at small schools—Murray State, Austin Peay. He had Leigh Anne go out and sign up Michael for every summer basketball camp she could find.

Then Hugh Freeze called Michael and said that this guy who wrote scouting reports on high school football players was coming through town and had agreed, on Hugh's recommendation, to see him. Accustomed to just doing what he was told around Briarcrest, Michael jumped in the passenger seat of a teammate's car and allowed himself to be driven to the University of Memphis. He sat through fifteen long minutes of this strange little guy's questions without the faintest interest in the encounter. "I just wanted him to stop talking so I could leave," he said later. Under Michael's mute gaze, Tom Lemming finally stopped talking. Michael left the forms Lemming gave him, unfilled. And that, Michael thought, was that.

Only it wasn't. Lemming's private scouting report was sent to the head coach at more than one hundred Division I college football programs and so more than one hundred head college football coaches learned that this kid in Memphis, whom no one had ever heard of, was the most striking left tackle talent he'd seen since he first met Orlando Pace. And Orlando Pace was now being paid $10 million a year to play left tackle for the St. Louis Rams. It was only a week or so after Lemming's report went out that the Briarcrest Saints football team met for two weeks of spring practice. Hugh Freeze was there, of course, as he was the head coach and ran the practices. Tim Long was there, too, because he coached the offensive line. Like several of the coaches, Long was a Briarcrest parent, but was also a six five, 300-pound former left tackle at the University of Memphis, and a fifth-round draft pick of the Minnesota Vikings. At first sight, Long had been awed by Michael Oher's raw ability. "When I first saw him," he said, "I thought: this guy is going to make us all famous." But then he'd coached him in the final games of his junior year, after Michael was moved to right tackle on the offensive line, and Long wondered why he wasn't a better player. One game he had pulled Michael out and sat him on the bench because he thought the team was better off playing another guy.

The only other coach at Briarcrest Spring Practice with any experience of college or pro sports was Sean Tuohy. Hugh Freeze had asked Sean to help out as an assistant coach—which meant his usual role as coach to the coach and unofficial Life Counselor to the players. When Sean told Leigh Anne he planned to coach football, she had laughed at the idea of it: her husband didn't know a first down from a free throw. And it was true: the first thing Sean learned about coaching football was that you shouldn't do it in a BMW. He came home the first day and told Leigh Anne, "I need to buy a pickup truck; I'm the only one without a pickup truck." A few days later he bought one.

That first afternoon of spring practice, Sean rolled up in his new truck to find the players lined up and stretching. The other coaches were there already. But there was this other, highly unusual cluster of identically dressed men: college football coaches who had turned up to watch practice. They stood to one side, but you could tell them by their identical dark slacks and coaching shirts with their school's emblem emblazoned on the chest: University of Michigan, Clemson University, University of Southern Mississippi, University of Tennessee, Florida State University. They weren't head coaches, just assistants. But still. College coaches of any sort weren't in the habit of coming to watch Briarcrest players. The Briarcrest football field was in the middle of nowhere and Michigan was in the middle of another nowhere. The Clemson guy mentioned to one of the Briarcrest coaches that he had driven eight hours just to be there. Few of the players had any idea, at first, why they were there. The coaches knew why, because Hugh Freeze had just told them, but they were still as surprised as the players. Carly Powers, the athletic director, said, "Big Mike hadn't been very good. You could tell he hadn't played before. The only thing he had going for him was his size." Tim Long said, "I don't know why they were there. I guess his size just got him noticed."

The most complicated set of social rules on the planet—the rules that govern the interaction of college football coaches and high school prospects—forbade the coaches from speaking directly to a high school junior until August before his senior year. They were allowed to visit his school twice, and watch him from a distance. So the coaches made a point of not saying anything directly; they just sat off to the side and stared. "I'll never forget it," said Tim Long. "We did calisthenics and agility. Then board drill, right away. We're ten minutes into it. Michael's first up."

The board drill—so named for the thin ten-foot-long board laid on the ground before it begins—is among the most violent drills in football. The offensive lineman takes his stance in the middle of the board and faces the defensive lineman. At the sound of the whistle, they do whatever they must to drive the other fellow off the end of the board. Facing off against Michael Oher during a football game was one thing: he was often unsure where to go, you more than likely had help from teammates, and, if you didn't, there was plenty of room to run and hide. Getting onto the board across from him, for a fight to the death, was something else. No one on the team wanted to do it.

At length, out stepped the team's biggest and most powerful defensive lineman, Joseph Crone. He was six two, maybe 270 pounds, and a candidate to attend college on a football scholarship. To him this new mission, going hat-on-hat with Big Mike, had the flavor of heroism. "The reason I stepped up," said Crone, "is that I didn't think anyone else wanted to go up against him. Because he was such a big guy."

Crone still didn't think of Michael Oher as an exceptional football player. But if he hadn't been a force on the field, Crone thought, it was only because he had no idea what he was supposed to do there. And Crone noticed that he had improved the past season and, by the final game, looked very good indeed. "He was figuring it out," said Crone. "How to move his feet, where to put his hands. How to get onto people so they couldn't get away." But even if Big Mike had no idea what he was doing on a football field, Crone found him an awesome physical specimen. He had a picture in his mind of the few opposing players who had made the mistake of being fallen upon by Big Mike. "They looked like pressed pennies," he said. "They'd get up and their backs would be one giant grass stain. I couldn't imagine being on the other side of the ball going against Mike." Now, by default, he was.

The two players dropped into their stances, with the eyes of the SEC, the Big Ten, Conference USA, and the ACC upon them. Joseph Crone's mind was working overtime: "I'm sitting there thinking, *Man, this guy is* HUGE. *I got to get low on him. I got to drive my feet.*"

"Best on best!" shouted Hugh Freeze, and blew his whistle.

When it was over—and it was over in a flash—the five coaches broke formation and made what appeared to be urgent private phone calls. Briarcrest athletic director Carly Powers turned to his left and found that one of the coaches, in his bid to separate himself from the others, had wandered up beside him. "He was whispering into his phone, '*My God, you've got to see this!*'" said Powers. The Clemson coach, Brad Scott (he was the former head football coach at the University of South Carolina), actually ran out onto the field, handed his card to Hugh Freeze, and said, "I seen all I need to see." If Michael Oher wanted a full scholarship to Clemson, it was his. "Then," says Tim Long, "the Clemson guy got in his car and drove eight or nine hours back home."

Hugh Freeze was as impressed, and surprised, as anyone: it could have been a training film. Big Mike had picked up 270 pounds and dealt with them as he might have dealt with thin air. "Joseph was a *man*. And Michael treated him like he was a hundred-pound weakling. And Joseph fought him! Those first two steps—they were as quick as any running back's. And when that body hits you, it's just an amazing force. And once he's on you, you can't get off of him. He kept his ol' back flat and just rose up as he took Joseph down the field."

Sean, who had been standing off to one side, walked over to Joseph and patted him on the helmet: he felt sorry for the kid. ("He just smashed me," said Crone. "I was like, 'God, that wasn't a fun experience.'") Sean knew one of the assistant coaches, Rip Scherer of Southern Miss—he'd once been the head football coach at the University of Memphis. Southern Miss was the poor cousin in this gathering of representatives from elite college football teams. Scherer, looking a little low, now walked over to Sean and said, "Well, we're obviously not going to be able to sign him. Who else you got?" In a single play Michael Oher had established himself as too rich for the blood of Southern Miss. "It was strange that day," said Tim Long. "His moment came and he was on. It was like he'd always been that good."

After that, the coaches came in platoons. Arkansas, Notre Dame, Ole Miss, Miami, Nebraska, Oklahoma State, Ohio State, and on and on. First, they were merely assistant coaches, but the assistant coaches would get on their cell phones—"no, you have to come see this"—and the top brass would dutifully materialize. "It got so I couldn't wait to get to practice to see who was there that day," said Tim Long. "You get there late and someone would say, 'Oops, you just missed Bob Stoopes.'" (Stoopes is the head football coach of the University of Oklahoma.) One afternoon the Briarcrest players and coaches looked up and saw the strange sight of Tennessee's most famous coach, Phil Fulmer, from the University of Tennessee, not walking but *run-*

ning to their practice. If ever there was a body not designed to move at speed it was Fulmer's. "I'd seen Phil Fulmer on TV," said Joseph Crone, who knew the moment he saw Fulmer that he was in for yet another unpleasant board drill. "But I'd never seen him in person." Fulmer had been in Memphis for a speech, and was meant to be on a plane back to Knoxville. Before he'd boarded, his recruiter had called and told him about this once-in-a-lifetime sight, and Fulmer decided he'd rather miss his flight. Then he drove the twenty miles out to the Briarcrest field—and parked in the wrong lot. "It's a hundred and fifty degrees," recalls Tim Long. "And there's Phil Fulmer racing across the parking lot. He's running down this dirt road. He gets there huffing and puffing, and says, 'I was told I need to see this for myself.'"

Fulmer watched Michael Oher for half an hour and then turned to Long and said, "He's the best in the nation." Which is what *USA Today* was about to say—thanks largely to Tom Lemming. In the middle of spring practice, Michael Oher became a pre-season First Team High School All-American. From that moment on, Hugh Freeze had to give up pretty much everything he was doing, and retire to his office to deal with the long line of college football coaches who wanted to spend quality time at the Briarcrest Christian School. "I feel there wasn't a coach in the country who did not call or come in person," he said. "Washington, Oregon, Oregon State. I mean, these people were calling from everywhere and asking, 'Coach, do we have a shot?' All spring practice I had one college head coach in my office, and another waiting outside." When the coaches weren't at practice, they were stalking the hallways of Briarcrest. "The best way I can describe it," said Joseph Crone, "is it was like a group of vultures trying to get their prey."

They were predatory by nature but they often came just to say they had seen *it*, in the spirit of tourists making their first trip to the Grand Canyon. The people at Briarcrest had trouble thinking of themselves as an athletic tourist attraction, and they had their own curiosities. Carly Powers asked one of the coaches: "What makes Michael so good?" And his answer was: "He's a freak of nature." Steve Simpson had one of the coaches in his office and took the occasion to ask, "What has you all so excited?" "He said you just don't see kids who are that big and that athletic." Two of the SEC head coaches told Tim Long that Michael Oher was the best offensive lineman they had ever seen. All but one of them would take away only memories, but even these, to some, were worth the trip. "The first time I saw Mike," said Stacey Searles, who coached the offensive line at LSU, "he was in a three-on-three Oklahoma Drill. He was just dominating people. I'd seen him from a distance and thought, 'Wow, that's a good-looking kid.' He has as much strength and size and agility and power as any lineman I'd ever seen. Then I got closer and said, *Oh my*. He was a freak of nature—for somebody to be that big, that powerful, that fast, and that talented. Every two or three years there is a kid who jumps out at you, and he was that kid."

Tim Long, who had been a star in high school, and in college, and had played in the NFL, had never seen anything like it. Sean Tuohy, who had been the most highly recruited basketball player in the state of Louisiana his senior year in high school, had never seen anything like it. Sean was mystified: "I was under the impression Michael sucked at football," he said. "I was trying to get him a basketball scholarship." Now he'd nip into Briarcrest for one reason or another and couldn't get to where he was going without hitting some big-time college football recruiter. One day he walks into Hugh Freeze's office just in time to hear Hugh tell the coach from the University of Missouri, "I don't want to be this way, but you got no shot at him. You're wasting your time here." Another time he'd squeezed a few minutes out of Hugh's schedule to meet to discuss some personal business—probably how to cover the tuition of one of the black players—when the football recruiter from the University of Florida barged in.

"I want to see Oher," he said. He pronounced it like the airport. "O-Hair."

"It's not O-Hair," said Sean. "It's Oher. Like a boat oar. "

As it was against the rules for the recruiters to speak to Michael before the start of his senior year, the Florida guy was literally there just to see Michael. Hugh told the Florida guy that Michael was in class, but he could go down and see him when class let out. Just before the bell rang, the three men—Hugh, Sean, the Florida guy—set out down the hallways in the direction of the classroom. The Florida guy was scrolling through the messages on his BlackBerry when the bell rang, and the door opened in front of him—

and so he didn't see Michael until he was right on top of him. When he looked up, Michael was two feet away: a wall of a human being. The Florida guy actually gave this little jump and a horror-movie gasp: *Uuuuuu!*

He'd seen Michael Oher. "That's when he started dialing," said Sean. "He was dialing so fast." Like the others, he knew he couldn't say a word to Michael; but he had *seen* him. With Michael just looking on, patiently, the Florida guy turned to Hugh Freeze and said, "You tell Michael Oher that the University of Florida is very interested in offering him a football scholarship." Then he walked away but not so far that Sean couldn't hear him, as he hissed into his cell phone: "Coach, you have got to come see this guy. No, you have to come see this guy." Reduced by NCAA regulations to a single sense, the coaches fetishized that sense. "Once you saw him on the hoof," said Kurt Roper, who led the Ole Miss recruiting effort at first, "you said . . . '*Wow!* This guy passes the look test. This guy looks like a big-time SEC lineman. And he's a *junior in high school.*' " Ole Miss had just sent a pair of offensive linemen to the NFL: Chris Spencer, a first-round draft pick of the Seattle Seahawks, and Marcus Johnson, a second-round pick of the Minnesota Vikings. And yet Roper had never seen a lineman of Michael Oher's caliber. "He was *by far* the best guy I'd ever seen," he said.

The frenzy over the player who would become the most highly sought after offensive lineman in the nation had begun, and it had only just begun. And no one had a very clear idea of who he was, where he came from, who his parents were—or even, truth be told, if he was a very good football player. Within two weeks Michael was both as famous and as unknown as a high school football player can be. There wasn't an offensive line coach in the country who wasn't aware of him, and a lot of the head coaches of the bigger football schools had seen him in the flesh. And yet the most basic details of his life were a mystery. One day in spring practice he made this point, inadvertently. He finished yet another board drill, flattened poor Joseph Crone yet again, and went down on one knee, and just stayed there. He was usually the first up and around, jumping on the balls of his feet, like a man half his size. Sean walked over to him.

"You doin' all right?" he asked.

"Pops," said Michael, "my dad died."

Before practice Big Tony had called the Briarcrest office to say that he'd just learned Michael's daddy had been murdered—thrown off an overpass on the west side of Memphis. *Three months ago*. It had been on the evening news—"Man Thrown Off Bridge"—but the man hadn't been identified. When he finally was, no one knew or cared how it happened. "I didn't even know he had a dad," said Sean. "I thought: *I'm sure Leigh Anne knows all this*." It followed from this that Leigh Anne would deal with whatever it meant inside of Michael Oher, as she was the only one who was allowed inside.

"How do you feel about that?" asked Sean. "Want to take practice off?"

"No."

"When did it happen?"

"Three months ago. But they just told me."

Sean thought that was strange. So did Michael.

"Why do you think they didn't want me to know?" he asked.

And that was all he said about it. He just took it inside him and filed it away in whatever place he kept for such data. Briarcrest had all these people—tutors, teachers, coaches—who thought of themselves as intimately involved with Big Mike's progress, and they were. The teachers who worked there thought that one of the ways a Christian school was superior to a public school was the depth of the spiritual connection between the teachers and the pupils. "It's hard to bond over calculus," said Dr. Pat Williams, a teacher who had been at Briarcrest since its founding. "But it's not hard to bond over 'Will you pray for my family?'" And yet Big Mike didn't think the fact that his father had been killed—or anything else about himself—worth mentioning to anyone but Sean.

He stayed on one knee a long time. Sean went over to Hugh and told him to keep Michael out of action for a spell. Sean called Leigh Anne—the Center for Emotional Involvement. When Michael walked in the door that evening, Leigh Anne took him aside and told him how sorry she was to hear about his dad. "And I hope this doesn't sound callous and cold to you," she said. "But you didn't know the man." Michael acknowledged that was true. Leigh Anne said, "You know, this might be better, because one way or another you are going to have money, and you know that he would have found you and made claims upon you."

That Michael's fortune might come to him from the game of football, rather than the last will and testament of Sean Tuohy, was suddenly thinkable. The first person, credible to Sean, to hint that Michael Oher might have a real future in football was Nick Saban, the head coach at LSU, fresh off a national championship. Michael was on the Briarcrest basketball court, playing a pickup game, when Saban walked into the school. Saban of course couldn't speak to the boy, but he didn't need to. He'd seen his tape. Now Saban watched him as he moved around on the basketball court. When Michael dribbled the ball between his legs, drove to the basket and rose up and dunked, Saban balked. There was no way, he said, that Michael Oher weighed more than 285 pounds. He demanded to see the boy on a scale. That was easy: Briarcrest had bought a new scale, just for him. When Saban saw that Michael tipped the scale at 345 pounds, he said, "If he isn't a top fifteen pick in the NFL draft three years from now, someone done him wrong."

In the frenzy, Hugh Freeze learned exactly what he had on his hands. Not just a big ol' lineman. Not some cement block, interchangeable with other cement blocks of similar dimensions. A future NFL left tackle. "All of those college coaches," said Hugh, "and I mean every last one of them, said, 'He'll play on Sundays. At left tackle.'"

That is what had them all so excited: Michael Oher fit as perfectly as any high school player they had ever seen the job description of NFL left tackle. And left tackle, as guardian of the quarterback's blind side, had become one of the most highly compensated jobs in the game. Hugh had played Michael on defense at first, and then, when that didn't work, moved him to right tackle. And so Michael Oher had never actually played left tackle. That was understandable: the left tackle wasn't a big deal in high school because the passing game, and thus the pass rush, weren't quite so important. Hugh now understood that in big-time college football, and in the NFL, the left tackle was some kind of huge deal. You find the freak of nature who can play the position brilliantly and you have one of the most valuable commodities in professional sports.

After spring practice Hugh informed the boy who had been playing left tackle that he was being moved to right tackle. Michael Oher was taking over his position.

CHAPTER FIVE

DEATH OF A LINEMAN

A BOY HAD COLLIDED WITH AN EVENT. THE BOY WAS IN MANY WAYS unlikely. He had never thought of himself as a football player, and didn't have the first idea what the fuss was all about. The event was a shift in football strategy that raised, dramatically, the value of the one role on the football field the boy was uniquely suited to play. Of course, any kid in America in 2004 thought to have a shot at a professional football career was going to get his share of attention. But if Michael Oher had been just any ordinary offensive lineman he wouldn't have been viewed as a future NFL player. It was the existence of the new prototype—or, more accurately, the stereotype—of the NFL left tackle that made him so interesting to football coaches. They took one look at him and knew exactly what he was born to do. The market for football players had reshaped the offensive line and, in effect, broken out this one position and treated it as almost a separate occupation: What caused *that*?

The answer lay buried in the history of football strategy. Football history, like personal history, is cleaner and more orderly in retrospect than it is at the time. It tends not to have crisp beginnings and endings. It progresses an accident at a time. As the left tackle position evolved, it experienced as many false starts and dead ends and random mutations and unnatural selections as the other little evolutions deep inside football. But the Oakland Coliseum, on December 28, 1975, was, in retrospect, a seminal moment.

The playoff game is in its final minutes, and the Cincinnati Bengals trail the Oakland Raiders 31–28. The Bengals have the ball on the Raiders' thirty-seven-yard line and are driving furiously. High up in the Coliseum, in the Bengals' wing of the press box, an assistant coach named Bill Walsh selects the next play. Walsh knows that whatever play he calls, he won't be able to change it. There won't be time. The Bengals' head coach, the legendary Paul Brown, wants to be seen to call the plays and has created a time-consuming "process" to preserve the illusion. Invisible and unacknowledged, Walsh relays the play over the phone to a fellow assistant coach on the sidelines, Bill Johnson. Johnson whispers the play to Brown. And then Brown, all eyes in the crowd on him, pulls aside a player, barks out his instructions, and pushes him out onto the field to tell the quarterback. Bill Walsh runs the Cincinnati offense; Paul Brown seems to. It doesn't bother Walsh, much. The press box offers what he calls "the clinical atmosphere" in which he thrives. Looking down from the press box one can more easily see what goes right, and what goes wrong. And he is about to see his play go very wrong.

It begins promisingly enough. Wide receiver Charley Joiner cuts across the middle and breaks free. Bengals quarterback Kenny Anderson is the league's most accurate passer and seldom misses an open target. Then a familiar shadow rises behind him. Oakland has a blind side pass rusher, named Ted Hendricks and known as "the Mad Stork." All day long Walsh has fretted about what might happen if the Bengals need to pass, and the Mad Stork knows they need to pass; all day long he's worried about just this moment. "We tried to have a running back pick Hendricks up," he says. "And he did. Most of the time." Now Joiner's open, and Kenny Anderson is about to release the ball when out of nowhere—*Bam!* The Mad Stork buries him. And just like that it's over. The moment the Mad Stork slips the running back's block, the Bengals' season is as good as done.

"I made up my mind right then," said Walsh, "there had to be a better way. And if I was ever in that situation again, I'd handle the blind side rush differently."

It took six years before he found himself in that situation again—calling plays in a playoff game that must account for a great blind side pass rusher. But when he did, the situation was far more alarming.

Now it's January 3, 1981. Walsh drives with a friend to Candlestick Park, before his first and possibly last playoff game as an NFL head coach. His team, the San Francisco 49ers, is about to face the New York Giants, with a newly energized defense coached by Bill Parcells. The Giants' rookie linebacker Lawrence Taylor presents the greatest systematic threat Walsh's offense has ever faced; how Walsh copes with it will inform the future of football strategy. Walsh's coaching career is still something of an iffy proposition—six months earlier Walsh decided to quit football altogether, then reversed himself. He's still in an odd place, professionally: the most innovative offensive mind of his generation and nobody understands what he's thought up. Lose this game and they might never know.

The week before, the Giants had won their first playoff game against the favored Philadelphia Eagles. The Eagles' head coach, Dick Vermeil, was a good friend of Walsh's. "I talked to Dick before their game," said Walsh, "and asked him how he was going to handle Lawrence Taylor. He said, 'Stan can take him. Stan can get out there.' " (Stan was the Eagles' left tackle, Stan Walters.) "Well, Stan didn't get out there." And Stan Walters was no chump. He'd been to the Pro Bowl twice and the year before, 1980, had not allowed a single quarterback sack. Taylor ate him alive, and seemed to take special pleasure in the havoc he created inside the mind of Eagles quarterback Ron Jaworski. In describing his signature hammer blow, Taylor said, "I hit Jaworski that way—with an over-the-head ax job. I thought his dick was going to drop in the dirt." Watching tape of Taylor, Walsh worked overtime to answer the question: how to keep this beast off the back of his new young quarterback? It wasn't Joe Montana's body parts that Walsh was worried about. It was his ability to run this intricate little passing game, Walsh's greatest creation.

Walsh took an unusual view of quarterbacks: he thought they were only as good as the system they played in. After they'd led their team to victory, people pointed to their air of confidence, their cool under pressure, and the other intangible virtues of the presumably born leader. If they led their teams to Super Bowls, these prima donnas became all but irreplaceable, in the public mind. The intangibles were nice, thought Walsh, but they weren't the reason quarterbacks succeeded or failed. "The performance of a quarterback must be manipulated," said Walsh. "To a degree coaching can make a quarterback, and it certainly is the most important factor for his success. The design of the team's offense is the key to a quarterback's performance. One has to be tuned to the other." His offense would make heroes of his quarterbacks. But that didn't mean he had to believe in them personally.

Walsh's career to that point had been as quixotic as his view of the football offense. He'd played minor college ball, at San Jose State. As a coach he had bounced back and forth between college and the pros without sticking in either place. One year he was an assistant with the Oakland Raiders, the next he was the head coach of something called the San Jose Apaches in a chaotic semi-pro league soon to implode. When he arrived in Cincinnati in 1968, at the age of thirty-seven, to run the passing game for Bengals head coach Paul Brown, he faced a new problem: comically inadequate football players. "We were an AFL expansion team," said Walsh, "and you just didn't get any quality players. We got the dregs, players who never should have been in pro football." The newfound Bengals clearly weren't going to frighten or push anyone off the line of scrimmage. If they were going to move the ball, they were going to need to pass the ball.

But the Bengals' small players were all, by NFL standards, as defective as the big ones. His new quarterback, Virgil Carter, was a case in point. Carter wasn't able to get the ball more than about 20 yards downfield in any form other than a slow desperate wobble. Walsh's job, as he saw it, was to create a system that suited Virgil Carter's talents: guile, nimbleness, and an ability to throw accurately, as long as he didn't have to throw far. "We couldn't dominate anyone with the run, so Virgil became our central performer," he said later. "And so that's how it all started. When I was forced to use Virgil."

Walsh's solution to Carter's weak arm was to teach him to use the field in a new way. He spread the field horizontally; that is, from sideline to sideline. He had the receivers run short routes timed precisely to the steps of the quarterback. If Carter took a three-step drop, they ran one sort of route; if Carter took a five-step drop, they ran another. Carter didn't wait for his receivers to come open but threw to where he expected them to be—usually just a few yards away. The process was further speeded up by reducing the number of decisions the quarterback was forced to make. His presumed precision means that he doesn't need to pay nearly so much attention to the defensive formation. His short, timed passes, if executed properly, can be completed against any defense. On any given play there might be as many as five Bengals receivers running pass patterns. But when Virgil Carter came to the line of scrimmage, he had already made up his mind to which side of the field he would throw, so he had reduced the five potential receivers to a short list of three: a primary, an alternate, and an outlet. He saw how the defense had lined up and made a pre-snap decision about the viability of his primary receiver. And so, as he dropped back to pass, he had at most one decision to make: alternate or outlet?

By its very nature the enterprise demanded tedious repetition: for ball and receiver to arrive on a patch of turf the size of a welcome mat at the same moment, their timing had to be precise, and to be precise it had to be second nature. At first Walsh had a problem finding the extraordinary amount of time he needed to practice with his quarterbacks and receivers. "Paul Brown didn't want us out on the field so long," he said, "so I'd sneak out with them during lunch." It was more like a handoff on the other side of the line of scrimmage than an aerial attack, and his players at first found it strange. "He'd show up every Monday with this high school play he'd thought up and we'd laugh at it all week," said Bengals receiver Chip Myers. "That Sunday, it'd work three times."

Walsh's father had been a talented auto mechanic and he had expected his son to join him in the family business. Walsh moved on, but something of his father lingered in him. His offense felt *engineered*. The virtues it exalted above all others were precision, consistency, and predictability. Walsh had created the contraption to compensate for the deficiencies of his quarterback, but an offense based on a lot of short, well-timed passes turned out to offer surprising inherent advantages. First, it delivered the ball into a runner's hands on the other side of the line of scrimmage, thus removing the biggest defensive beasts from the space between him and the goal line. The pass had always been viewed as a complement to the run, but it could apparently function as a substitute as well.

Next, by shortening—and timing—the passing game, Walsh reduced its two biggest risks: interceptions and incompletion. "Our argument was that the chance of a completion drops dramatically over twelve yards," said Walsh. "So, we would throw a ten-yard pass. Our formula was that we should get at least half our passing yardage from the run *after* the catch."

Finally, the Walsh plan addressed the football coach's visceral fear of an offense based on the passing game. For such an offense to be viable, lots of people need to go out for a pass. Walsh did not usually feel that five receivers was necessary, but he needed, at a minimum, three. But the more people who go out for a pass, the fewer who remain to block for the quarterback. The defense, alert to the pass, already is more than usually intent on killing the quarterback. By reducing the amount of time the quarterback held the ball, Walsh had minimized the risk that they would succeed. He had infused the passing game with two new qualities: dullness and safety. "People made fun of it," Walsh said. "They thought if you weren't throwing the ball twenty yards downfield, you weren't throwing the ball. They called it a nickel-and-dime offense."

In 1971, Virgil Carter, who had never completed as many as half of his passes, somehow led the entire league in completion percentage (62.2) and bumped his yards per attempt from 5.9 to 7.3. The Bengals surprised everyone and won their division. The next year Carter gave way to Ken Anderson, a little known passer out of even less well known Augustana College, who hadn't completed even half his passes in college. In Walsh's offense, Kenny Anderson did even better than Virgil Carter. When he saw Anderson play, Walsh later said, he realized that the offense he had designed to compensate for a weak-armed quarterback had a more general effectiveness; this passing game of his could survive on very little talent, but it could also exploit better material. In 1974, Anderson led the league in completion percentage and total yards and yards per attempt (8.13). After the Mad Stork ended the 1975 season, and Paul Brown retired, Walsh expected to take over as head coach. Brown had several times refused other NFL teams permission to interview Walsh for their head coaching jobs, without bothering to mention their interest to Walsh. Instead, Brown had told Walsh that he didn't think he'd ever make a good NFL head coach. Now Brown did his part to make his prediction come true, by arranging for another coach to replace him. "The selection of head coaches in the NFL always has been a mystery to me," said Walsh not long afterwards. "I expect to be a head coach. I want to be a head coach. He really *is* the game. Everybody else are production people in his show."

Walsh left Cincinnati in anger, to run the offense for the San Diego Chargers. There he inherited a struggling quarterback named Dan Fouts. In Walsh's passing system, Fouts went on to lead the league in completion percentage. Walsh himself quickly moved on to become a head football coach at Stanford University. He coached the Cardinal for two seasons, 1977 and 1978. In 1977, Stanford quarterback Guy Benjamin led the nation in passing and won the Sammy Baugh Award given to the nation's top college passer. In 1978, his replacement, Steve Dils, did the same. In 1979, Walsh, now forty-nine years old, finally was named an NFL head coach, of the team with the league's lowest payroll and the league's worst record, the San Francisco 49ers.

The 49ers also had, by most statistical measures, one of the NFL's worst quarterbacks, Steve Deberg. The year before Walsh arrived, Deberg, a recent tenth-round draft choice, had engineered the lowest scoring offense in the entire NFL. In leading his team to a 2–14 record, Deberg threw 302 passes and completed 137 of them, or 45.4 percent, not counting the 22 he delivered into the hands of the opposing team. The next year, in Bill Walsh's system of well-timed passes, the seemingly inept Deberg threw more passes (578) than any quarterback in the history of the NFL. His completion rate rose to an astonishing 60 percent, and he also completed more passes than any quarterback in the history of the NFL. Deberg also cut his interception rate in half and threw for more than an extra yard on each passing attempt (5.2 to 6.32). The transformation of Steve Deberg—and the 49er offense—

amounted to a football miracle. But if anyone noticed, Walsh didn't hear about it.

In a pattern now familiar in Walsh's offenses, a quarterback who seemed to deserve a raise was instead handed a pink slip. Walsh replaced Deberg in 1980 with a quarterback drafted in the third round who everyone said was too small and had too weak an arm to play in the NFL: Joe Montana. The next two years, Montana led the NFL in completion percentage (64.5 and 63.7) and also in avoiding interceptions. He would become, by general consensus, the finest quarterback ever to play the game. How good was he really? That's hard to know, because his coach held a magic wand, and every quarterback over whose head that wand passed instantly looked better than he'd ever been. When Joe Montana's play became sloppy during the 1987 season, Walsh replaced him, temporarily, with Steve Young—whose sensational performance caused a lot of 49er fans to wonder, and to feel guilty for wondering, if maybe Steve Young was even better than Joe Montana.

The performance of Walsh's quarterbacks suggested a radical thought: that in the most effective passing attack in the NFL, and on one of the most successful teams in the history of pro football, the quarterbacks were fungible. The system was the star. Walsh had imported into pro football the spirit of a Japanese auto plant—Total Quality Management. A lot of people in and around pro football were uncomfortable with the idea, and the benching of Joe Montana, for them, was the final straw. "Walsh was wanting to bench him and play his other guy," hollered former star quarterback Terry Bradshaw, doing his best to speak for the man on the street, "because if Young can go in there and do it, then Walsh looks like another genius again. You know, he really believes that genius tag. But the genius really wears number sixteen [Montana's number]. That's the genius, and he [Walsh] was messing with him."

And yet when Young eventually took over the San Francisco 49er offense for good, he led the league in passing five out of his first six years, won two Super Bowls, and wound up with his face on a bust in the Hall of Fame. Perhaps because Young had played for other NFL teams, he appreciated better than most what Walsh had brought to the passing game. "When I was at Tampa," Young told sports writer Glenn Dickey, after he took over the 49ers quarterback job, "the coaches told me to hold the ball until the receiver came open. By that time everybody was on top of me. Now I have a progression of receivers, and I hit the first one who's open. It might be only a three yard gain, and maybe I could have waited and hit a receiver another ten yards down the field, but I've completed the pass, moved the ball, and added to the frustration of defensive linemen trying to stop me."

Young, like Montana, came to be viewed as a born star whose success in pro football was inevitable. But before Young arrived there were others, and no one in their right minds mistook them for first-tier NFL quarterbacks. In 1986, for instance, Jeff Kemp, Dartmouth College graduate and son of future vice-presidential candidate Jack, stepped in for the injured Montana for ten games. Kemp was five eleven and had trouble seeing over the heads of his blockers. To clear the view, Walsh had the linemen go out after the pass rushers rather than fall back, as they typically would do. The tactic was less effective in delaying the rush but it did, momentarily, create a window through which Kemp might glimpse the field. The bill for his view arrived milliseconds after he released the football, when some monster hammered him into the ground. In his career leading up to the moment he replaced Joe Montana—a career spent entirely with the Los Angeles Rams—Kemp had completed fewer than half his passes. That year in San Francisco he completed nearly 60 percent of his passes, for an impressive 7.77 yards per attempt, and posted one of the highest passer ratings in the NFL. Then Kemp, too, was injured. His replacement was a fellow named Mike Moroski, so obscure that any question concerning his NFL career would be considered out of bounds in a game of Trivial Pursuit. Moroski had been with the 49ers for exactly two weeks before he became, by default, their starting quarterback. He completed 57.5 percent of *his* passes.

Eventually people must have noticed. As Walsh performed miracle after miracle with his quarterbacks, a more general trend emerged in NFL strategy: away from the run and toward the pass.* In 1978, NFL teams passed 42 percent of the time and ran the ball 58 percent of the time. Each year, right through until the mid-1990s, they passed more and ran less until the ratios were almost exactly reversed: in 1995, NFL teams passed 59 percent of the time and ran 41 percent of the time. It's not hard to see why; the passing game was improving, and the running game was stagnant. Every year NFL teams ran the ball thousands of times, and every year the league averaged between 3.9 and 4.1 yards per carry. With just the tiniest, seemingly random variations from year to year, the yield from this mill was monotonously consistent going all the way back to 1960. Some teams did a bit better, of course, and some did a bit worse. The league as a whole, however, never figured out how to make the running game yield even a fraction of a yard more than it always had. It was possible that the running game awaited some innovative coach to figure out how to make it work more efficiently. And it could be that the steel industry is just awaiting the CEO who can find gold in its mills.

The passing game behaved like an altogether different and more promising business. In 1960, an NFL pass netted you, on average, 4.6 yards. That was better than running the ball, but then you had to consider that a pass was still twice as likely to cost you the ball. Quarterbacks threw interceptions a bit more than 6 percent of the time while running backs

---

* I'm grateful to Ben Alamar for both his thoughts on this subject and for doing most of the actual work. Alamar, a professor of sports management at Menlo College, did his first football research as a graduate student. He sought to answer the question: which is more likely to lead to team success, a good running attack or a good passing attack? And he found that a team with a relatively strong passing attack was far more likely to make the NFL playoffs. He tried to get a statistics or economics journal to publish his study, but found no takers. Five years later, to fill the void in interest in his football research, Alamar founded the *Journal of Quantitative Analyses in Sports.* Today he is employed as a consultant to an actual NFL team.

But Alamar is a special case; there are only a handful of people engaged in the statistical analysis of football players, and football strategies, and they don't meet and argue and review each other's work, the way baseball people do. (The Society of American Baseball Research has thousands of members and a tradition of peer review and annual conferences, and has, in recent years, supplied Major League Baseball front offices with a great deal of brain power. Its founder, Bill James, has a World Series ring from his work with the 2004 Boston Red Sox.) No doubt there are plenty of reasons for the relative paucity of football research, but a big one is that inquiring minds have been discouraged by the messiness of the game. It's relatively easy to assign credit and blame on a baseball field. On a football field, there is no such thing as individual achievement. A quarterback throws an interception and it might be his own fault; but it might also be the fault of the receiver who ran the wrong route, or the blocker who allowed him to be hit as he threw. Twenty-two players are involved in every football play. To value precisely the activity of any one of them, it is first necessary to account for the actions of the other twenty-one.

fumbled the ball only about 3 percent of the time. The trade-off must have seemed unappealing to NFL coaches, as passing attempts per game actually fell a bit through the 1960s. By 1975, teams were throwing the ball, on average, just 24 times each game. Then something happened: teams began to pass more each year than they had the year before until, by the early 1990s, NFL quarterbacks were throwing the ball, on average, 34 times per game. All else being equal, this should have been a disaster for those quarterbacks. In a business with normal returns, the more you produce of a good the less you can sell it for. The passing game didn't exhibit normal returns. From a yield of 4.6 yards each throw, the average gain climbed steadily from the late 1970s until the early 1990s, until it settled in at around 7 yards per passing attempt. Each attempt was significantly more likely to be caught by a receiver. Right through the 1960s, NFL quarterbacks hit on fewer than 50 percent of their passes. In the 1970s, quarterbacks not only began to throw more often but to complete a higher percentage of their passes. Again, the trend was gradual but relentless, until the early 2000s when, on average, NFL quarterbacks made good on 60 percent of their throws.

The more closely you examined the passing business, the stranger it appeared. You might think, for instance, that the more the quarterback threw the ball, the less picky he'd be about where he threw it, and the more easily a defense could anticipate the pass and intercept it. Appar-

---

Still, as Alamar points out, there are all sorts of questions about football waiting to be answered as soon as someone bothers to collect the data. One example relevant to this story: how much does the performance of quarterbacks vary with the amount of time they spend in the pocket? A critical part of any passing game—another reason for the extreme importance of left tackles—is the amount of time a quarterback has to throw the ball. The difference between a quick decision-making quarterback and a slow one is typically fractions of a second: a difference impossible to see with the naked eye. In 2004, for example, the New York Giants lost to the Arizona Cardinals, and Giants quarterback Kurt Warner was sacked six times. The New York sports press, with just a couple of interesting exceptions, vilified the Giants' offensive line. Giants coach Tom Coughlin suspected another culprit. He stayed up that night reviewing game tape, and finally took out a stopwatch and put it on Kurt Warner: 2.5 seconds is a generous amount of time for an NFL quarterback to enjoy before he gets rid of the ball. Anything longer than 3 seconds is an eternity. On thirty of the thirty-seven pass plays the Giants ran against the Cardinals, Warner had held the ball 3.8 seconds or more. Coughlin left his offensive line intact, but the next day he benched Warner and installed rookie Eli Manning in his place.

"Time in the pocket and the rate at which the quarterback is under pressure are the two most important aspects of a team's performance (both offensively and defensively)," says Alamar. And yet no record of it is kept.

ently not: the more often NFL quarterbacks put the ball up in the air, the less likely it was to be intercepted. From the late 1970s until the mid-1990s, the interception rate fell steadily—from 6 percent all the way down to 3 percent. By 1995, a quarterback was no more likely to be intercepted than a runner was to fumble the ball. The running game was a dull, barely profitable business that exhibited little potential for growth. The passing game looked like a booming software company: the more quarterbacks produced, the bigger their profit margins. Adding to the mystery, the passing boom occurred as the number of teams in the league, and the number of games each team played, expanded. There were twice as many NFL quarterbacks in 1995 as there were in 1960, and more nearly always means worse. In this peculiar instance, more meant better. In 1960, NFL quarterbacks threw 7,583 passes and completed 49.6 percent of them, while throwing 470 interceptions (6.2 percent of all passes were intercepted). In 2005, NFL quarterbacks threw 16,430 passes, completed 59.5 percent of them, and had 507 of them intercepted (only 3.1 percent of all passes were intercepted).

An obvious reason for the boom in the passing game is the changes made to the rules of the NFL game. In 1978, NFL linemen were permitted, for the first time in history, to use their hands when they blocked. Overnight the image of the lineman with his elbows stuck out in imitation of a coat hanger became charmingly antiquated. That same year defensive backs were forbidden to make contact with receivers more than five yards beyond the line of scrimmage. Both rule changes helped the passing game along. But rule changes alone didn't begin to explain why a system of passing created before the changes had proven so effective: they don't explain Bill Walsh's success with quarterbacks. What seems to have happened is that NFL offenses began to pass the ball more effectively, the new passing attacks pleased the crowds and were good for business, and so NFL rulemakers made a point of encouraging them. As Indianapolis Colts general manager Bill Polian, who sat on the committee to change the rules, puts it, "Innovation drove the rule changes rather than the other way around."

And the 1970s and early 1980s were a golden era for innovation in the passing game. The football field is usually a tightly strung ecosystem, an efficient economy: there is seldom a free lunch on it. Of course there are the weaknesses and strengths of individual players. The other team might have an inept cornerback, for instance, and the smart coach will know how to exploit him. *Systematic* opportunity is rare. Yet Walsh had stumbled upon a systematic opportunity. The short, precisely timed passing game might not offer an entirely free lunch, but the discount to the retail price was steep. Bill Polian remembers when he first studied the 49ers' offense on tape, in 1986. Then the general manager of the AFC Champion Buffalo Bills, he was waiting to see which team in the soon-to-be-played NFC Championship game he would face in the Super Bowl, Walsh's 49ers or Bill Parcells's New York Giants. What he saw on the tape persuaded him that Bill Walsh's passing game would change football. "That was the Eureka moment for me," he said.

The Bills subsequently borrowed liberally from Walsh, as did the Colts once Polian moved there. As did many other teams, covertly. An astonishing number of Walsh's assistants—Andy Reid, Mike Sherman, Steve Mariucci, George Seifert, John Gruden, Mike Shanahan, Denny Green, Gary Kubiak—left to become NFL head coaches. When, in the mid-1990s, Brett Favre of the Green Bay Packers stepped onto center stage and took over the role of God's gift to the quarterbacking position, a Walsh disciple (Packer head coach and former Walsh assistant Mike Holmgren) stood behind the curtain pulling the strings. The story wasn't quite as simple as Bill Walsh created this offense—which came to be called "the West Coast offense"*—and everyone

---

* There's an arcane dispute waiting for anyone who wants to have one about the meaning of the phrase "West Coast offense." According to Paul Zimmerman, the term came from a piece he wrote for *Sports Illustrated*; it referred to the passing game created by Sid Gilman, and adopted by Don Coryell, at the San Diego Chargers, and others, including Walsh, mistakenly applied it to Walsh's offense. The full intellectual history of the passing game is beyond the scope of this book, but Gilman was obviously central to it. "A football field is 53 and a 1/3 yards wide by 100," Gilman told the *Houston Post*, in what in the mid-1960s counted as a radical observation. "We felt we should take advantage of the fact that the football field was that wide and that long. So our formations reflected the fact that we were going to put our outside ends wide enough so

else ripped it off. But it was close: by the late 1990s, every NFL team had a rhythm passing game. "In that sense," says Bill Polian of the Indianapolis Colts, "everyone in the NFL today runs Bill Walsh's offense. Because the rhythm passing game is all Walsh."

This single strand of the history of the game—the strand that would become the rope tied around Michael Oher's waist and haul him up in the world—is clearer than most. Over time, the statistics of NFL quarterbacks, on average, came to resemble the statistics of Bill Walsh's quarterbacks—because other coaches borrowed heavily from Walsh. The passing game was transformed from a risky business with returns not all that much greater than the running game to a clearly superior way to move the football down the field. As a result, the players most important to the passing game became, relatively, a great deal more valuable. The force that pulled on the rope around Michael Oher's waist was the mind of Bill Walsh.

But on the afternoon of January 3, 1981, that mind had not been fully appreciated. It hadn't infected anything except a few quarterbacks. Football strategy has no inevitable path it must follow. Walsh still had no sense that his ideas were likely to be pilfered, or that they were even recognized as ideas. The drift of the game was in his favor—"The rule changes played right into our hands," he said—but hardly inexorable. The only proof of any concept in the NFL was a championship ring. Walsh knew he couldn't win with

---

that we could take advantage of the entire width of the field. And then we were going to throw the ball far enough so that we forced people to cover the width AND the length." Gilman was the first pro football coach to spread the field and treat the pass as the primary offensive weapon, and Walsh studied his work closely. "I think the difference between me and a lot of other people was that other people really weren't willing to pick up on what Sid was doing," Walsh told me. "Except for [Raider coach] Al Davis. Because it was complex."

Walsh and Coryell followed in Gilman's footsteps to a fork in the road, then set out in different directions: Coryell went deep and Walsh went wide. In Coryell's system, the first receiver the quarterback looked for was the receiver going long: the high-risk option. The quarterbacks who played for Coryell passed for many yards, but also threw a lot of interceptions, and took a lot of punishment. To enable the receivers to get downfield they held the ball longer and gave pass rushers more time to get to them. This was the big difference in Walsh's approach from previous innovators of the passing game: it stripped a lot of the risk out of passing. It was more reliable and less explosive, more mechanical and less obviously artistic. It was also more appealing to other coaches and general managers looking for a passing game to steal. If "West Coast offense" came to

offense alone any more than a defensive-minded coach could win with defense alone. And defense, to Walsh's mind, was not a strategic challenge but a matter of finding better players. That was something that he hadn't been able to do. Toward the end of the 1980 season, after yet another close loss, in which his team had scored a surprising number of points, Walsh had made up his mind to quit. "I spent the five hour flight home sitting by myself," he later wrote. "I looked out the window so no one could see me break down. It was too much for anyone. I was emotionally, mentally, and physically exhausted. I decided I would resign as soon as the season ended; I believed I had done as much as I could do and the job was just too much for me."

He had lasted into the 1981 season, just, but a successful regular season wasn't enough. He was still at risk of winding up a cliché of free market capitalism: the inventor whose brainchild would lead to profit for others and nothing for himself. For fifteen seasons he had performed miracles with quarterbacks. He had just done something truly extraordinary: take the worst offense in the NFL and, in two years, turn it into the seventh best. And still no one knew. "If I had stopped then," he said, "it [his passing game] would have been discarded. There wasn't anyone else. Everyone was just watching to see how we would do. If it worked, nobody said anything. If it didn't work, everyone said, 'Look, that shows this stuff

---

refer to Walsh's passing game, and not Coryell's, it may have been because the spread of Walsh's demanded a catch phrase.

People who wish to stress Coryell's importance point to the success of his Hall of Fame quarterback Dan Fouts. The trouble with this is that Walsh coached Fouts first. When Walsh arrived in San Diego in 1976, says Fouts, "I was a mess. I was on my way to being cut or traded or whatever." A year under Walsh, and Fouts was on his way to stardom. After Walsh left in 1977, and Coryell took over, in 1978, Fouts indeed passed more frequently, and for more yards, and probably had a lot more fun than he had under Walsh—but he also threw a lot more interceptions. Fouts is reluctant to credit Walsh or Coryell alone for his success: both were instrumental. "I don't know who gets the credit," he says. "There's only one Moses, but I'm not sure there's a Moses here." But Howard Mudd, who coached the Chargers' offensive line at the time, and watched Fouts's transformation, has no such ambivalence. "Bill Walsh *made* Dan Fouts," Mudd says. "He stopped reading all over the field. He was looking for the player to be open rather than reading the defense. He rehearsed this *constantly*. Walsh created a new efficiency. And that efficiency turned Dan around totally."

Both Mudd and Fouts note that Coryell, after he came to San Diego, preserved an important element of Walsh's passing game: the emphasis on routes timed precisely to the quarterback's movements. "That was the beauty of that offense," says Fouts. "The rhythm and the timing follows from the steps the quarterback takes."

doesn't work.' "* He'd brought to the NFL passing game the precision and efficiency of a Japanese auto factory. And now, at the very moment he was ready to export to America, Godzilla had arrived to tear the factory apart.

Inside football, the argument between brains and brawn never has been settled, and probably never will be. The argument less and less found its way into words off the field, but on the field it reprised itself in action and strategy, over and over again. And on the chilly wet afternoon in Candlestick Park, it was about to play out in an extreme form, with Walsh as the brains and Bill Parcells as the brawn. Parcells was deeply suspicious of the overt use of intellect on a football sideline. He knew that Walsh claimed to script the first 25 plays of every game in advance, but later said "that scripting was a bunch of bullshit. They never got past number eight." And Parcells's influence in football, as measured by the number of his assistants who would go on to coach other teams, was nearly as great as Walsh's: Bill Belichick, Al Groh, Tom Coughlin, Sean Payton. (By 2006, two thirds of the teams in the NFL had been run by a coaching descendant of Walsh or Parcells.) After Parcells later won his first Super Bowl, in 1986, he said his style of football "never had anything to prove. It's the fancy-pants stuff that needs to prove itself." Walsh was the latest embodiment of fancy-pants. In 1981, people were starting to take notice of his new and improved little passing game, but Parcells had something new and improved, too: a passing game destructomatic called Lawrence Taylor. Just as Walsh was lowering the risk of throwing the ball, Parcells was raising the risk to the men who threw it.

---

* The bias against the pass was deeply ingrained in football. It was illegal until 1906, and even then severely restricted. It wasn't until 1933 that a quarterback was allowed to throw a forward pass from anywhere behind the line of scrimmage. Once legalized it was disdained, in large part because it had been legalized to make the game safer, and a big point in the game's favor, to those who played it, was its unsafety. Right up until the mid-1940s, in a rearguard attempt to slow the spread of wussiness, roughing the passer was actually encouraged. A small-college coach named Elmer Berry who had used an innovative passing attack to sneak up and beat bigger schools got so worked up about the anti-pass sentiment that he penned a counterblast, called *The Forward Pass in Football*. "Apparently many regard the forward pass simply as a valuable threat, something for occasional use, something to take a chance with, something the possibility of which makes the real game still workable," Berry wrote in 1921. "To a large degree this has been the attitude of the larger colleges. In general they have frowned upon the forward pass; opposed it, sneered at it, called it basketball and done what they could to retard its adoption. It has taken away from them the advantage of numbers, weight and power, made the game one of brains, speed and strategy—even, if you please, of luck—and rendered the outcome of their 'practice' games with smaller colleges uncertain."

At the end of the 1981 season Taylor was for Parcells still a shiny new toy with a complicated control panel that he was figuring out how to use. No matter what Parcells told his rookie linebacker to do, Taylor's instinct was to find the quarterback and kill him. Later in his career Taylor enjoyed letting people think he had a gift for freelancing, but during his rookie year, at least, he often didn't know what he was meant to do—and so, unable to think up a better idea, he just went after the passer. The sixth game of that season, against the St. Louis Cardinals, was a case in point. "The deal was," said Parcells, "that whichever side the tight end lined up on, the linebacker facing him was supposed to drop back into pass coverage. Usually the tight end lined up on the right side, and Lawrence blitzed. But early in the game they moved the tight end over to the left, to deal with Lawrence. He rushes anyway, and sacks the quarterback. I went over and said, 'Lawrence, they got the tight end on your side, you need to be back in coverage.' He says, 'Oh yeah, Coach, oh yeah.' I said, 'Watch out, 'cause they gonna do that again.' 'Yeah, yeah, Coach, okay. I'm ready.' Third quarter they do it again, they put the tight end on his side . . . *and Lawrence blitzes again.* This time he hits the quarterback, knocks the ball out of his hands, and [defensive end] George Martin picks it up and runs for a touchdown. Everyone's jumping on top of each other in the end zone and I'm pissed. I went and found him on the bench and he sees me and says, 'I didn't do it again, did I?' I said, 'Lawrence, we don't even *have* what you're doing.' And he says, 'Well, we better put it in on Monday, Coach, 'cause it works!' "

And Parcells loved it! "I'm a little Neanderthal," Parcells said. "I think defense is the key to any sport. That was my intent when I started coaching. That's what I wanted to coach. Not football. Football *defense.* It's not glamorous to those who are into what's aesthetically pleasing. But it's glamorous to *me.* 'Cause I think defense is the key to the game." It went without saying that the key to defense was passion and violence.

Walsh's temperament—and his football interests—couldn't have been more different. He preferred offense because offense was strategic. "There's just so much to offense that a coach really does have control of," he said. "Defense is just a matter of having the personnel." As a rookie NFL head coach, Bill Walsh was able to stand on the sideline in the pose of a man before a fire with a glass of port in one hand and a volume of Matthew Arnold's essays in the other. He kept about him a degree of calm that led *Los Angeles Times* columnist Jim Murray to write of him, "you half expect his headset is playing Mozart." Parcells lived out his emotional life inside the game; Walsh aimed to cleanse himself of emotion before the game ever started. The effort was immense, as he had a great deal of emotion to dispose of, and after some games he could be seen brushing tears from his eyes. But once "The Star-Spangled Banner" began to play, he said, "I'd tell myself, 'Here you go. Start pulling away, start computerizing. You must think clearly and *remove yourself.*' . . . It was like watching a game through a window."

Lawrence Taylor was a problem new to Walsh. Lawrence Taylor smashed the window. Walsh's system enabled Joe Montana to get rid of the ball faster than anyone in football, and normally that was fast enough. Now it wasn't. "Taylor was so quick," said Walsh, "that no matter how quickly we executed, he could still get there." To leave some running back or tight end to deal with Taylor was out of the question: Walsh needed his tight ends out spreading the field, and Taylor ate running backs for breakfast. The next most obvious candidate to block Taylor was the left tackle, as he lined up closest to the point where Taylor crossed the line of scrimmage. But the 49ers' left tackle, Dan Audick, was six two, 250 pounds, and even less well designed to handle Taylor than the Eagles' Stan Walters. "It's when I started to play left tackle," Audick said, "that the coaches were just starting to discover that they needed their best lineman at left tackle. I think they just wanted me to play the position as a kind of final experiment to verify their hypothesis" (Audick might not have been big or fast, but he was charming).

Walsh had brought his left tackle problem on himself. When he'd arrived in San Francisco, he had a very promising young left tackle, Ron Singleton. But then, as Walsh later put it, "Ron decided that he should be a marquee player, and subsequently sounded off in the locker room about how he should have been receiving credit and publicity." Walsh could put up, just, with his quarterbacks prancing around like superstars, but he had no space in his brain for the idea of linemen as celebrities. Singleton took the outlandish step of hiring an agent, who demanded the outrageous sum of $90,000 a year. When Walsh refused to pay it, the agent told people that Walsh was unwilling to negotiate because Singleton was black. That's when Walsh flipped. He had a staffer go to Singleton's locker, toss his belongings in a cardboard box, drive over to Singleton's house, and leave them on the doorstep. "That's how he knew he was fired," said Walsh. "He opened his front door and found the cardboard box." The player, or the agent, had misjudged the coach. Walsh's problem with Singleton's exalted self-image had nothing to do with the color of his skin but with the position he played. The man was a *lineman.*

In the end, Walsh decided that the episode had been a turning point for his team. Parting so unsentimentally with his left tackle showed everyone that he was not to be trifled with. It set a certain tone. On the other hand . . . who was going to block Lawrence Taylor?

I hit Jaworski that way—with an over-the-head ax job. I thought his dick was going to drop in the dirt.

The system was all about rhythm, and rhythm was precisely what you didn't have when you heard Taylor's footsteps behind you. Walsh needed to stop Taylor in his tracks, take him out of the game. Searching his locker room for a solution, he settled on a man named John Ayers. Ayers played left guard. He was six five, 270 pounds, and quick-footed. He grew up in Canyon, a small ranching town in west Texas, and in the off season he still worked as a cowboy, branding and castrating bulls, which was probably good practice. "John was born fifty years too late," said his wife, Laurel. "He'd have been a cowboy on a ranch. For twenty dollars a day. And been just as happy." Ayers said almost nothing and did what he was told and everyone liked him and few really knew him. He didn't think more than twice about how little he was paid, and it didn't occur to him to promote himself. "He was always in the background," said his wife. "He preferred it that way. He preferred the anonymity." He was, in short, Bill Walsh's idea of an offensive lineman. When Walsh spoke of his linemen, he sounded like a sea captain describing ships. "He had a low center of gravity," he said of Ayers. "You couldn't get his feet up off the ground. He had great balance. He had *ballast.*"

On each passing play Ayers would first check to make sure that no other Giant was blitzing up the middle, then skip backwards and to his left and meet the onrushing Taylor. Walsh thought he was quick enough to get in front of Taylor; the ballast would do the rest.

Informed that he would be dealing, from his left guard position, with this linebacker coming off the edge, Ayers was at first puzzled. Then he watched tapes of Lawrence Taylor. "They said there's this rookie linebacker who's tearing up the league," he told the *New York Times*. "I said, 'Well, good, that's the fullback's problem.' Then I took a look at him and said, 'Well, maybe the fullback can't get it done.'" His wife looked at tape with him. "I was scared to death that he had that assignment," she said. "All we heard about the week before the game was this big bad Lawrence Taylor."

On January 3, 1981, Bill Walsh drove to Candlestick Park, changed into his coaching shirt, met with the trainers and his coaches, then said a few low-key words to the players. He didn't feel there was any point in trying to motivate them at that point; mainly he was trying to calm them down. ("Whenever I tried to give an inspirational talk before the game, the other team would score first, so I didn't see the numbers in it.") Then he lined up to listen to "The Star-Spangled Banner." The rain began to fall and the field became such a mess that, after the kickoff, teams of men in dark blue windbreakers ran around replacing the divots. When Joe Montana took his position under the center, the wedges of grass were still strewn around him like cheap toupees. Walsh has made no secret of his general game plan: the night before he had informed the television announcers, Pat Summerall and John Madden, that he intended to throw the ball on 17 of the first 22 plays. He knew that Parcells knew, and Parcells knew that he knew, just as Walsh knew that on most of those 17 passing plays Lawrence Taylor would be coming for Joe Montana. And if they somehow hadn't surmised as much, Taylor would remind them, well in advance. "When Lawrence is pass-rushing," Giants defensive back Beasley Reece said, "he telegraphs it. It's like a cop putting sirens on top of his car. Lawrence puts a light on his helmet. His hands are flopping and his arms are swinging. He looks at the blocker the minute he attacks and destroys the blocker. Then he goes after the quarterback."

John Ayers's job was to look over and see if Taylor's hands were flopping. If he saw Taylor preparing to charge, he stepped back to meet him. It was only a matter of how the carefully planned collision ended: John Ayers is the one surprise. How he turns out, Walsh thought, would determine the outcome of the game.

On the first play from scrimmage Montana drops back, and Taylor comes. For a moment the field in front of him is empty. Then, out of nowhere, a figure appears and . . . *Pow!*

It was as if Taylor had run into the side of a house. What he had run into was 270 pounds of cowboy, who trained each off season by harnessing himself to a six-foot-tall tractor tire and hauling it sideways behind him for miles around a freshly ploughed field. The training showed. On every passing play Taylor looked like a man who had gone to get his quart of vanilla ice cream only to yank on the freezer door and find it locked. "It was the first time I'd seen it," he said. "It was the first time they'd brought the guard back to meet me. There was nothing I could do but try to run him over." He didn't run him over: the first pass was thrown. And the next. And the next. Watching Walsh's offense attack Parcells's defense was like watching a giant icicle plunging into a volcano. Steam rose, and you couldn't tell at first whether the icicle had melted or the fire had been extinguished.

Then the air cleared. At halftime the 49ers led 24–10 and Montana had completed 15 of 22 passes for 276 yards and two touchdowns. He'd picked to pieces the NFL's most dangerous defense. Montana once observed of Walsh's passing attack that "if you missed perfect, you wound up with great." He missed perfect on this day, but not by much. He threw a careless interception, and once took off from the pocket when he didn't really need to—and was chased down from behind by Lawrence Taylor. Otherwise, he played like a kid who'd been given the answers to the test in advance. "I'd never seen us execute like that," he said after the game. "That's why it didn't look tough for us. But it was. Our line was stopping them, and when I got that time, things became easy." The threat from the blind side had, thanks to John Ayers, vanished. "I couldn't figure out what to do with him," said Taylor, much later.

When Bill Parcells looked up at the end of the game, the scoreboard read 38–24, but it hadn't been as close as that. His defense hadn't allowed 38 points in any game all season, and they were lucky to have allowed only 38 today. Parcells was appalled, at not only the outcome but the interpretation of the outcome—that the difference in the game had been Walsh's strategy. There was no chance that some *left guard* was shutting down LT. "That would never have worked on a fast track," he said. "The only reason it worked was that the field was so bad that nobody could rush the passer. It was a mud pile. It was a slow track. If that was AstroTurf that would have never worked." And in the future, he would make damn sure it wouldn't work even in a mud pile. Later, when he watched the tape of the game, Parcells saw the weakness of Walsh's strategy. When Ayers dropped back, he left a hole in the middle of the line. Had the Giants blitzed a middle linebacker, he'd have had a clear path to Joe Montana. They never did. "We learned to deal with that as we went on," said Parcells. "We blitzed [Harry] Carson and teams stopped doing that. What they eventually had to do is slide the line to Taylor. We knew that unless they were extremely gifted at the left tackle position, they would have to compensate for him." And if they had to compensate for their left tackle, they created weakness elsewhere, and the game was half-won.

After the game Bill Walsh smiled sheepishly and told the television audience that he had suspected the game was won the minute he saw that his offense could throw the ball. The next week, in an NFC Championship game far more famous than this one, his team will beat the Dallas Cowboys. Two weeks later, with the lowest payroll in the NFL, they will win the Super Bowl. People wanted proof that this offense worked: he'd taken a team that had been 2–14 two years before to a championship. Q.E.D. But it was here, after they beat the Giants, and dealt with Lawrence Taylor and all that he implied, that Walsh came to a pair of conclusions about his football team. The first was that he needed to find himself a player like Lawrence Taylor to terrorize opposing quarterbacks. The second was that he needed to use his first pick of the next amateur draft to find a left tackle because, as Bill Parcells observed, the only way to handle this monster coming off the edge without disrupting the rhythm of the new passing attack was to have a left tackle with the physical ability to deal with him. The old left tackle was coming to the end of his natural life. Dan Audick was crushed when he lost his job after winning a Super Bowl, but he understood: the left tackle was no longer going to be just another lineman. In some ways he wouldn't be a lineman at all but a highly skilled player who happened never to get his hands on the ball. Bill Walsh had made the quarterback a lot more valuable, and so the man who protected the quarterback was going to be a whole lot more valuable, too. Whoever he was, he was going to have to be special. The old idea was about to die.

But it lived for this one last day. On this final day there was no need to compensate for Lawrence Taylor. John Ayers acted as an impenetrable wall between Taylor and his quarterback right to the end of the game. "My husband loved Joe Montana," said Laurel Ayers. "He was not going to let Joe Montana get hit by Lawrence Taylor, or get hurt." It was Taylor who finally relented. "It was obvious," said the 49ers' line coach, Bob McKittrick, right after the game. "You could see how frustrated Taylor was getting out there as the game progressed. I don't want to put him down, but he was quitting out there." Ayers, on the other hand, was a profile in toughness and pass-blocking technique. He was, for that one moment, the critical component of Bill Walsh's passing attack, and hardly a soul in Candlestick Park noticed. He was a reminder that what sets football apart from other sports is that what you don't see is often the most important thing. What John Ayers was doing seemed routine. But to the few who knew, and watched, it was a thing of beauty.

The ball is snapped and John Ayers sees Taylor coming, and slides quickly back one step and to his left. And as he slides, he steps to meet his future. He's stepping into 1985, when the turf will be fast and he won't be able to deal with Lawrence Taylor. . . . Another quick step, back and left, and it's 1986, and he's injured and on the sidelines when the Giants send Joe Montana to the hospital and the 49ers home on the way to their own Super Bowl victory. . . . A third quick step and he crouches like one power forward denying another access to the hoop. But now it's 1987 and Coach Bill Walsh is advising John Ayers to retire. Ayers ignores the advice and then learns that Walsh won't invite him back to training camp. . . . He takes his final quick step back and left and times his blow, to stop dead in his tracks the most terrifying force ever launched at an NFL quarterback. "I don't think I've ever played against a football player who had more drive and intensity to get to the quarterback," John Ayers will say, after it's all over, and he's been given the game ball by his teammates. "It was almost like he was possessed." . . . But now it's 1995, and John Ayers has just died of cancer, at forty-two, and left behind a wife and two children. Joe Montana charters a plane to fly a dozen teammates to Amarillo, Texas, to serve as pallbearers. At the funeral of John Ayers the letter of tribute from Bill Walsh is read aloud.

—

CHAPTER SIX

INVENTING MICHAEL

BY THE TIME THE BRIARCREST CHRISTIAN SCHOOL SAINTS OPENED their 2004 season, Michael Oher had spent four months growing accustomed to the idea that he was a football star. He'd been featured in the *Memphis Commercial Appeal*, attended summer camps for elite football prospects at LSU, Ole Miss, North Carolina State, and the University of Oklahoma, and turned down invitations to summer at another fifty or so Division I football programs. He'd received more than a thousand letters from college football programs, and many dozens of Federal Express packages—and so he had learned, among other things, that when the letter came by FedEx it contained the offer of a full scholarship. The only major football school that hadn't offered him a full scholarship was Penn State. He'd received, additionally, four months of frantic private tutoring from both his head coach Hugh Freeze and his offensive line coach Tim Long, who had been drafted in 1985 by the Minnesota Vikings to play left tackle. (Injuries cut short Long's NFL career. He played pre-season games with the Vikings, the San Francisco 49ers, and the Indianapolis Colts, and just three regular season games, in 1987, with the 49ers.) In practices before the first game, Sean Tuohy thought Michael looked like a different football player—which is to say he almost looked as if he knew what he was doing. "Tim doesn't take any credit for it," said Sean, "but something he said to him changed everything. He showed him how to use his hands."

The technique Long taught Michael was called "getting fit." A lineman the size and power of Michel Oher needed only to get his hands on his defender to ruin his day. He was so strong, and his hands so big, that there was no opponent—certainly not in high school, probably not even in college—who, once hooked, could wriggle free. It was of course illegal for an offensive lineman to grab a defender broadly, sumo-style; the lineman had to master the art of grabbing narrowly, of keeping his hands in close, and seizing his opponent near the breastplate of his shoulder pads. That's what Tim Long taught Michael Oher to do: get fit. "Fire to fit," became Hugh Freeze's mantra: fire off the line of scrimmage and get fit on the defender before he knows what's hit him.

The college football coaches of America had taken one look at Michael Oher and had seen a future NFL left tackle. Sean and Leigh Anne Tuohy had their doubts. Michael had wandered into their lives, moved into their home, and quickly become entirely dependent on them. He was meant to be a football player but, until everyone started telling him he was a star football player, he had shown hardly any interest in football. When he'd been thrown into games during his junior year, he had spent most of his time wandering around the field in search of someone to fall over. He'd looked completely lost, and passive. The left tackle might be the one guy on the field whose job was to reduce the level of violence. But even the left tackle, if he was to succeed, needed to play with aggression. And the few people who had paid attention on the few occasions when Michael played in football games hadn't seen even a hint of aggression.

Michael's first test was not an official game, but a pre-season scrimmage at home, against a team from Munford, twenty-five miles outside of Memphis. Leigh Anne took her usual seat in the stands, on the fifty-yard line, two rows from the top, right beneath the "N" in "SAINTS." She sat in a cluster of players' mothers, all of whom had definite views about the quality of Briarcrest's coaching and football strategy. They kept a cell phone handy just in case, as Leigh Anne put it, "we had any opinions or thoughts on the game that we felt Hugh or Sean needed to know." She was the coach in the skybox, and already she watched football games in a way few Americans did: focused on the offensive line. A play would end and she would have missed entirely what had happened to the ball. "I don't know about 'keeping his pad level down' and 'getting fit' and all these key little nichey phrases that the football coaches use to talk about what linemen do," she said. "All I can tell is if Michael's laying on top of somebody. And if he's spreadeagled on top of somebody, that's good."

Sean also took his place, a few yards down the sidelines from Hugh Freeze, where he could get a different view of the action than the head coach. Hugh, who fully grasped Sean's near-magical ability to boost the confidence of teen-aged boys, had taught him football just so that he might put him in charge of the Briarcrest quarterbacks. Sean still kept one eye on Michael, but tonight he missed the signs. From the first play of the game the Munford defensive end who lined up directly across from Michael targeted him for special ridicule. The Munford player was about six two and couldn't have weighed more than 220 pounds, and yet he wouldn't shut up. Every play, he had something nasty to say.

Hey fat ass, I'm a kill you!

Hey fat ass! Fat people can't play football! I'm a run your fat ass over!

It was the last game of Michael Oher's football career in which the opposing team wouldn't have the first clue who he was. He didn't yet have an impressive highlight reel of game film to precede him, and the folks up in Munford apparently didn't read either the Memphis newspapers or Tom Lemming's newsletter. Michael's body was indeed wide, but deceptively so. Leigh Anne had just remeasured him for a pair of slacks and found he had a 50-inch waist and a 32-inch inseam. He had some fat on him, but his width was mainly bone and muscle—he didn't need all 50 inches in the waist of his pants, but pants any smaller in the waist failed to accommodate his thighs. His teammates and coaches now understood that Michael Oher, even by national football standards, was a physical oddity. "He's the biggest player anyone's ever seen, and he may be the fastest player on our team in the ten-yard dash," said Terio Franklin, the Briarcrest linebacker and kick returner with whom Michael briefly lived. Too wide for anyone to imagine him solid and too big for anyone to imagine him fast, Michael Oher had, one last time, the element of surprise. "Force equals mass times acceleration," Coach Hugh Freeze liked to say. "And when Michael's mass hits you at Michael's speed, it's just an amazing and unexpected force."

The Munford scouting report hadn't picked up Michael's size and speed. The Munford defensive end who lined up across from Michael Oher obviously took one look at him and saw a high school football cliché: the fat kid they stuck on the offensive line because there was no place else to put him except the tuba section of the band.

Hey fat ass! I'm a put your fat ass in the dirt!

The more he went on, the angrier Michael became, and yet no one noticed, possibly because no one was prepared to imagine the rage inside Michael Oher. Hugh Freeze ordered up plays that called for Michael to block a linebacker, or to pull and sweep around the right end, and leave the defensive end across from him alone. The first quarter and a half of the scrimmage was uneventful—until Hugh Freeze called a different sort of play.

Leigh Anne could always tell when something angered Michael. "I can tell by his body language," she said. "You piss Michael off and he looks more like a bull in his stance." Early in the scrimmage he had a bull-like demeanor, but he hadn't done anything out of anger. Leigh Anne rose from her seat to beat the crowd to the concessions stand, and so had her back to the action when the people in the stands around her began to laugh.

"Where's he taking him?" she heard someone say.

"He's not letting go of that kid!" shouted someone else.

She turned around in time to see twenty football players running down one side of the field, after the Briarcrest running back with the ball. On the other side of the field Briarcrest's No. 74 was racing at speed in the opposite direction, with a defensive end in his arms.

From his place on the sideline Sean watched in amazement. Hugh had called a running play, around the right end, away from Michael's side. Michael's job was simply to take the kid who had been jabbering at him and wall him off. Just keep him away from the ball carrier. Instead, he'd fired off the line of scrimmage and gotten fit. Once he had his hands inside the Munford player's shoulder pads, he lifted him off the ground. It was a perfectly legal block, with unusual consequences. He drove the Munford player straight down the field for 15 yards, then took a hard left, toward the Munford sidelines. "The Munford kid's feet were hitting the ground every four steps, like a cartoon character," said Sean. As the kid strained to get his feet back on the ground, Michael ran him the next 25 or so yards to the Munford bench. When he got there he didn't stop, but piled right through it, knocking over the bench, several more Munford players, and scattering the team. He didn't skip a beat. Encircling the football field was a cinder track. He blocked the kid across the 10-yard-wide track, and then across the grass on the other side of the cinder track.

That's where Sean lost sight of him. What appeared to be the entire Munford football team leaped on top of Michael, and the officials raced over to peel them off. All Sean could make out was a huge pile of bodies. "Then Michael gets up," says Sean. "And it's like watching Gulliver. Bodies flying everywhere. Flags flying everywhere. And then the referee comes over to scream at us."

All the officials knew Sean Tuohy, both as the former star point guard at Ole Miss and as the current radio color man for the Memphis Grizzlies. They read the Memphis sports pages, and so they also knew of Michael Oher, newly heralded as the hottest football recruit to come out of Memphis in some time who, for some strange reason, was now living with Sean Tuohy. Looking for a grown-up to complain to, an official sprinted back across the field. He made straight for Sean.

"Coach Tuohy!" he hollered.

Sean stepped out onto the field. "What's goin' on?"

"Coach Tuohy, he just can't do that."

"Did the whistle blow?" asked Sean, who could have made a good living as a tort lawyer.

The whistle had not blown. The Briarcrest running back had kept his feet for a conveniently long time.

"No," said the referee. "But he's got to let go of him when he gets him to the sidelines. He can't just keep on running with him."

"C'mon," said Sean. "The play wasn't over."

"Sean," said the ref. "He took that boy across the track."

"Okay," said Sean. "I'll talk to him."

Beyond the Munford bench, the cinder track, and the stretch of grass, was a chain-link fence.

"So what's the penalty?" someone else asked.

"Excessive blocking."

As the referee walked off the 15-yard penalty, Sean hollered at Michael to get his ass to the bench, and Michael trotted over, with an air of perfect detachment. He couldn't have seemed less interested in the ruckus. "Everyone's freaking out," said Sean, "the refs are screaming, their whole team is wanting to fight, and he's totally calm, like he's out for a Sunday stroll." Technically, it was Hugh's job to talk to Michael, as, since Michael's apotheosis, Hugh had taken a special interest in the offensive line. But in Hugh's view, Michael was merely doing what he'd taught him to do: block until the whistle blows. Upon reflection, thought Hugh, "You tell Michael, 'I want you to block until the whistle blows.' Well, he takes that real literal."

Sean and Tim Long took Michael off to one side. "You can't do that, Michael," said Long, struggling to keep a straight face. "These guys are after you, and now you've made a scene." Long had never heard of a lineman penalized for "excessive blocking," but then he'd never seen a block quite so dramatic as this one. For his first time as a volunteer football coach Tim was having difficulty swallowing his desire to giggle. ("I'd never seen that before—the lineman takes his man fifteen yards down the middle of the field, and then he decides to turn him left and take him all the way to his sidelines and through the bench.") Sean wasn't laughing; Sean had his stern face on. This incident fell into the ever-expanding category of Things Michael Oher Needed to Understand to Succeed. When Long was finished, Sean explained to Michael that he was now a famous football recruit, and bigger than anyone on just about any football field on earth. Even if he was an offensive lineman, he had to play as if everyone in the stadium was watching his every move. No matter how rude or dirty the opposing player might be, Michael had to swallow his desire for such obvious revenge. He could win, he could dominate, he could even humiliate. He just shouldn't attract the attention of the legal authorities.

Michael listened to Sean's little speech without responding except to grunt "okay." He was still eerily calm, as if this whole fuss didn't really concern him. Finishing his lecture, Sean looked over at the Munford bench: Michael had picked up a 220-pound defensive end and moved him at least 60 yards. In *seconds*.

"Michael," said Sean. "Where were you taking him, anyway?"

"I was gonna put him on the bus," said Michael.

Parked on the other side of the chain-link fence was, in fact, the Munford team bus.

"The *bus*?" asked Sean.

"I got tired of him talking," said Michael. "It was time for him to go home."

Sean thought he must be joking. He wasn't. Michael had thought it all through in advance; he'd been waiting nearly half a football game to do just exactly what he had very nearly done. To pick up this trash-talking defensive end and take him not *to* the chain-link fence but *through* the chain-link fence. To the bus. And then put him on the bus. Sean began to laugh.

"How far did you get?" asked Sean.

"I got him up against the fence," said Michael. Now Michael began to chuckle.

"What did that guy say while you were taking him to the bus?" asked Sean.

"Nothin'!" said Michael. "He was just hanging on for dear life."

As the laughter rose up in him, Sean thought: *there might be a fire in this belly after all.* He didn't worry much what might happen if that fire was misdirected, off the football field. He figured football could channel it, usefully.

THE QUESTION ASKED about Michael Oher by the Washington Redskins' quarterback still hadn't been answered to anyone's satisfaction: *Who was this kid?* Collins Tuohy, Michael's age and soon to be crowned Homecoming Queen of Michael's Briarcrest class, was now also functioning, in effect, as

Michael's sister. And Collins thought Michael's identity was a work in progress. At school a year ago you couldn't get him to take his eyes off the floor. Now she'd catch him smiling and laughing and bantering with other kids in the halls and, in general, playing Big Man on Campus. He'd told the track coach he wanted to try the long jump, as the shot put and discus were too easy. He'd told the football coaches that he was tired of blocking the opposing team's extra points: he was going to try to catch one. The senior class was planning a skit. Three of the girls intended to perform a song-and-dance routine, and they were looking for a striking-looking male lead singer. They'd asked Michael to play the part and he'd shocked everyone by agreeing to do it. "After hearing, 'you're so good,' 'you're so good,' 'you're so good,' " said Collins, "he's started thinking, maybe I *am* good."

As Leigh Anne gradually took over the management of Michael's life, she noticed changes, too. He was a lot more talkative, and a bit more sure of himself, at least on the surface. His point of view began to intrude on the narrative. He now wanted things, and acknowledged that he wanted them, and the first thing he said he wanted was a driver's license. She handed him the driver's test prep books, and agreed to take him to the Memphis Department of Motor Vehicles, but immediately there was a problem: he couldn't prove who he was. To get a driver's license he needed two forms of identification. He didn't have so much as a YMCA membership card on him, and he swore that his mother, wherever she was, didn't have anything either. Leigh Anne thought that the hospital where he was born must have preserved some record of the event, but Michael didn't know where he'd been born. "We started with nothing," said Leigh Anne. "There wasn't a shred of evidence he even existed." She put the problem to Hugh Freeze, and Hugh told her that it was the easiest thing in the world to drive out to the Social Security Administration Office and get a Social Security card. He'd done it himself.

So that's how they began, with the two of them driving out to the Memphis suburbs, and asking a man behind a government computer for proof of Michael's existence. "To get a Social Security card," the man explained patiently, "you need to have a birth certificate." Leigh Anne tried to explain that they only needed the card so that they might obtain a driver's license, but the man remained firm: with so many terrorists on the loose he couldn't be handing out Social Security cards to people without other personal identification. Leigh Anne was born knowing how to play the damsel in distress; after she'd done it, the man agreed to help them, on the condition that Leigh Anne provide some evidence that Michael attended school in Memphis. Back they drove to Briarcrest, the only institution Leigh Anne could think of that recognized Michael's existence. Steve Simpson kindly printed Michael a school I.D. and wrote a letter identifying Michael Jerome Oher as a Briarcrest student. Then they went back to the Social Security office, where the man behind the desk looked at the dummied-up Briarcrest I.D. and got cold feet. He'd said any form of I.D. but he didn't mean *any* form of I.D. He meant something a bit more . . . official.

"Look at me," said Leigh Anne. "We have nothing. He's had seven addresses and he's gone to fifteen different schools. He doesn't know the names of his brothers and sisters. He's never committed a crime so we don't even have a criminal record. We . . . have . . . *nothing.*" The man behind the desk either had a soft spot for a pretty woman in desperate circumstances or a hunch that he'd be much safer, long term, if he just gave this lady whatever she wanted. In any case, he began to punch the buttons on his computer. "You know why I'm going to do this," he said. "I'm going to do this because I want to know why a short white blond lady has got a big black kid in here trying to get him a driver's license." So Leigh Anne told him the story, and the man went looking in his computer for evidence of the existence of Michael Oher. She finished her story before he found the evidence. After a few minutes of searching, he looked up and said: "There's no such person as Michael Jerome Oher."

Michael just sat there in silence. Leigh Anne begged the man to keep looking: did he have anything even close? He tried spelling Oher in various ways; he tried spelling Michael in various ways. Finally he said, "There's a Michael Jerome *Williams.*"

"That's me," said Michael.

It is? thought Leigh Anne, but said nothing.

"You've been issued six Social Security cards in the last eighteen months," said the man from Social Security. He wasn't happy about it.

Leigh Anne had no idea what that was about—"someone was probably selling them on the Internet"—and neither did Michael. To the Social Security administrator she said, "I promise if you give us just one more, it'll be the last time we ask." Grudgingly, and a bit suspiciously, the man printed out a Social Security card. Only when they were outside did Leigh Anne stop to look at it: "Michael Jerome Williams Junior," it read.

"Who the hell is Michael Jerome Williams?" she asked.

"That's my dad," said Michael. He didn't find anything interesting about that fact, and so didn't elaborate.

She now had a Social Security card that said his name was Michael Jerome Williams and a student I.D. that said his name was Michael Jerome Oher. Leigh Anne explained to Michael: No matter how nice the people at the Memphis DMV are, they aren't going to accept these as two forms of legal identification for one boy. She told him that if he wanted a driver's license she was going to have to visit his mother, and see if she had a birth certificate. "She doesn't have any birth certificate," said Michael. "She doesn't have anything." Since Michael had moved in, Leigh Anne had pestered Michael to go and visit his mother. Occasionally, and grudgingly, Michael went, or said he did; but as he had never let any of the Tuohys near his old inner-city home, they couldn't be sure. The drawbridge might come down between white and black Memphis, but Michael insisted on crossing it alone. "Michael," Leigh Anne would say. "She is your mother. She will always be your mother. And you are never going to be able to look at me and say, 'You took me away from my mother.'" Now she said, "If you won't go, I will."

"No," he said. "I'll go."

He left and returned a few hours later. It was tattered and smeared, and he held it like a piece of trash, crumpled up in a tight ball in his hand, but he'd found a birth certificate. A boy named Michael Jerome Williams was indeed born in Memphis, on May 26, 1986.

"You told me your birthday was May 28," said Leigh Anne.

Michael looked at his birth certificate and frowned. "They must have got the date wrong," he said.

"They don't get the date wrong on birth certificates, Michael," said Leigh Anne.

"No, they got it wrong," he insisted.

She dropped the matter, and his birthday remained May 28. Armed with the Social Security card, the birth certificate, and the letter from Principal Simpson of the Briarcrest Christian School, they drove the next day to the Department of Motor Vehicles. This time they had Collins in tow. Collins had herself just turned seventeen and so was eligible to have the restrictions removed from her license. The DMV was for some reason miles east, outside the Memphis beltway, on a road lined with anemic maples, porn shops, and churches. They passed a porn shop and then a church and then another porn shop and another church; it was as if the people of Memphis had chosen this place to fight the war between animal nature and the instinct to subdue it. The DMV was a blue wooden shack in the woods, but there wasn't a trace of nature inside. It hummed with fluorescent lights and automated voices and the bells from the row of testing machines in the back. The walls were white cinder block, the floors speckled linoleum. At the front desk were four large black ladies. Leigh Anne handed all the documents over to one of them, who took one look at them and said in a slow drawl, "Uh-uh. This school letter is a *copy*. You got to have an *original*."

And so they left Collins to become a fully authorized grown-up driver, and raced the fifteen miles out to the Briarcrest Christian School, where Mr. Simpson met them in the parking lot, with the original of his letter embossed with the Briarcrest seal. They went back to the DMV, and the large black lady looked at the paperwork again. "Uh-uh," she said. "To apply for his license, he needs proof of residence, too." A phone or electric bill addressed to him, or someone whose name might plausibly be associated with his, that placed him more precisely in the world.

This was tricky. They had, right now, at home, boxes of letters addressed to Michael from college football coaches and boosters and just people who wanted to get to know the future star. They had a personal letter from Congressman Harold Ford Jr., who seemed to want to become Michael's friend, and a stack of letters from a football coach at the University of Alabama, who seemed prepared to offer his hand in marriage. Leigh Anne had long ago quit counting the letters: more than a thousand, fewer than ten thousand. The trouble was they were all addressed to "Michael Oher," who, legally, didn't exist. The only thing to do was to drive west across the city and find Michael's mother and, God willing, some piece of mail with an address and a more useful name on it. It was now 3:30 p.m. and the DMV didn't let anyone through the door after four-thirty.

"Let's just pick this up another day," said Leigh Anne.

"No," said Michael. "I want to get my driver's license *today.*"

She'd never seen him so definite and purposeful. For the first time, when Leigh Anne said that she would accompany him to his mother's house, Michael didn't protest. Leaving Collins to stall the DMV, she and Michael took off for inner-city Memphis, at 90 miles per hour. Along the way Michael said, "No one in my whole family has ever had a driver's license." That's why it was so important for him to get his driver's license. It would make him different from his family.

At length, they roared up in front of the same redbrick public housing project where Leigh Anne had dropped him off after their day of shopping for clothes. Michael had phoned his mother en route to let her know they were on the way, and to ask her to find an old bill or something. Now the woman herself opened the door: she was very large and very black. Six foot one at least, with big bones and, Leigh Anne thought, a pretty face. Denise was her name but everyone called her "Dee Dee."

"How y'all doin today?"

She was drunk, or high, and slurring her words. She wore a muu-muu and a garish wig that Leigh Anne assumed she had thrown on when they'd called to tell her they were on their way. She didn't invite them in and Leigh Anne sensed that she didn't want to, either. If she had, Leigh Anne would have found only a single trace of the childhood of Michael Oher: a sentimental photograph of a little boy hugging a big-eyed tabby cat that he had taped to the wall in the room where as a little boy he had, on occasion, slept. The sun was setting, and behind her the small apartment was dark. Michael just stood away from her, keeping his distance.

"You better come over here and hug your mama!" she shouted at Michael.

Michael just walked over and stood there. He offered no resistance when she threw her arms around him, but he didn't respond in kind or, for that matter, utter a word. She hadn't bothered to go looking for an envelope with an address on it, and they were in a mad rush, so they didn't have time to talk. At Leigh Anne's request, Dee Dee went and found the key to her mailbox. They walked down together to the row of surprisingly large metal boxes. Dee Dee found hers, but just before she opened it, she said, "Oh, there's no telling what's in here." Then she yanked open the box and down came the avalanche: water bills, light bills, gas bills, phone bills, eviction notices. It looked to be about three months' worth of stuff, and when it was done falling out, a moraine of future trouble rose from the pavement. Leigh Anne needed only a single bill; she was spoiled for choice. She reached down and grabbed the one on top, thanked Dee Dee for her trouble, and drove 90 miles per hour with Michael back to the DMV. On the way, neither she nor Michael said a thing about what they'd just seen.

By the time they arrived at the DMV the doors were shut, but Collins had persuaded the ladies to hold it open just a few minutes more. There wasn't a soul in the place; when Michael walked to the testing area, he had it all to himself. Leigh Anne was now sufficiently exasperated to remind Michael what she had been telling him for weeks: "You have one chance to pass this test. I gave Collins one chance, and I'll give you one chance. I'm not coming down here again." Michael vanished behind the partition where Leigh Anne couldn't see him. For a moment there was only the hum of the fluorescent lights. Then she heard Michael in conversation with the ladies. She couldn't make out what they were saying, but he was clearly chattering up a storm. Then he went silent.

Moments later, Leigh Anne heard the first ominous sound: *Bing!* That would be the bell on the testing terminal signaling that he'd made a mistake. He was allowed to miss four questions; five and he'd fail, and they'd have to return and do this all over again. Which, despite her threats, she knew she would have to do. She took a seat against the white cinder-block wall beside the large sign with red letters that said APPLICANTS ONLY BEYOND THIS POINT, and began to pray.

She was uncomfortable leaving Michael alone to solve a problem by himself. She already assumed that his problems were *her* problems, for if they weren't, no problem ever would be solved. He was already, in this sense, her son. Her own extended family hadn't liked the idea of them taking Michael in, at least initially. ("The only one who could never handle it was Daddy," Leigh Anne said. "I truly think God took Daddy because He knew he couldn't handle it.") But then the more they came to know Michael, the less they fought it. Her mother, Virginia, was already playing the role of doting grandmother to Michael, and she and Michael clearly adored each other. Outside the family, the reaction was still mixed—"we knew people were going to have issues because we had a daughter exactly the same age," said Leigh Anne. She often found herself greeted in the shops and restaurants and schools of East Memphis with the same leading line: "How have you *handled* it?"

What the woman—it was nearly always a woman—who asked Leigh Anne the question meant was, *How have you handled having your gorgeous, nubile, seventeen-year-old daughter living under the same roof with a huge young black man the same age?*

Leigh Anne explained about fifty times that Michael's relationship to both Collins and Sean Junior was so much like that of a sibling that you'd never guess they hadn't grown up together. Michael and Sean Junior would shut the door to Michael's room for hours and compete: video games, miniature basketball, and whatever else they could find that leveled the playing field between a four-foot six-inch, 85-pound ten-year-old boy and a six-foot five-inch, 350-pound teenager. Michael and Collins would bicker and squabble just the way teen-aged brothers and sisters have since they were first created. As Leigh Anne's feelings for Michael developed, the questions people asked became offensive to her. She'd been taking care of his material needs for a good year and a half, and his emotional ones, to the extent he wanted them taken care of, for almost as long. "I love him as if I birthed him," she said. About the hundredth time someone asked her how she handled his sexual urges, Leigh Anne snapped. "You just need to mind your own business. You worry about your life and I'll worry about mine," she'd said. Word must have gotten around because after that no one asked.

Bing!

They now faced a problem far more difficult than mere social disapproval. At the end of Michael's junior year, Leigh Anne had ordered up his Briarcrest transcripts. No one at Briarcrest had said anything to her about his grades, and so she assumed they must be at least barely acceptable. They weren't. He had a cumulative GPA of 1.56 going into his senior year, and the NCAA required a 2.56. Out of a class of 161 students, he ranked 161st. The expensive private school was not much better than the worst sort of public one in filling the void: the empty space in the life of a child who had no one at home to take care of him. He was being described in the Memphis papers as the next great college football star, but to be the next great college football star you had to get to college, and there was little chance of that. Just to graduate from Briarcrest he needed eight more full credits—and there were only seven periods in the day! Most kids only took five classes, and had free periods for the other two. "The numbers don't add up," she said. "If he got an A in every class he still wouldn't qualify."

Bing!

When she saw Michael's grades, steam came out of her ears. She marched into Briarcrest and hollered at a bunch of people, starting with the principal. The Briarcrest Christian School was just shuffling him along without ever intending for him to graduate. "This going-on-faith thing isn't working," she said. "They just kind of hoped it would happen. That's bull. This isn't a faith thing; this is a tangible thing." She signed him up to take seven classes, plus before-school Bible Study—which counted toward graduation but not for the NCAA. She called every one of the teachers and told them that they were now to deal directly with her. He'd leave the house each morning at 6:00 a.m. and be in class straight through until 3:30 p.m. When she saw how many books he'd need, she realized he was going to need an industrial-strength backpack to carry them in. North Face, she thought, might do the trick ("It gets to the top of Everest," she thought) and so she went out and bought him a North Face backpack. Michael had taken one look at it and said, "I don't want to take that to school."

"Why not?" she'd asked.

"That's the one all the little rich kids carry," he'd said.

"Michael," she'd said. "You *are* a little rich kid."

And he'd taken the backpack to school.

Bing!

The first test of Michael's senior year was a quiz on the summer reading. Bunyan's *The Pilgrim's Progress* had been assigned. Michael was incapable of reading it himself. She and Sean had taken turns every night that summer reading it aloud to him. It took two months and nearly killed them both: Sean hadn't read a book cover to cover since—well, possibly ever. John Grisham had been at Ole Miss Law School when Sean was dazzling people on the Ole Miss basketball court. Grisham was a Sean Tuohy fan and sent Sean signed copies of his thrillers. They just piled up in Sean's clothes closet, unread. Now Sean was up half the night, every other night, reading *The Pilgrim's Progress . . . aloud.* They had gone over every passage of the book with Michael before the test. Leigh Anne thought he'd score a perfect 100. He got a 59. After that first day of school he brought the test score home with him, along with a long reading list, and an assignment to write a term paper. At that point Leigh Anne had turned to Sean, and Sean said, "Don't look at me. I majored in basketball."

She took over Michael's academic life. Every day, without fail, she went through his North Face backpack. He'd fail a quiz or get a D on a paper and never think it worth mentioning. He wouldn't throw away his papers and test grades but he wouldn't volunteer them, either. She'd find the paper balled up at the bottom of the backpack. That was their biggest problem at first: he wouldn't tell you when there was a problem. He had the most intense desire to please, without the ability to do the things that pleased. He had spent his whole life treating his mind as a problem to be covered up. He had grown so accustomed to not sharing a thing about himself, or perhaps never being asked about himself, that he didn't even know how to begin.

He now called her "Mama." (Except when he was pissed off at her for making him do something he didn't want to do, in which case he called her "Ms. Tuohy.") When he felt vulnerable, he came to her. She was now, without a doubt, the person on earth in whom Michael was most likely to confide. And in the last thirty-six hours she had learned that she didn't know either his name or his birthday! Information about himself he viewed either as so totally without value, or so very precious, that it shouldn't be shared with others. In the Briarcrest locker room before and after his basketball games, he changed in a bathroom stall. He was the single most private person she had ever met. Every now and again when Michael suspected he might have revealed something about himself to her, or after Leigh Anne had made some observation about him, he'd smile and say, "You think you really know me, don't you?"

All of which raised a question: what was he hiding? The thought had crossed Leigh Anne's mind: *maybe he's gay.*

She didn't know a lot of gay people. White Evangelical Christian Memphis—which is to say most of East Memphis—wasn't really designed to make black people feel comfortable in it, but if you had a choice of being black in East Memphis, or being gay in East Memphis, you'd think at least twice about it. White Memphis life was organized around the churches, and the churches, at any rate most of them, viewed homosexuality as either a sin to be expiated or a disease to be treated. The vast and fast-growing Grace Evangelical Church that the Tuohys had been instrumental in creating was no softer on homosexuality than any other. Black people were perfectly welcome at Grace Evan—it's just that none but Michael Oher ever came. Gay people, unless they were looking to be cured, were not.

Bing!

When Leigh Anne heard the fifth and final mistake she stopped praying and started cursing. "Shit!" she said, and then she began to curse him: *Why couldn't he study? Why didn't he learn? What more could she possibly do?* Then she heard another sound—of the large black woman who'd stayed behind to administer the test.

"Congratulations, Michael!" said a cheery voice. "You've passed the test. You come on over here and have your picture made!"

A few minutes later Michael emerged with one of the ladies, climbed into Sean's BMW 745, and zipped off for a fifteen-minute test drive. When he returned, they handed him the first driver's license anyone in his family had ever owned. On the way out the door, one of the ladies shouted after him, "Don't you forget, I'm gonna have that NFL sideline pass off you!"

THERE WAS A new force in Michael Oher's life: a woman paying extremely close attention to him who had an eye for detail, a nose for trouble, the heart of a lion, and the will of a storm trooper. A mother. "When I moved in with Leigh Anne and Sean, I felt loved," said Michael, "like part of a family. In the other houses I didn't feel like part of the family. I didn't feel like they wanted me there." The feeling was good for Michael and it was also, oddly enough, good for the Briarcrest Christian School football team. The team came out for their first real game in early September 2004. The opponent was Melrose, a public school that would wind up in the state championship game in the division for Tennessee's biggest schools. The game was in the Liberty Bowl, and it was, from the point of view of the Michael Oher fan club, deflating. At the half, Melrose led 8–0 and went on to win 16–6. Afterwards, Hugh came up to the suite where Leigh Anne and a few of the other mothers and coaches' wives had watched the game. "So what'd you think?" he asked Leigh Anne, not actually expecting her to have a critical thought.

"I think you have the number one left tackle in America and you ran the ball right eighty percent of the time," said Leigh Anne, sharply. "I don't know a lot about football but that just doesn't make a lot of sense to me."

Hugh Freeze's authority on football matters was seldom questioned. Hugh had his own style, and it was, by high school and even some college standards, extremely complicated. He ran flea-flickers and fumblerooskis and double reverses and a seemingly endless variety of passing plays involving as many receivers as possible. He had one play where the quarterback hit the running back with a little screen in the middle of the field, the running back pitched it back to a wide receiver looping through the backfield, and the wide receiver chucked it 30 yards downfield to the quarterback. Of course every pro and college and even high school team has a trick play or three they can go to from time to time. The difference was that Hugh went to them routinely.

He had all these elaborate plays, in part, to compensate for what he saw as Briarcrest's systematic lack of brute force. From time to time he'd get a talented running back or quarterback, but he always found his team overmatched on the line of scrimmage. He couldn't power his way to victory, so he set out to trick his way to victory, and he had done it, often. He'd led the Briarcrest Christian School Saints to five of the previous six Tennessee State Championship games and, in the bargain, raised the money for a brand-new million-dollar football complex ten miles outside of town, a thirty-thousand-dollar boom on which to place his end zone cameras, and not one but two sets of uniforms (120 green helmets *and* 120 gold helmets). He had six paid assistant coaches and three volunteers: a former NFL offensive lineman, a former All-SEC defensive end, and a former All-SEC point guard. The only reason he didn't charter a jet to fly his team to their away games in Nashville is that Sean talked him out of it, on the grounds that it might upset some of the more academically inclined people at Briarcrest who wondered where the football program found all this money. Hugh had just turned thirty-five years old and Sean was willing to bet that by the time he was forty-five, he'd be the head football coach at a major college. Hugh would make that bet, too. "He's so absolutely cocky," said Sean, "that if you don't love him like a brother, you absolutely hate him."

Sean and Leigh Anne both loved Hugh like a brother; on the other hand, Leigh Anne had watched the game and thought: *Hugh doesn't know how to use his most precious football asset.* He had done all his fancy stuff and it hadn't worked. Only toward the end of that game did he pound the ball over Michael's side of the field where—lo and behold—huge holes opened up. After Leigh Anne said what she said, Hugh went silent, turned to Sean, and said, "Sean, I think it's time for me to leave." With that he walked out—and wouldn't answer his cell phone when Sean called him. They'd played that game on a Saturday and so the next morning, of course, everyone went to church. After church, Hugh met in his million-dollar football field house with his ten assistant coaches to review film of the game. The lights went down; the room was solemn. For the first hour or so, Hugh didn't say a word about the outrageous challenge to his authority. Then they came to a play where Michael missed a block. Hugh froze the film.

"Now look at that block Michael Oher just made," he said. "Call Leigh Anne Tuohy about *that* one."

"I can call her all you want, Hugh," said Sean. "But she's right."

Leigh Anne had just fired the first shot in a war that was waiting to happen. After the film, Hugh got up and showed the coaches the game plan for the following week: a chalkboard that was already a blizzard of new formations and new plays. Tim Long sat in the front row and could no longer contain himself. Long had played in the NFL, and yet he had the classic lineman personality: he laid low, said little, followed orders, and insisted on his own relative unimportance. He was six five, 300 pounds, and yet had spent the past two years feeling intimidated by five-foot ten-inch Hugh Freeze, who had maybe played in high school. "He's the sharpest football guy I've ever known, so I just got so I felt kinda inferior to him," said Long. The night before, depressed after the loss to Melrose, Long had flipped on the TV. The movie *Tin Cup* was on, and he sat and watched the whole thing until one in the morning. Why weren't they running the ball behind Michael Oher? He had never seen an offensive lineman who was such a force of nature that he might control an entire football game, if used properly. Now he had. In two years Long had never had the nerve to get up in front of the coaches and speak. Now he did.

"Coach Freeze, I got something to say," he said.

"All right," said Hugh.

Long rose. "I'm not a man of many words," he said. "But last night I watched *Tin Cup*. And I watched that boy par the entire back nine using nothing but a seven-iron."

He let that sink in.

"Well, that's nice, Tim," Sean said from the back of the room. "But what the hell are you talking about?"

"We can win football games running *one* play," Long replied.

"All right, Tim," said Hugh. "What play would that be?"

"Coach Freeze," said Tim. "I think we can run Gap."

The play was called Gap because each lineman was responsible for his own gap, defined as the space between his inside eye and the head of the defender inside of him (the eye and the defender closest to the center). The quarterback handed the ball to the running back. The running back ran at the right butt cheek of the left tackle, Michael's gap, and followed it as far as it would take him. Michael's job was simply to run straight down the field and destroy everything in front of him.

Michael had brought to Briarcrest an argument that ran right through football on every level—high school, college, the NFL. It was the argument Bill Walsh met when he first stressed the passing game as it had never before been stressed. It was the argument between the football fundamentalists and the football liberals. The fundamentalists reduce football to a game of brute force—and some of them do it so well that they appear to have found the secret to football success. The liberals minimize the importance of brute force and seek to overcome brute force with guile—and some of them do it so well that they, too, appear to have found the key to football success. That was Hugh: small, blond, looking nothing like a football coach but every ounce the crafty chess master, or the military strategist. Whatever his politics, Hugh was, by nature, a football liberal.

Sean Tuohy thought there was another reason, apart from his desire to win, why Hugh made everything so complicated: the pleasure of thinking up new things. "Hugh thinks football is supposed to be fun," said Sean. "We've got a quarterback who is average at best. No running back. No speed at receiver. And Hugh wants to run the triple reverse."

Hugh wanted to run a triple reverse because in his seven years as head coach of the Briarcrest Christian School Hugh had never had a player he could count on to physically overpower the bigger kids from the bigger schools. Now he had one of the most awesome forces ever to walk onto a

Tennessee football field; and he didn't at first grasp the implications of that. He thought he could keep coaching the way he had always coached, and win a state championship. He was furious at Leigh Anne because, as he later put it, "she don't know what she's talking about, so she should keep her mouth shut. She was speaking out of ignorance. Fact being, the entire first half, whenever we went Michael's side, Michael was going the wrong way. He lost focus, or wasn't thinking." To which he added: "When you're on the sidelines you don't know what's happening. It took me until halftime to figure it out." Now he had this giant looking down at him telling him he should give the ball to the goddamn running back and let God's gift to head football coaches escort him to the end zone.

"All right," said Hugh.

But he didn't mean it. It took him a full two weeks to suppress his true nature and coach football in a way he'd never coached before. ("It had to be his idea," said Long.) Briarcrest won the next two games, but against weak opponents. The fourth game they faced another big public school, called Treadwell. Treadwell had just humiliated another white Christian school about the size and caliber of Briarcrest, the Harding Academy; and the Treadwell coach, and several Treadwell players, were quoted in the Memphis newspaper saying that they had taken care of one of the Christian schools and didn't think the other would be much of a problem. Hugh had a problem on his hands: Treadwell was better than Briarcrest, if he played the style of football he preferred to play. Every one of Treadwell's skill players would have started on the Briarcrest team. If they were going to win, he'd have to change; and all the coaches knew it. The day before that game, Tim Long came to practice with a 7-iron tucked in his belt.

On Friday night, the players donned their green helmets. There was a reason for this: the light uniforms made them look fast, the dark uniforms made them look big. In his dark green helmet and his dark green uniform, Michael Oher looked about nine feet tall and eight feet wide. Before the game, Hugh gathered together not just his players and coaches but also the offensive line coach from LSU, Stacey Searles, fresh off a national championship, who had come to see Michael play. Hugh loved to give pre-game speeches. "I feel that's the gift God gave me," he said. "I feel that is what I was really gifted at. I never would be emotional during the week. I'd save it all for right before the game." Now he began to speak.

"I don't *mind* that their coach said in the newspaper that they gonna beat us," he started out, then paused for effect. "What I *mind* is that they compared us to Harding." He let that sink in. (The fact that Harding Academy of Memphis was, from ten paces, indistinguishable from the Briarcrest Christian School of Memphis was what made the comparison so deeply, and unforgivably, insulting.) "So what we gonna do when we get the ball, on the first play, is we're gonna run Gap."

"The second play we're gonna run Gap," he said. Now his players were looking at each other. There wasn't a soul in that locker room who didn't know what he meant: the taboo weapon would finally be deployed. Michael Oher would be pointed at the opposition and fired. The Briarcrest Christian School was about to go nuclear.

"Then we're gonna run Gap again," said Hugh. He could feel the thrill in the air.

"The fourth play, we're gonna run Gap."

"The fifth play," he continued, then looked around the room. "What are we gonna run?"

"Gap!" they all screamed. They could be heard by the fans outside the field house, 50 yards away.

"And the sixth play?"

"GAP!!"

"And the seventh play?"

"GAP!!!!!"

Hugh then went quiet, and led them in the prayer that always concluded these pre-game locker-room talks. The players repeated after him:

"For we can . . ." *For we can . . .*

"Do all things . . ." *Do all things . . .*

"Through Jesus Christ . . ." *Through Jesus Christ . . .*

"Who strengthens us . . ." *Who strengthens us . . .*

"Each and every day . . ." *Each and every day . . .*

"And may God . . ." *And may God . . .*

"Bless the Saints!!!" they screamed together at the tops of their lungs. At which point the line coach from LSU could no longer contain himself, and shouted: "Somebody's got to find me a helmet! I got to play tonight."

With that, the team ran out onto the field. Seven plays into the game the score was 14–0 and they had done nothing but give the ball to their stumpy five three running back—"the Oompaloompah," Sean called him—and told him to follow Michael Oher's right butt cheek. The Treadwell defensive lineman across from Michael weighed 365 pounds, but they were the wrong sort of pounds, and Michael blasted them away before moving on to destroy other targets. They ran that same play over and over again. By the time they were done, the Briarcrest offense would know that one play better than a football team ever knew a play. And because they knew it so well, they ran it with conviction and confidence; the entire team moved like a single well-thrown spear, knowing that the head of the spear was among the most terrifying sights on an American high school football field.

The LSU line coach, Stacey Searles, had never seen anything like it. Between plays, Michael was as impressive as during them. He skipped and fidgeted and jumped around like a 165-pound man. *He walked on the balls of his feet.* Running on and off the field he moved like a running back. There was nothing lumbering about him; it was as if when gravity was doling out its assignments, Michael wasn't paying attention. The LSU coach finally turned to Sean and asked, "How many three-hundred-forty-five-pound guys skip?"

By the end of the first half, Briarcrest had scored 40 points. When Sean looked down the sidelines, he saw Hugh shaking his head sadly. "This ain't any fun," he said. And, for Hugh, it wasn't. For the fans in the stands inclined to watch offensive line play, or the viewers of the game films, the sight of Michael Oher operating at full force, with a simple assignment and a definite purpose, was a unique experience. They saw things they had never before seen. They saw defenders, at the snap of the ball, turn and run in the opposite direction. They saw defensive ends assigned to rush the quarterback run to the sidelines to avoid having to make contact with this awesome force in charge of protecting the quarterback. They saw a single offensive lineman determine the outcome of a football game. Tim Long, the former NFL lineman long accustomed to the idea that offensive linemen were built to be ignored, experienced football nirvana. "What was so much fun," he said later, "was when he would take a guy and run him right off the field. He ran one guy right out of the back of the end zone. He just went completely out of the picture."

They beat Treadwell 59–20, with Michael sitting out the last quarter, and the chicken necks—which was what they'd dubbed the freshmen and sophomores—on the field. *God Bless!!!!* read the Briarcrest scoreboard. "That was the defining moment for us," said Hugh. "From that moment we decided that this is what we're going to do and teams are going to have to stop this. No matter what defenses they presented, no matter what blitzes. We were running Gap."

The next game they faced a bigger and tougher public school, Carver High, to whom they had lost badly the year before. Carver had a tough little 200-pound nose tackle who had lived in the Briarcrest backfield. He lined up between the guard and the center and raced through the gap before the Briarcrest lineman could get to him. He'd created total havoc; and this year he was back, bigger and better. Hugh wanted to discourage the kid before he caused trouble again.

Hugh now understood that Michael learned much more quickly from pictures than from words or charts. There was no point drawing up X's and O's on the chalkboard for him. Before the game he showed Michael tapes of the previous year's game, to illustrate the nature of the problem. On the first play of the game Michael moved down from left tackle to left guard, and positioned himself directly across from the kid—who wore No. 30. Hugh had called for a quarterback sneak. He'd told Michael, "I don't want you to block number thirty. I don't want him to go under you. I want him to go for a ride." At the snap of the ball the kid tried to do his usual trick, and jumped into the gap between the center and Michael, but Michael was too quick. He got up under No. 30 and for the next few seconds the nose tackle looked like a man riding a tsunami: arms flailing madly, legs kicking wildly. You could almost hear him gasping for air. Ten yards downfield he was delivered, violently, back to the earth, where he vanished for several seconds beneath Michael, until Michael, with the indolence of an heir to a great fortune getting out of bed in the morning, lifted himself off the flattened body. On the second play Michael lined up at guard again and Hugh called another quarterback sneak. At the snap of the ball No. 30 just threw himself flat on the ground. After that Michael moved back to left tackle, and No. 30 did his best to remain inconspicuous.

They beat Carver and then played Christian Brothers, a school five times the size of Briarcrest and a perennial Tennessee football powerhouse. Across the line from Michael were a defensive end and a linebacker who were Division I college football prospects; the linebacker, Chris Mosby, would later sign to play linebacker for the University of Kentucky. Still they ran Gap, straight into the strength of the defense. Nine plays into the game, Michael went out after Mosby and pancaked him. Mosby left the game and never returned. "The Christian Brothers' game finished my thought process," said Hugh Freeze. "When I saw Michael doing what he was doing to those guys, I thought, 'You know, we just might line up behind him and win a state championship. And really not have to do anything else.' Mosby was the best player we saw. And he wanted no part of him. I've never seen a lineman have that effect, and I tell you what, I coached against Chad Clifton and Will Ofenheusle."*

The funny thing was how unappreciated Michael remained. He was the driving factor in every game and the average fan would have had to force himself to pay attention to him, because the average fan watched the ball. Oh, he might notice that small, slow-running backs were waltzing over the left tackle for 15 yards each carry. He might notice, after the play, how many times Briarcrest's No. 74 was lifting himself off the ground to reveal a previously invisible opponent flat on the grass beneath him. But he wouldn't really understand. Even Michael's own teammates didn't understand his consequences until they watched game film. "In games you'd be too caught

* Clifton is now the left tackle for the Green Bay Packers, and Ofenheusle, a star left tackle for the University of Tennessee, was drafted in 2003 by the New York Jets.

up," said Terio Franklin. "But you'd look at the tape and you'd see he'd be knocking down three, four people on every play."

It took even Hugh Freeze several games to understand that a single offensive lineman, all by himself, could change the ecosystem on the football field. In response to Michael, the other team simply abandoned any hope of getting to the quarterback. In response to Michael, the other team stacked their players in all sorts of strange ways to compensate—thus creating openings elsewhere. Only after the fact, on film, could one fully appreciate the effect of this kind of power. Even the officials were unprepared; Michael dominated the opposition so thoroughly that the officials assumed he must be cheating, and they hurled their yellow flags at that assumption. As Tim Long put it, "The referees would see him killing everyone and try to level the playing field." Midway through the season, Hugh began to take the officials aside before the game and say, "Let me tell you three things about my number seventy-four. My number seventy-four doesn't hold. My number seventy-four will block until the whistle blows. And my number seventy-four is the quickest player on either team. He's not offside; he's the first off the ball." He asked the officials to watch, rather than assume. And when they watched, they saw that Hugh was right.

It wasn't until near the end of the season that an opposing team came up with a strategy for dealing with this new force. Briarcrest's archrival was the Evangelical Christian School (ECS). The two schools met every year in what Sean had dubbed the "Jesus Bowl," and in the 2004 Jesus Bowl ECS sent players to simply tackle Michael Oher, so he couldn't escort a running back down the field. They'd assign a player, or sometimes two, to the job, and the strategy worked; ECS won that game. Afterwards Hugh thought, *That's just got to be illegal, you can't just tackle an offensive lineman.* He called the Tennessee Secondary School Athletic Association and found a perplexed authority, who told him, "Well, we never really thought about it, 'cause why would a defensive player tackle an offensive lineman?" As they'd never heard of anyone doing it, they weren't going to do anything to prevent it. The tactic presented Hugh with about the only chance he had all season to outsmart the opposition. He told Michael, "If they come low, fall on them as heavily as you can, with your arms splayed wide, so they can't call you for holding. If they try to take you head-on, destroy them." Hugh then stacked the left side of the line with extra blockers; they would serve as the downfield escort for the running back, after he had scampered through the large hole where Michael, and the defenders who tackled him, had been.

They made it into the playoffs in early December and found themselves just three games away from the state championship. The first game was against Harding Academy. The Harding coach, Paul Simmons, had taken one look at Michael Oher and seen a player unlike any big man his teams had ever faced. There was simply no way they could win if they didn't do something a little strange. "Our whole goal was to keep Michael Oher from blocking more than one person," said Simmons. He told his six two, 230-pound defensive end to take Michael out below the knees; if he went for his knees, he should be able to bring him down all by himself. "For a defensive end to cut block an offensive lineman is unheard of," said Simmons. "But if Michael buried the defensive end and only the defensive end, that was a victory for us." Michael still opened a hole. ("Instead of having a freeway," said Simmons, "they just had a pretty good path.") And as the game went on, Micheal began to figure out how to use his hands to keep the defensive end away from his knees.

Briarcrest beat Harding, barely, and then faced a team from across the state, Notre Dame. Notre Dame had the ball first. Hugh sent Michael out on defense. He lined up at nose tackle; but the moment the Notre Dame offense broke huddle and came to the line, he backed up and became a middle line-backer, 350 pounds rocking back and forth preparing to charge. The Notre Dame quarterback called time-out and ran to the sidelines to ask his coach what to do about it; the coach didn't really know. The game was never close.

The state championship game was played six hours away in Nashville, in Vanderbilt Stadium. It was a rematch of the Jesus Bowl—the Briarcrest Christian School against the Evangelical Christian School—but it didn't take long to see that Jesus was keeping his distance. Before the first half was over, one of the ECS players had been penalized for calling the referee a motherfucker, and one of the Briarcrest players had been flagged for skipping around the field gleefully, hollering, "We're gonna beat their fucking ass! We're gonna beat their fucking ass!" The problem on both sides was a total lack of balance, caused by Michael Oher, which was odd in view of ECS's victory in their first meeting earlier in the season. But Hugh had succeeded in neutralizing the strategy of tackling Michael, and keeping him on the line of scrimmage. Michael still opened a big hole, but he was no longer available to escort the running back downfield, and so Hugh simply lined up a couple of extra blockers on Michael's side to deal with the downfield tacklers. ECS gave it up, and played him straight. As Briarcrest marched downfield to score the first touchdown, the ECS coach, Jim Heinz, grasped that he was up against an unstoppable force. "Whatever Michael Oher wanted to do," said Heinz, "he did."

At some point early in the game, Hugh Freeze decided he didn't fully enjoy the sight of his team simply rolling over the opposition to the state championship. The truth was, he'd grown weary of winning with brute force; when that force was Michael Oher, it was too easy. In the middle of the second quarter, Briarcrest had the ball first and goal on the ECS ten-yard line. They were leading, 10–0, and if they punched this one into the end zone, the game would be as good as over. Hugh saw Sean walking up the sidelines, no doubt to tell him to just keep running Gap over Michael's right butt cheek until they scored. Hugh sent in the play before he could get there.

"What'd you call?" asked Sean.

"Coach Tuohy, you just don't want to know," said Hugh.

"Hugh, we can just run off tackle three times and score," Sean begged.

"Coach Tuohy, that's not near as much fun," said Hugh. He'd been holding back for two and a half months now and he couldn't hold back any longer. "It was my one season in my coaching career where I didn't feel like myself," Hugh said. When his gut told him that no one in Vanderbilt Stadium expected him to run a trick play—well, that's when you ran a trick play. And his gut now told him that there wasn't a soul in Vanderbilt Stadium who expected him to do anything but run right behind Michael Oher.

When they broke the huddle, the short little fullback hid behind the right guard—when Hugh taught his fullbacks how to run the fumblerooski, he told them, "You should be sniffing the right guard's butt." When they got to the line the fullback squatted down, nose to the guard's rear end, and remained hidden from the defense. Apart from the center, who was on the ball, the Briarcrest offensive linemen never even bothered to drop down into their stances. They stood tall, as if unready for the snap but in fact obscuring the defense's view of their backfield. The center snapped the ball to the quarterback, who walked a step to his right, handed the ball between the legs of the squatting fullback (who buried it in his stomach), and then sprinted out as if running an option play. (This handoff was a wrinkle Hugh had added; in a true fumblerooski, the quarterback puts the ball on the ground, creating a "fumble" that the guard picks up and runs with.) The right guard, right tackle, and halfback all sprinted right with the quarterback. Believing that the quarterback still had the ball, the defense—already slow to react because the play was so bizarre—chased after him. The fullback waited until the coast cleared and then stood up and raced in the opposite direction, around the left end, where his left guard and left tackle waited to escort him downfield.

Everyone did what he was supposed to do, except for Michael Oher. For some reason known only to himself, Michael just stood there from the start of the play until the end. The Briarcrest fullback got as far as the one-yard line before he was pushed out of bounds, by the man Michael should have blocked. On the next play they scored, but Sean was waiting for Michael when he trotted off the field.

"Michael, all you had to do was give that guy a little push and we'd have scored," he said. "What were you thinking?"

"Man, I know," said Michael. "But it was such a great play. I just wanted to watch."

Hugh Freeze had Michael playing the entire game not only left tackle on offense but also at nose tackle on defense. This ensured, among other things, that ECS players spent even more time than usual beneath him. Trailing 17–0, ECS ran a sweep. The ECS fullback led the ECS halfback around the end, and looked for someone to block. The fullback was a five eight, 165-pound gamer named Clarky Norton. Clarky, as it happened, was the son of friends of Sean and Leigh Anne Tuohy, and spent a lot of time inside the Tuohys' home. Clarky's job was to pick up the first defender he saw as he came around the right end. Expecting to encounter an ordinary-sized human, he ran straight into No. 74. "Everything went black for a moment," said Clarky. "Then he goes to throw me on the ground and I think, 'Oh my God, he's gonna kill me.' " But then Michael peered through the face mask and saw the boy he'd dined beside not two weeks before. Their eyes met. "Oh. Hey, Clarky," said Michael, and carefully picked Clarky up and moved him out of harm's way, before running down the ball carrier. "I was like, 'Thank God for the Tuohy family,' " Clarky later said, "because I was about to die."

The season had begun with an act of vengeance; it ended with that act of mercy. A few of the ECS players, frustrated and ungrateful, in effect quit playing the game and turned their energies directly on the player most responsible for their unhappiness. As Briarcrest ran out the clock, the ECS defenders lunged at Michael's knees and tried to take him out. It was dangerous, unsportsmanlike, and probably also un-Christian; and after a few plays of this Michael walked over to an official and asked him to make them stop. The official had no sympathy. "Son," he said. "You been whipping everybody out here all night long. Why don't you just go back to the huddle and let this game be over with." A few minutes later, the Briarcrest Christian School Saints were state champions. Michael Oher was, by general consensus, the best football player in the state of Tennessee. The easy part was over.

CHAPTER SEVEN

THE PASTA COACH

A SURPRISINGLY LONG TIME BEFORE THE BRIARCREST CHRISTIAN School Saints bulldozed their way to a Tennessee State Championship, Leigh Anne mailed the Tuohy family Christmas card. At the end of December 2004, she and Sean would become Michael's legal guardians, but even without the imprimatur of law Michael felt so much a part of the family that she couldn't imagine him out of the Christmas picture. Leigh Anne did everything two months before it needed to be done, and her Christmas card was no exception. She snapped the portrait of her three perfect children in October, and sent it out to several hundred friends and distant relatives, without it ever occurring to her that most of the recipients would have no idea about the strange new addition to the family. A few weeks later, the phone rang late one night. It was a North Carolina cousin.

"All right," he blurted into the phone. "I've just had my fifth beer. Who *the hell* is this black kid in y'all's Christmas card?"

She sprang the relationship on the college football coaches of America in the same take-it-or-leave-it spirit, without comment or explanation. She virtually dared them to ask who she thought she was to harbor the nation's most highly prized lineman. They'd fly into Memphis from all over the country thinking they were coming to sell another poor black kid with raw talent, few strings attached, and the usual vulnerabilities. What they found waiting for them, in effect, was an extremely well connected rich kid who was nearly impossible to impress—and guarded by a warrior princess.

Michael Oher didn't want money or shoes or clothes or cars. Sean and Leigh Anne bought him pretty much whatever he asked for, and his share in the Tuohy estate came to millions. He didn't want to see the NBA games at the FedEx Forum; Sean, who announced the games, had a season pass, courtside. He didn't want free plane tickets, or a fifty-yard line seat for the national championship college football game between USC and Oklahoma. A private jet would fly him to the Orange Bowl or anywhere else for that matter, and Fred Smith's corporate suite would host him once inside. Smith, the founder and CEO of Federal Express, as well as the Orange Bowl's sponsor, was a good friend of the Tuohys. Collins Tuohy was dating his son.

As half the college football coaches in America gathered on his front lawn, Sean assumed the same pose that he had adopted at the end of basketball games when he had the ball in his hands with six seconds to go and his team was down by a point. He feigned indifference. To avoid the appearance of interest, he required all college coaches to approach Michael not through him but through Hugh Freeze. This provided him with an alibi without actually fooling anyone. Everywhere they looked, the college football coaches of America saw evidence of Sean Tuohy's devotion to his alma mater, the University of Mississippi. He and Leigh Anne were building a second home in Oxford, just off campus, on the assumption that Collins would follow her mother's footsteps and become an Ole Miss cheerleader and leading member of the ancient Kappa Delta sorority. When the coaches walked into the living room of the Tuohys' lovely Memphis home, the first thing they saw was the Rebel Christmas tree: red and blue branches festooned with nothing but Ole Miss ornaments. On their way out they passed, in the front yard, a little stone statue of what at first appeared a gnome but, upon closer inspection, proved to be the Ole Miss mascot, "Colonel Rebel." A statue of Santa Claus joined him at Christmas, a giant Easter Bunny came out for Easter, but Colonel Rebel was the statue for all seasons. Sean himself was so well known as an Ole Miss alumnus that a Memphis radio station, on the eve of the University of Memphis–Ole Miss football game, stole his Rebel gnome, hid it, and offered a prize to whichever listener found it first. Leigh Anne and Sean had both been the first members of their families to go to Ole Miss, but their lives were as intertwined with the place as if they'd founded it.

Hugh Freeze, for his part, quickly complicated the wooing of Michael Oher by entering into talks to join the coaching staff at the University of Tennessee. Hugh didn't even pretend not to care where Michael played college football; he let Michael know early and often his opinion that the University of Tennessee was the place for him. Further expanding the web of intrigue surrounding Michael was Justin Sparks, the Briarcrest placekicker. Justin's parents, Robert and Linda Sparks, had family ties to Oklahoma State and Mississippi State, and a lot more money than the Tuohys. The Sparkses' Hawker-800 dwarfed Sean's small plane—which Leigh Anne had dubbed *Air Taco*. The Hawker-800 flew Michael to all Sparks-affiliated schools. And because Justin Sparks could kick a football so well, the number of Sparks-affiliated schools quickly expanded. Justin flew to LSU's summer football camp, and Michael flew with him. North Carolina State was the first to offer Justin a football scholarship and, with direct private jet service established between Memphis and Raleigh, North Carolina State became, to Michael Oher, an appealing place to play football.

But the web around Michael was tightly strung. Inside it, every move triggered a countermove. Nanoseconds after North Carolina State made its offer to Justin, Leigh Anne called the Ole Miss football coach, David Cutcliffe, and told him that if he wanted Michael Oher, he had better offer a scholarship to Justin, too. Cutcliffe quickly did.

During the five months between the start of his senior year and the day—February 1, 2005—when prized college football recruits announced their decisions, Michael Oher was surrounded by people intensely interested in that decision. In what came to be, perhaps inadvertently, a kind of Ole Miss pincer movement, Leigh Anne had brought in Sue Mitchell to tutor Michael every night. Miss Sue, as she was known, had spent her career as a teacher in the Memphis public schools. Now in her mid-fifties, and retired, Miss Sue's only remaining school tie was with Ole Miss, from which she had graduated. Every night for five hours, six nights a week, Miss Sue and Michael worked together. They grew very close. And the closer they grew, the more Miss Sue felt she had to let Michael know what a mistake he'd be making if he didn't go to Ole Miss. On the night before he was making his official visit to Tennessee, for instance, Miss Sue told him that he had to be very careful in Knoxville, Tennessee, as she'd just learned from a good friend acquainted with the mystery novelist Patricia Cornwell that Knoxville, Tennessee, was used by the FBI to study the effects of the soil on decomposing human body parts.

"They bury a hand and let it sit for six weeks, then dig it up and see what it looks like," she explained. "These body parts are just below the surface of Knoxville, but the main thing is where they store them, when they aren't burying them. Right underneath the football field!" When the coaches took him out on the field before the game, she said, Michael should pay less attention to the 107,000 people dressed in orange and cheering him at the top of their lungs than to the hands and feet of dead people set to poke up through the turf. She ended her speech with a cheery, "But it's your decision where you play football. Don't let me 'influence' you!"

Michael, for his part, did an excellent imitation of a ditzy debutante unable to decide which of the fifteen eager young men in her parlor she wanted to escort her to the ball. He of course told Leigh Anne and Sean that he really liked Ole Miss—but only after Leigh Anne and Sean explained to him that, if he had any intention of going to Ole Miss, they really ought to go through the process of formally adopting him, so that the many gifts they had already bestowed on him might be construed not as boosters' graft but parental love. Then he flew off to a Fellowship of Christian Athletes camp at the University of Oklahoma.

A few weeks later, a Memphis news station rolled into a Briarcrest football practice to ask Michael where he might like to go to college. "I really can see myself going to Oklahoma," Michael said, provoking a frenzy on the Oklahoma football fan Web sites, and instigating a number of calls from Oklahoma coaches. He made further, unofficial visits to Mississippi State, Oklahoma State, North Carolina State, Tennessee, LSU, and Ole Miss.

After he'd told the Memphis television audience that Oklahoma was now "at the top of my list," he told Hugh Freeze that it was his "lifetime dream" to go to Tennessee. After he'd shared with his coach his love of Tennessee, he told Robert Sparks how much he also liked Oklahoma State and Mississippi State. And after North Carolina State became the first school to offer Justin Sparks a football scholarship, Michael told the N.C. State coaches how much he liked the idea of playing football for them, too.

The head coaches weren't allowed to visit Michael in Memphis until the end of the Briarcrest football season, but they were allowed to call him whenever they wanted to—which turned out to be whenever Michael would pick up the phone. He had a lifetime of homework to finish, he had football to play, and no hours in the day to waste chitchatting with the head football coach from schools in states he couldn't find on a map.

Sean Tuohy and Hugh Freeze agreed that on Wednesday night each week Michael should go to Hugh's house and receive phone calls. The coaches soon learned that Wednesday night was the night to find Michael Oher, and Hugh soon learned that any coach who happened to get Michael on the phone wound up thinking that Michael might like to play for him. For instance, the recruiter from Alabama, Sparky Woods, called, and Michael, who had not shown the faintest interest in Alabama, jumped on the phone with him and said how much he liked the idea of paying Alabama an official visit. As Michael was allowed to make only five official visits, he was telling the Alabama coach that he was on his short list of five. "If the coaches *ever* got Michael on the phone," Hugh said, "he was going to lead 'em on. Every one of those coaches came away thinking Michael Oher wanted to play for him."

But Michael didn't want to play for them; he merely wanted to fly to see them. Flying on private planes, Michael developed the opinion that pretty much anyplace in America he wanted to go was a delightful day trip from Memphis. One Friday afternoon, Sean came home to find Michael walking out of the house, with the air of a man going for a stroll down the block.

"Where you going?" Sean asked.

"N.C. State," said Michael. He had accepted the school's invitation to make an "official visit." Michael was allowed to make as many unofficial visits to N.C. State as he wanted and to those he could fly in Mr. Sparks's jet. But North Carolina State picked up the tab for the official visit, and they flew their recruits commercial. Sean knew this, and wondered why Michael was leaving the house empty-handed. The boy didn't have so much as a toothbrush on him.

"Where your bags?" asked Sean.

"Not taking any," said Michael. "I'm coming back today."

Sean explained that when you took an official visit, you flew commercial, and when you flew commercial, the miles between the Tuohy home and the North Carolina State football stadium took a lot longer to travel. Michael might need to change planes, and he'd certainly need to accommodate the airlines' schedules. A boy leaving Memphis on Saturday morning for a football game that afternoon in Raleigh, North Carolina, had no choice but to spend the night somewhere other than Memphis.

When Sean had finished, Michael turned around, marched back into the house, and said, "Then I'm not going."

Sean couldn't let that happen. Not turning up for an official visit to N.C. State would give the impression the fix was in for Ole Miss. He hollered at Michael to pack his bag and get his ass to the airport, and Michael did.

The wooing of Michael Oher was pure southern ritual: everyone knew, or thought they knew, everyone else's darker motives, and what didn't get said was far more important than what did. The men seized formal control of the process. The women, acting behind the scenes, assumed they were actually in charge. Of all the people around there was really only one who spoke his mind directly, and advertised his own naked self-interest: eleven-year-old Sean Junior. The first coach through the Tuohy home, Ole Miss assistant coach Kurt Roper, noticed right away that his prized recruit had a special feeling for this little kid. When Roper arrived, he asked Michael to show him around, and they wound up in his room, with Roper reduced to onlooker while Michael and Sean Junior engaged in some endless contest involving miniature basketballs. "You could tell just watching them shoot around," said Roper. "Those two were like brothers." And just in case he didn't pick up on this little kid's importance, Michael muttered something about how Roper "really ought to talk to SJ, because he's gonna have a say in where I go."

When Roper took Michael back downstairs for the sales pitch, Sean Junior followed. At the end of the pitch, to which Michael listened wordlessly, Sean Junior stood up. He didn't raise his hand but he might as well have. "Can I ask my question?" he asked. His voice cracked. He now had this squeaky drawl, to go with his big slow smile and straight black hair falling down over his eyes. He was the sort of little kid grown women took one look at and said, "Oh, isn't he just the *sweetest* thing you ever saw!"

"Uh, sure."

With that, Sean Junior took off on a surprisingly insistent rap. He explained how important it was for him to be near Michael, and how concerned he was that once Michael committed himself to some big-time college football program, he'd become totally inaccessible. Then came the question: if Michael Oher agreed to play football for Ole Miss, what level of access would be granted to his little brother?

"How about we get you an all-access pass?" said the Ole Miss recruiter.

"That'd be good."

LEIGH ANNE'S FIRST impression of the college coaches of America was that none of them had the first idea what he was getting into. Michael Oher was so far from being qualified to go to college that there was hardly any point to the discussion. Added to that was the obvious question: even if he somehow qualified to attend college, without the elaborate support system she had created for him, how would he cope once he got there? She wasn't worried about the spirit but the letter of higher education. School she viewed mostly as something you did well in so you could (a) play sports and (b) get out of it and make something of yourself in the wider world. In the wider world Michael was lost, and would remain lost no matter how much Shakespeare they made him read.

Michael wasn't stupid. He was ignorant, but a lot of people mistook ignorance for stupidity, and knowingness for intelligence. He'd been denied the life experience that led to knowingness, which every other kid at Briar-crest took for granted. Leigh Anne was now making it her personal respon-sibility to introduce him to the most basic facts of life, the sort of things any normal person would have learned by osmosis. "Every day I try to make sure he knows something he doesn't know," she said. "If you ask him, 'Where should I shop for a girl to impress her?' he'll tell you, 'Tiffany's.' I'll go through the whole golf game. He can tell you what six under is, and what's a birdie and what's par. I want him to know the difference between Monet and Matisse."

Restaurant dining was a subject unto itself. "You don't know how com-plicated it all is until you go with someone who has no idea," she said. When she took him to an Italian restaurant, she didn't order for two. She ordered up the entire menu, "just to show him what they were." Michael thus learned to distinguish pesto from alfredo, and puttanesca from marinara.

The trouble was that there really was no end to the quotidian details of upper-class American life bafflingly new to Michael Oher. Every time he turned around, he bumped into a thing with which he should have been completely familiar and wasn't. One day they were leaving the house to go to a track meet. It would be a three-hour flight on *Air Taco* and Michael needed to bring his North Face backpack so he could study on the road. They were still in the driveway when Leigh Anne noticed he didn't have it with him.

"Michael," she said, "go and get your backpack."

"I don't know where it is," he said.

"It's in the foyer," she said. "Just go in and get it."

He left the car reluctantly and returned to the house. She waited several long minutes, then followed him inside to see what on earth had gone wrong. Coming through the front door she found the backpack where it had been, in the foyer. There was no sign of Michael, and she walked through the house until she came upon him near the back door, loitering uneasily. He looked up at her and asked, "What's a foyer?" It took a minute to explain, as her explanations amounted to little lectures on the general subject. ("It's an entry hall some places. A foy-er some places. A foy-yay other places, depending on where you are in the South.") When she was done, Michael just shook his head.

"But let me tell you something," Leigh Anne said. "He absorbed it. He absorbed *everything*." More and more, as Michael put it, "I feel smarter. 'Cause I know what things are."

Leigh Anne Tuohy was trying to do for one boy what economists had been trying to do, with little success, for less developed countries for the last fifty years. Kick him out of one growth path and onto another. Jump-start him. She had already satisfied his most basic needs: food, clothing, shelter, transportation, and health care. He had pouted for three days after she had taken him to get the vaccines he should have had as a child. It was amazing he hadn't already died some nineteenth-century death from, say, the mumps. (When she tried to get him a flu shot the second year in a row, he said, "You white people are obsessed with that flu shot. You don't need one every year.") Now she was moving on to what she interpreted as his cultural deficiencies. She had watched her own penniless husband turn his athletic triumphs into business success and, indeed, a happy life. But there was nothing inevitable about the process; you needed to know how to translate one narrow kind of success into another, much broader kind. To Sean, the skill came naturally. It would never come naturally to Michael, but it might come unnaturally, if she worked on him. She would make him completely at home in white Christian entrepreneurial Memphis, but in the way that a blind man became comfortable in a well-furnished room. He'd memorize the contents of the room so perfectly that his blindness became irrelevant.

To others it might seem silly, or beside the point, for Michael to know how to read a wine list, or score a golf game, or distinguish between Gucci and Chanel, but to Leigh Anne it didn't seem silly at all. He had to know all sorts of ridiculous little things if he was ever going to feel at ease in their world. The rich world. It was one thing when she first met Michael and took him out to buy clothes—she could see why she shouldn't impose her tastes on a stranger. It was another matter entirely now that Michael was, in effect, her child. "I'm trying to make him more preppy," she said. "He just looks so nice in a Ralph Lauren sports jacket."

He went through phases where he wore headbands and throwback jerseys and pants that drooped down the back of his ass, and Sean had tried to explain to her that "yes, it's a thug look, but it's an *organized* thug look, a *high-priced* thug look." She didn't buy it; she fought back; and she took it as one of many small victories in the great war when Michael's friend Terio Franklin from Briarcrest called her one day and said, "Mizz Tuohy, I need some of those shirts with alligators on them—can you get me some?"

In every city in America, rich white kids worked overtime to look and sound like black kids from the ghetto. In Leigh Anne's new world, black kids were crossing the line from the other direction.

She wasn't shy, either, about impressing upon Michael the important distinctions within the white world, and a sense of his new social class. One morning she and Collins and Michael set out on a little trip to Alabama. On their way they stopped at a McDonald's. As they waited for their food, a scruffy-looking man came through in a pickup truck with a gun rack and some dead animal in the bed of his truck. "Lord, he's such a redneck," said Collins. Ten minutes down the road, Michael asked, "What's a redneck?" Collins tried to explain but couldn't quite get it across until she said, "Thomas Trubride is a redneck."*

Trubride was a Briarcrest classmate of theirs. "Thomas Trubride is a good guy," Michael said.

"A redneck is just someone who drives a pickup truck with guns in it," said Leigh Anne.

"That doesn't sound too bad to me," said Michael.

"It's not bad," said Leigh Anne. "It's just not who we are."

Increasingly, it wasn't. In many ways Michael was coming to resemble a naturalized citizen of East Memphis. Every Sunday he attended Grace Evangelical Church, and he was always the first one dressed to go in the morning. His grades had improved, dramatically, thanks to Miss Sue. At the end of the first semester he'd come home from the Briarcrest Christian School with four A's, two B's, and a C. The school's report cards included the students'

* Not his real name.

cumulative class ranking. Up until then Michael had always finished dead last. On the strength of the first semester of his senior year, in a class of 163 students, he placed 162nd. "He's started making his move!" shouted Sean, gleefully. "He's picking them off one at a time, like Sergeant York."

But it wasn't just his grades. He had a family that loved him, and would take care of him, and *he was coming to take their love for granted.* Leigh Anne got these little hints of Michael's security in the relationship. For instance, one afternoon she received a phone call from the store manager of one of Sean's Taco Bells on the other side of Memphis. "Mizz Tuohy," the man drawled, "there is a big ol' black kid here who says we need to serve him for free 'cause he's your son." She had treated Michael as she treated their other two children, which is to say she lavished upon him most of the material comforts and spiritual guidance known to mankind. "A year ago he didn't have a bed to sleep in and wouldn't look you in the eye," said Sean. "Now he's got a car, money in his pocket, and everyone knows who he is." No wonder he got better at football his senior year, thought Leigh Anne. He was charging off the ball with confidence because he was arriving at the football field with confidence.

A year and a half into the reeducation of Michael Oher she felt, for the first time, almost relaxed. One night she realized that for the first time since she began to feel responsible for Michael, she was worried about nothing. "It was nine at night and Sean was traveling with the Grizzlies," she said. "I was sitting alone in bed with the remote in my lap. I could hear Miss Sue working away with Michael at the kitchen table. And I thought: I am so happy. I don't have to worry. I don't have to do *anything.*"

Not long after that, she went out for her afternoon walk. The sky couldn't decide whether to rain or snow; it was a winter day not so very different from the one on which she had first met Michael. She was motoring along at a fantastic clip when her cell phone rang: "Mom, you have to come home," Collins shouted into the phone. "There's been an accident."

All Collins knew was that Michael had been driving Sean Junior out to Briarcrest to play basketball when Michael's truck collided with another car. Collins and Leigh Anne drove out together, but the accident had created a traffic jam, and they couldn't get within a half-mile of it. When Leigh Anne saw they couldn't drive any closer, she left Collins with the car and took off at a sprint. The first thing she saw was Michael's truck, totaled. Then Michael, sitting on the side of the road, crying.

When she got to him, he was sobbing so violently that she could barely understand what he was saying. She grabbed his cheeks in her hands and said, "Michael, listen to me, this could happen to anybody." Then she understood what he was saying: "SJ needs you. Go over to SJ." Then she saw Sean Junior stretched out on the ground on the other side of the mangled truck. She ran to him in a panic. His face was an unrecognizable mass of swollen, oozing flesh. She wasn't entirely sure it was him until he spoke. "Mom," he said, "will the blood come out of my shirt?"

She laughed; how badly hurt could he be if he was worried about his shirt? She sent Michael home and climbed in the ambulance with SJ. And Michael kept right on sobbing. "I just wished it was me going to the hospital instead of SJ," he said later.

At the hospital, the doctors said they were amazed that Sean Junior hadn't been more seriously injured. His face was bruised, and incredibly swollen—"I never knew a human face could do that," said Leigh Anne. "I never knew lips could swell like that." But his bones were perfectly intact. Michael's truck had skidded on the ice across the divide at 25 miles per hour and crashed head-on into the big van, also traveling at 25 miles per hour. The driver of the van was fine, and so was Michael, but no four and a half foot tall boy should have been sitting in the front seat: the airbag had exploded directly into Sean Junior's face. The doctors saw this kind of thing fairly often, and in every other case the airbag busted the little kid's nose or cheekbones, and usually took out a bunch of teeth in the bargain.

Leigh Anne listened to the doctors discuss how bizarrely lucky Sean Junior had been in his collision with the airbag. Then she went back home and relayed the conversation to Michael, who held out his arm. An ugly burn mark ran right down the fearsome length of it. "I stopped it," he said.

In Michael Oher's file at the Briarcrest Christian School were the results of a test he had been given, by the Memphis City School system, at some point during the eighth grade. The test was designed to measure his aptitude for a variety of careers. It showed that he had an aptitude for almost nothing. He scored in the 3rd percentile in spatial relations. In a category called "the ability to learn," he had scored in the 5th percentile. But there was one quality he possessed in an extreme form, and in whatever test the public school system had used to measure it, Michael Oher had scored in the 90th percentile. The quality was labeled "Protective Instincts."

AROUND THE TIME of the accident, the head coaches of the schools on Michael's short list came for their formal visits, or tried to. Urban Meyer was named the new head coach at the University of Florida and called Hugh Freeze every single day for the next two weeks, hoping to be invited into the Tuohy home. Leigh Anne picked up the home phone once a week to find Mark Richt, the head football coach from the University of Georgia. One week Richt finally said to her, "Look, if I have any shot at all, I'll be there in an hour and a half." "I have to be honest with you," said Leigh Anne. "I have no desire to go to Athens, Georgia, every Saturday to watch my son play football." Richt graciously thanked her for not wasting his time, and promised not to pester her further. Some of the coaches gave up; more of them slinked into Briarcrest and found Michael there. But they all knew they remained outside the circle of trust. Michael formally decided who to have into the house, but Leigh Anne was never far away from the decision. In the end, they chose three: Nick Saban of LSU; Phil Fulmer of Tennessee; and David Cutcliffe of Ole Miss.

The assistant coaches of all three universities had spent the previous six months loitering in the vicinity of the Tuohy home and Briarcrest. Trooper Taylor, the recruiter from the University of Tennessee, might as well have had season tickets to Michael Oher's Briarcrest basketball games. "I just love watching high school basketball," he leaned over and told Sean Junior during one of the games. And who could argue the point, when he traveled six hours from Knoxville to do it? Now the head coaches arrived to close the deal with Michael, with the ceremonial air of great chefs condescending to grill the beef, after their sous-chefs had done the marinating.

Sean made a show of not being present when the coaches turned up in his living room (*See? I don't care!*). It was left to Leigh Anne to receive the famous football coaches with a big smile that disguised her gritted teeth. Leigh Anne didn't have Sean's ability to fake it. Sean could pretend all he wanted, but Michael simply *could not function* without the elaborate support system she had built for him: private tutors, constant monitoring, and a steady drip-drip-drip Chinese cultural reeducation program, administered by herself, to assimilate him into their world. ("The Chinese government would have shot her at some point," said Sean, "'cause after she finished telling everyone else what to do, she would have tried to tell them what to do, too.")

Leigh Anne reasoned that, if Michael was going to be part of the family, he had to know what the family knew and behave as the family behaved. Ole Miss was an hour away, and she had, on her fingertips, every pullable string inside the place. The chancellor was a friend, the athletic director called Sean for advice, the locals, who still remembered Sean as the Great White Point Guard, asked him for his autograph. Leigh Anne could be as sweet as the day is long, and seldom did she need to be anything but sweet. But if her friends at Ole Miss didn't take care of her little 350-pound baby she could, and would, have their asses in a sling. She liked knowing that.

The first to enter was Nick Saban, of LSU, fresh off winning the national championship. He was at a serious disadvantage with Michael, however, because Michael had already visited LSU and been entertained for a lurid evening by a few of LSU's star football players. Michael refused to go into the details of the night, but when he came home his eyes were big and round. To Leigh Anne he said simply, "Mom, that's a *bad* place down there." Leigh didn't want to know what had happened—she could guess—but she did ask Michael what they fed him: raw seafood. "I don't think he ate anything the whole weekend," she said.

With Michael's official visit to Ole Miss coming up, she picked up the phone, called Ole Miss recruiter Kurt Roper, and said, "I am faxing you a list of what Michael likes and what he doesn't like and you use it like a frickin' road map." Leigh Anne's list was straightforward and exact: "Don't take him to some titty bar and give him shots of tequila. Don't put him with guys who want to show him how to have sex in eighty-five different positions. Don't feed him a steak: he *hates* steak. Take him to Ole Venice [a restaurant in Oxford] and feed him Fettuccine Alfredo with chicken. Take him to a movie—and not *The Texas Chainsaw Massacre* because he'll just hide his face in his hands the whole time. And then let him go to bed." And the people at Ole Miss had done exactly that. And Michael had come home and said what a fine time he had had—and how Ole Miss wasn't at all like LSU.

Then Nick Saban arrived. Waiting for him were the Tuohys minus Sean, plus Miss Sue, Coach Hugh Freeze, and Briarcrest principal Steve Simpson—who Sean thought would get a kick out of being included. Whatever damage LSU had done to its reputation with Michael on his visit to the place was immediately forgotten—at least by Leigh Anne. Saban came into the house in his Armani suit and Gucci dress shoes and made a point of being polite to every single person in the room. Then he looked around, as if soaking in every last detail of the Olde English and Country French furnishings, and said, "What a lovely home. I just love those window treatments." *I just love those window treatments.* He didn't say, "I just love the way you put together the Windsor valances with the draw drapes," but he might as well have. Right then Leigh Anne decided that if Nick Saban wasn't the most polished and charming football coach in America, she was ready to marry whoever was.

Saban sat down beside the Ole Miss Christmas tree and explained to Michael how he, and LSU, planned to make him not merely a great NFL player but also a college graduate. Michael said not one word. "These coaches would come into the house to talk to him," said Collins, who watched the whole process with disguised but intense interest, "and he was like a stone. The coaches talked the *whole* time." Ten minutes into the soliloquy Hugh Freeze rose, offered a big yawn, and announced that he really had to leave to go spend some time with his family.

Leigh Anne seethed. This was nothing more than the University of Tennessee spitting on LSU. "It was so *rude*," she said. "And he did it because LSU hadn't offered him a coaching job." Saban's response—to not miss a beat, to not take obvious offense—caused Leigh Anne to think even more highly of him. Now *that* was good manners. He knew everything from the names of the people who would tutor Michael to the place on campus where Michael would do his laundry. And he addressed his remarks not only to Michael but also to Leigh Anne. Michael didn't have any questions for him but Leigh Anne did; and he answered them beautifully.

When he was done, Sean Junior stepped out into the living room. "Um, can I ask my question?" he said, then explained his concern about having access to his beloved older brother—and revealed that the recruiter from Ole Miss had offered to give him an all-access pass.

The LSU coach smiled his charming smile and said that Sean Junior could have a pass that said he was welcome in the LSU locker room, even if Michael didn't play football for LSU. And if Michael did play football for LSU, they'd make sure SJ had the adjoining locker.

"Hmm," said Sean Junior. "That'd be good."

On Saban's way out the door, Michael finally had a question, and it was a pointed one:

"You staying?" he asked, offhandedly.

There were rumors in the air that Saban was being offered NFL jobs. There was no point in going to LSU to play football for the incredibly charming Nick Saban if Nick Saban wasn't going to be there. "I've been offered several NFL head coaching jobs since I've been at LSU," replied Saban, "and haven't taken one yet." Then he left and Collins turned to Leigh Anne and said, "That was a *great* political answer." (Three weeks later, the Miami Dolphins announced Nick Saban as their new head coach.)

Michael's next visitor was meant to be Ole Miss's David Cutcliffe. He was due to arrive in the living room on a Sunday, but he was fired the Friday before. *Oops!* The news didn't travel fast, it traveled instantaneously. Moments after Cutcliffe's dismissal, the Tuohys' home phone began to ring. The first caller was LSU's director of athletics, Skip Bertman, to say that even though Nick Saban had just announced he was leaving to coach the Miami Dolphins, and LSU no longer had a football coach, LSU was of course still extremely interested in having Michael Oher play for LSU. The next call came from Phil Fulmer, head coach of the University of Tennessee Volunteers, who was scheduled to visit Michael in a couple of weeks. Now, Fulmer said, he'd be coming right over.

Since the spring football practice that doubled as Michael's coming-out party, Phil Fulmer had become perfectly obsessed with Michael Oher. When the University of Tennessee traveled to play Ole Miss, Fulmer took his entire team on a wide detour to the middle of nowhere, to practice at the Briarcrest Christian School. His plan had been to roll up to Briarcrest in the Volunteers' swanky team buses, and, offensive lineman leading the charge, have the entire team surround Michael Oher and give him a cheer. Even more shrewdly, Fulmer staged his tableau on the very Friday that Michael was meant to make his official visit to Ole Miss. Michael was to become, in effect, Ole Miss's property at 3:00 p.m. sharp. Fulmer planned to arrive just before that, and detain him.

It didn't work out that way. Just before 3:00, Fulmer called the Ole Miss recruiter, Kurt Roper, said his team bus was stuck in Memphis traffic, and persuaded Roper to wait until 3:30 to take Michael away. (In the small world of big-time football, assistant coaches know better than to annoy head coaches; a year later, Fulmer hired Roper at Tennessee.) Roper informed Leigh Anne who, of course, was furious. She told Roper that if Fulmer's bus came even one minute past 3:30 he was to take off. Caught between a rock and a hard place, Roper succumbed to the rock: Fulmer's buses rolled into Briarcrest at 3:31, just in time to pass Roper driving in the other direction, with Michael in the car.

Now Fulmer was coming alone, more or less. He started his official visit to Michael Oher, accompanied by his offensive line coach and his recruiting coordinator, at Briarcrest. Hugh Freeze found Michael and pulled him out of class, and Michael was immediately struck by how happy the Tennessee coaches, and Hugh Freeze, seemed about the firing of the Ole Miss football coach. That afternoon Fulmer happened to be giving a talk at the Tennessee high school football awards ceremony, at which Michael Oher would be named Player of the Year. Michael needed to go home and don a jacket and tie, but Fulmer asked if he could pick him up there and give him a lift. Michael never said no to anyone, and he didn't say no to Fulmer.

A few hours later, Fulmer was greeted at the Tuohys' front door by Ole Miss alumna Miss Sue. Neglecting to mention the human remains buried under his football field, Miss Sue asked him into the house. Miss Sue offered the Tennessee coach a seat in the chair beside the Ole Miss Christmas tree, which he declined. "I'll just stand here and wait," he said. Miss Sue took one look at Fulmer. He didn't have the slightest interest in saying so much as hello to her. He just stood there, awkwardly, in the blue blazer and khaki pants combo familiar to every little boy whose mama dressed him up for church. She decided he was a hick. He might be the head coach of the University of Tennessee but he didn't have half the wit or charm of Nick Saban, not to mention his looks. ("I happen to think Nick Saban is a *very* good looking man.")

Seconds later Collins raced down the stairs, a giant pair of black slacks in hand, chased by Michael, in his underpants, hollering at the top of his lungs, "Give me my pants!" He caught her in the living room, tucked her under his arm as if she were a football, looked up, and saw the head coach of the University of Tennessee. If Fulmer was disturbed by the scene, he didn't show it.

"Michael wasn't impressed by anyone who walked through our door," said Collins. "He just thought: 'Oh, here comes someone else I don't want to talk to who's trying to tell me why I need to go to their school.' " Now, airborne, she looked up at the Tennessee head football coach, said hello, and explained, "Michael is trying to wear *black* pants with his blue blazer to the awards ceremony. Tell him that doesn't match."

Collins watched Fulmer stand there, uneasily. She assumed he was trying to decide if he should agree with Michael or tell the truth. He told the truth. It had no effect.

Fulmer took Michael, in his black pants and blue blazer, away to the banquet, during which Michael had many pictures of his oddly dressed self taken by many newspapers. Afterwards, Fulmer insisted on driving him back home. This time when he and his entourage of assistant coaches walked through the door, Leigh Anne was waiting for them.

Phil Fulmer may not have thought Miss Sue worthy of his attention but he quickly set about ingratiating himself with Leigh Anne. He didn't notice her Windsor valances and draw drapes. He noticed the swimming pool. ("Y'all gotta pond! Ooooo, look at that pool out there.") Then he started making promises, and there wasn't much, it seemed to Leigh Anne, that the coach wouldn't promise if it meant getting Michael Oher to play for the University of Tennessee. To allay her concerns that she knew absolutely no one in Knoxville, Tennessee, he offered the Fulmer guesthouse as a home away from home. To make her feel better about the fact that Michael might be too far away to get home for Thanksgiving, he suggested they all have Thanksgiving dinner together, at the Fulmers'. Every year!

He couldn't be nicer in his own hokey way, thought Leigh Anne, kind of like the Andy Griffith character in *Mayberry R.F.D.* He couldn't have been phonier, thought Collins, who walked away and said, "That was just a lot of good ol' country boy hoopla. He was blowing a lot of smoke up our butt." Leigh Anne didn't see the point of thinking ill of a football coach just trying his best to get what he most desperately wanted, but it did cross her mind that "the difference between Phil Fulmer and Nick Saban was the difference between dealing with the town mayor and dealing with the White House."

The town mayor, for a start, didn't know when to leave. These visits usually lasted a couple of hours. It was ten o clock at night and neither Fulmer nor his retinue showed any signs of tiring. Finally Leigh Anne realized that he was waiting to have a word with the man of the house—so she got on the phone and told Sean to quit hiding and come home, so she could go to bed.

While they waited, Sean Junior seized the moment to take the floor. "Can I ask my question?" he said.

Maybe it was Coach Fulmer's demotic southern manner, or maybe it was just that SJ was growing bolder with age and experience. But this time he put his question bluntly. "What I want to know," he said, after explaining the access he'd been promised to various SEC football locker rooms, "is what's in it for me?"

"Locker room, hell," boomed Fulmer. "You ever been to a UT football game, son?" He set the scene: *one hundred and seven thousand* people all dressed in orange and screaming at the top of their lungs. The band forming a capital T on the field before the game. The Tennessee football team bursting out of the locker room and running through the T, led by none other than Phil Fulmer. When he'd finished, he said: "First home game is on national television. It's me and you running through the T, arm-in-arm."

"And I'll have the other arm," said his recruiting director, Trooper Taylor.

"That'd be good," said Sean Junior.

And so it was that Sean Senior returned home to find in his living room a very self-satisfied Tennessee football coach. He knew that Fulmer knew that there were only three schools left standing: Ole Miss, LSU, and Tennessee. Ole Miss had just fired its coach, and LSU had just lost theirs to the Miami Dolphins. That left Fulmer as the last man standing. Fulmer gave Sean his pitch—"the minute Michael walks on campus he's my starting left tackle"—and then told him, in the spirit of Grant consoling Lee, that he understood completely that such a prominent Ole Miss Rebel might have trouble watching his son become a Tennessee Volunteer. "Phil," said Sean, "if Archie can sit in the Tennessee stands for four years, I can sit in the Tennessee stands for four years."

Archie was Archie Manning, the Ole Miss football legend whose son Peyton had just been named the MVP of the NFL. Before that he had spurned his father's alma mater, Ole Miss, to go to Tennessee, where he had one of the greatest careers in the history of college quarterbacking. After Peyton announced he was going to Tennessee, the Manning family had *death threats.* Ten years later, there were still large numbers of Ole Miss alums with whom Archie Manning was no longer on speaking terms. Leigh Anne heard the exchange and said, "That's fine. But I don't look good in orange so I'm not wearing it."

With that, Phil Fulmer, his assistant coaches, and Hugh Freeze walked out the front door. Fulmer asked Michael to walk him to the car, and Michael—who never said no—walked him to the car. A minute became two minutes became three minutes. Sean turned to Leigh Anne and asked, "You think he's telling Fulmer that he's going to UT right now?" Leigh Anne didn't even want to think about it. At length, Michael came back inside.

"Did you commit to Tennessee?" asked Sean.

Michael just looked at him, and walked upstairs and went to bed.

Sean didn't leave it at that, of course. He was perfectly happy to seem as if he had no control over the process; he wasn't at all happy actually to have no control. He picked up the phone and called his friend, and Phil Fulmer's agent, Jimmy Sexton. Fulmer had only been on the road five minutes and yet Sexton had already spoken to him. "I just hung up with Phil," he said, "and Phil thinks he has him."

At that moment Sean decided to drop his pose of indifference. "If he thinks he's going to Tennessee," he said, "he's not going to Tennessee. I'm going to get LSU back in here."

He couldn't make Michael go to Ole Miss without crossing some kind of line he didn't want to cross. But he had no official ties to LSU; there was nothing the slightest bit unethical about putting him on *Air Taco* to Baton Rouge. Sean was from Louisiana, knew people at LSU, and could control Michael's experience there, in a way he could not at Tennessee. Hugh Freeze must have sensed Sean's intent to upset his own best-laid plans. One night when it was just the two of them, Hugh finally broke and hollered at Sean: "Coach Tuohy, you got to let him go to Tennessee!"

But until Michael declared his intentions, Sean would do nothing at all. And, left alone, Michael didn't declare anything. "I know Michael better than anyone," said Sean. "And I would look at him and say: what is going on in that head?"

Michael flew off to San Antonio on *Air Taco* and played in Tom Lemming's U.S. Army All-American game. Lemming invited him after Hugh Freeze called and told him "it was Michael's lifelong dream to play in the Army all-star game," and that the reason he hadn't filled in the forms was that he was embarrassed by his penmanship. Sean thought Michael had fled his meeting with Lemming in haste because "he thought that to play he was going to have to join the Army." Lemming didn't actually believe any of this, but he had a last-minute need for someone to play center for the East squad.

Michael had never played center in his life, but he did the job beautifully. After the game, Lemming forgot his dark suspicions of Michael's character and declared in print that Michael Oher was far and away the nation's finest offensive line prospect. At the all-star game, ESPN reporters poked microphones into the faces of the nation's top prospects and asked them to declare their plans for college. Michael declined to answer.

Two weeks later, Ole Miss found itself another head coach. With USC about to play for the national championship, the USC defensive line coach, Ed Orgeron, formally agreed to replace David Cutcliffe. He flew to Mississippi for the press conference, where he announced that his first order of business was to persuade Michael Oher to become an Ole Miss Rebel. The press conference began in Oxford at one in the afternoon; at five Coach O was marching through the Tuohys' front door in Memphis. Memphis had never before seen or heard anything like him. This new coach had a neck that ran like a drainage pipe from his chin to his chest, and a chest that seemed to extend all the way down to his ankles. The ankles were thin and strangely feminine, and so the effect of the whole was of a great wooden barrel teetering on toothpicks. From the depths of the barrel emerged sounds so clotted and guttural that, when you first heard them, you did not recognize them as English, or, for that matter, human speech.

"YAAAWWW BEEE BAAWWW!"

Huh?

"YAAAWWW BEEE BAAWWW!"

That's what he bellowed as he burst through the door and got his first look at Michael in the flesh: "YAAAWWW BEEE BAAWWW!" ("You a big boy!") Then he gave Michael a huge bear hug, followed by the sales pitch.

Michael listened to the hearty Cajun coach for a good thirty minutes, as he listened to the other coaches, only in Coach O's case there was a twist: Michael couldn't understand a word he said. He seemed to be saying something about being a really good recruiter, who planned to turn the Ole Miss football program around, but that he needed a star recruit like Michael Oher to kick-start the process. "It was scary," said Michael later. "I never heard anything like that." Leigh Anne, Collins, and Sean Junior were equally lost. Only Sean, who grew up in southeast Louisiana, could understand what Coach O was trying to say. "Coach O is pure one hundred percent coon-ass," he explained, "and I grew up surrounded by coon-asses."

Still, as Michael never said anything to the coaches, or even signaled non-verbally his interest in what had been said, he was, in his way, Coach O's ideal listener. He sat in silence and pretended to understand. When Coach O finally finished, Michael asked his first sincere, formal question of the entire five months' recruiting process.

"What," he asked, "are you going to do for the kids that already committed to Ole Miss?"

"My jaw about hit the floor," said Collins, who had been fixing something in the kitchen. "Michael spoke!"

Coach O sensed, shrewdly, that there was a right answer and a wrong answer to this. "*Lemsday!*" he bellowed. "Let them stay!"

"That's all I want to know," said Michael. With that Coach O, who apparently had been forewarned, turned on Sean Junior, and beat him to the punch.

"All right big boy what you got for me?" he boomed. "I know you got something."

Even SJ was startled: word traveled fast. Apparently Coach O had heard that if he wanted to dance with Michael Oher, he'd need to pay the little fiddler. SJ's speech grew longer with each passing coach. He now explained that Ole Miss had initially offered a locker-room pass, but then LSU had topped that offer with the offer of not merely a locker-room pass but a locker. But then Coach Fulmer came along and tossed in his wild card: running with the team through the T in front of 107,000 screaming fans. When he was done, Coach O was ready to join the bidding war.

"Son," he said, in a grave tone. "First game of the season, you and Coach O will be walking through the Grove together."

"The Grove" was Ole Miss's answer to the T. Before each home game, tens of thousands of Rebel fans did not so much gather as swarm. They ate and drank and prepared their bodies for the chemical jolt of an SEC football game. The pre-game ritual climaxed with the Ole Miss players marching along a narrow brick path through the Grove that led to the stadium, known, more than a little hopefully, as "The Walk of Champions." The whole shebang was conducted in the spirit of an ancient rite, when it was in fact the brainchild of an Ole Miss football coach in the early 1980s.

"That'd be good," said Sean Junior.

On the way out the door, Coach O, obviously anxious to know what sort of impression he had made on Michael, asked Sean, "Whataamoo baadaat kwestON?" ("What did he mean by that question?")

"He wanted to know what you are going to do about Justin," said Sean. Justin was Justin Sparks, the Briarcrest placekicker and provider of jet transport to Michael, who was now planning on kicking for Ole Miss. Coach O signaled his relief with a smile and said, "Shaaa! Cudda tow me baaaa fo ahwak-n-heee." ("Sean! You could have told me that before I walked in here.")

"Don't worry. You gave him the right answer."

Actually, Michael was after something more important than the fate of his Briarcrest teammate. "I wanted to see what type of person he was," he said later. "If he's pulling scholarships that they'd promised kids, would you want to play for that kind of person? Be around that kind of person?" Coach O wasn't that kind of person, he decided; more interestingly, Coach O was the only coach who didn't promise him he'd crack the starting lineup his freshman year. Michael decided Coach O was all right.

The whole recruiting process had been interesting to Michael, in its way. It told him a lot about the people who had taken an interest in his future. His high school coach had used him to get himself a college football coaching job, and by the end he had taken to calling Hugh Freeze "The Snake." After Hugh laughed about it—this was the way their world worked—the nickname stuck. Michael had put Sean in a position to pressure him if he wanted, and Sean hadn't, at least not overtly. Leigh Anne and Miss Sue had pressured him plenty but for what seemed to him to be legitimate reasons—if he went too far away they couldn't take care of him, and he needed a lot of taking care of. Sean Junior was the most nakedly ambitious, but Michael sort of enjoyed the boy's naked ambition. "SJ worked it," said Michael, laughing.

"He had locker-room passes, trips through the T. If I'd a kept on, he'd a been playing on a team."

The Orange Bowl was the cherry on top of the process, at least for Sean Junior. The Tuohys went to the national championship game as a family, and Coach O had arranged for them to attend USC's pre-game practice. While it was against NCAA rules for Coach O to so much as wink at Michael Oher, there was nothing that said his players couldn't amuse Michael. At the end of the practice USC's two biggest stars, quarterback Matt Leinert and running back Reggie Bush, along with the entire USC offensive line, came over to Michael, surrounded him, and offered fulsome praise of Coach O. As he eavesdropped on their banter, Sean Senior noticed a pair of shocking facts: (1) Michael was bigger than *all* the USC linemen; and (2) Sean Junior had somehow wormed his way into the scrum, and was sidling up to Reggie Bush.

"Hey, Reggie," Sean Junior was saying. The future Heisman Trophy winner looked down, obviously a little surprised. *How did this little kid get in here?*

"Whazzup dawg?" said Reggie Bush.

"You know, that's my brother," said SJ, pointing to Michael.

"Oh really," said Reggie Bush, perhaps thinking two words would suffice to abort a weird conversation. They didn't.

"Can I have your sweatbands?" said Sean Junior.

On February 1, 2005, Michael Oher held a press conference to announce where he intended to go to college. He faced a bank of microphones and explained how he'd decided he'd go to Ole Miss, as that's where his family had gone. To hear him talk, you'd have thought he'd descended from generations of Ole Miss Rebels. He answered a few questions from reporters, without actually saying anything, and then went home and waited for all hell to break loose. Up in Indianapolis, the NCAA was about to hear a rumor that white families in the South were going into the ghetto, seizing poor black kids, and *adopting* them, so that they might play football for their SEC alma maters. But it was still weeks before the NCAA investigator would turn up in the Tuohy living room.

After his press conference, Michael had to attend to the important business of playing miniature basketball with Sean Junior. Up they went into SJ's room, whose walls were a shrine to his father's Ole Miss playing career: trophies, pictures, flags, newspaper articles. Over the bed was a beautifully framed basketball net, with bloodstains on its cords. This was the net Sean Senior had cut down on national television, right after he'd led Ole Miss to its first and only SEC Tournament Championship. The net said something that never would be put into words, about the relationship between Ole Miss and the Tuohys—that the school was less source of identity than foil. Sean was always the smallest man on the court, and he was forever taking cheap shots and rising bloodied from the floor. Blood dripped from his chin as he cut down the net, sullying and sanctifying his prize. The moment he'd come down from the rim, however, his coach had grabbed the net from him, and claimed it as the property of the University of Mississippi. Into the Ole Miss trophy case the net went. The next night Sean had gone out to a playground, cut down another net, broken into the Ole Miss trophy case, and swapped the net he'd stolen for the one he'd earned. "That's my blood," he said simply. "And so that's my net."

Under the bloody net Sean Junior and Michael resumed their endless struggle for supremacy in miniature basketball. SJ was far less interested in old school ties than his private haul of booty. "I was hoping to go to LSU," he said. "I had a locker and a field pass for the whole season." Special access to the hallowed ground of SEC football, inside the T and the Grove, was nice, but it didn't beat having his own locker in the locker room of the national champions. About Michael's motives, or his thinking, SJ could have cared less. He never prodded him with the questions that obsessed the grown-ups, because they never occurred to him. But now he was, faintly, curious.

"When d'you decide?" asked Sean Junior.

"Back in September," said Michael. As the wooing of Michael Oher had started, in earnest, in September and run all the way to February, a lot of other people's valuable time had been wasted: all along Michael had known he was going to Ole Miss. "It was running across my mind to go to Tennessee, because everyone was saying I shouldn't go to a place in transition," he said. "But deep down inside I wanted to go to Ole Miss. It just felt like home." It felt like home, of course, because home now felt a lot like Ole Miss.

"But," he now told the little boy he loved like a brother, "it was kind of cool having all those coaches around here."

"Uh-huh," said Sean Junior, and promptly lost what little interest he'd had.

CHAPTER EIGHT

CHARACTER COURSES

"THIS IS JOYCE THOMPSON, ASSISTANT DIRECTOR OF ENFORCEMENT at the NCAA. Today's date is March 30, 2005. And I am currently talking to prospective student-athlete Michael Oher. There are other individuals in the room at this time and I would like for them to state their names for the record."

"Sean Tuohy," said Sean.

So began the investigation of Michael Oher. Leigh Anne refused to participate, on the grounds that the whole thing was offensive. Collins was busy. Sean Junior failed to see the upside. But then, the upside was hard to see. Some college football coach, and quite possibly more than one college football coach, had gone to the NCAA and accused the Tuohys of abducting Michael and showering him with possessions in exchange for becoming the future left tackle of the Ole Miss Rebels. The NCAA had sent this lady to investigate. The lady was young, black, intelligent, childless, private school–educated, and with a manner and an accent that made her impossible to place as anything other than generically American. She had an off-the-rack professional quality about her, too, and if she didn't make a good living shining a faint light on the shady dealings between high school football players and the college boosters who love them, she probably could have made a better one reading the news at any local television station in the country.

She settled into one of Leigh Anne's antique English chairs and took in her surroundings. On a cabinet behind her stood a framed copy of the page in *USA Today* on which Michael Oher had just been named a First Team High School All-American football player. Joyce Thompson politely explained that she had come to find out if Michael Oher had violated any NCAA regulations. If he had, and she could prove it, he could put aside his football career for a while.

Then she switched on her tape recorder, and asked Michael for his name, address, phone number, and the names of the people with whom he lived. These he effortlessly supplied. It was the next question that tripped him up: "And who are your siblings?"

"Collins Tuohy and Sean Junior," said Michael.

She was about to move on but Sean, unbidden, jumped in. "That's his siblings *here*," he said. "He's got other siblings."

"And so who are your other siblings?" she asked.

Michael looked at her. "Uh—name 'em *all*?" he said, as if she had asked him to recite the Kama Sutra in the original Sanskrit.

Miss Joyce Thompson laughed. Yes, she said, could he please name them all. Michael sat with his hands folded in his lap—and now his fingers were extended. He was trying to count, without seeming to. It was humiliating not to be able to come out quickly with the names of his brothers and sisters, especially before this well-dressed, privately educated black lady from the NCAA.

"Marcus Oher. Andre Oher, Deljuan Oher," he blurted out.

The lady scribbled as fast as she could to keep up. "Deljuan?" she asked. "Can you spell that?"

"D . . . E . . . L . . ." the letters came slowly at first, then charged out of him in a wildly uncertain bull rush. "J-U-A-N?"

"Okay," she said, with a big smile.

"Rico Oher," he continued.

"Okay," she said.

"Carlos," he said.

"Okay," she said.

"John," he said.

"Okay," she said.

He'd stopped. Still staring at his hands in his lap, he repeated: *Marcus, Andre, Deljuan, Rico, Carlos, John.* He sounded like a small child reciting the alphabet from the beginning in an attempt to propel his mind to whatever follows "G."

"All brothers?" asked the lady from the NCAA.

Michael nodded and relaxed, and it was clear to Sean that he was going to seize on the finality in her voice to leave it at that. Marcus, Andre, Deljuan, Rico, Carlos, John. Sean didn't know how many there were, but he knew there were more than those six.

"No," said Sean. "We're not finished."

Michael thought. "Denise," he said, finally.

"Okay," said the lady from the NCAA, uneasily, putting pen back to notepad.

"Tyra," said Michael. Or, perhaps, "Tara."

"Tyra?" asked the NCAA lady. "T-Y-R-A?"

"Uhhhh . . ." He was unsure. "Yes," he finally said.

"Okay," she said, then began to laugh. "Are these still Oher?"

"Uhhhh—" said Michael, thinking for a moment. "Yes."

"He dudn't know that," said Sean. "Some are."

"Depthia," added Michael.

Sean watched Michael. He might not know the length of Michael's bloodlines but he knew the depth of his anxiety. Confronted by alien authority figures, Michael froze. He was more likely to tell this woman what he thought she wanted to hear than the truth.

"Depthia?" said the lady. "Can you spell that for me?"

"D—" Michael starts, and then gave up. "No."

"Oher or Williams?" asked the lady—because she knew that Michael's legal name was Michael Jerome Williams.

"Oher."

"They can't all be Oher!" said Sean. He knew that there were at least five different fathers.

"It *is Oher*," Michael insisted. Then he thought some more.

"Marcus Young," he said.

"Okay," said the NCAA lady. She was now shaking her head in wonder.

"David Young," said Michael.

"Okay," she said, scribbling away.

"How many's that?" asked Sean, with genuine curiosity.

"Thirteen," said the NCAA lady.

"*Thirteen?*" asked Michael. It was as if he couldn't imagine how she'd arrived at such an absurdly big number. Sean Senior took the list and handed it to Michael to study. Michael stared at this list for a very long time. As he did, the NCAA lady giggled nervously. Michael announced, "You put John down twice."

"So there's two Marcuses?" she said, taking back her list. "Not two Johns?"

That was right. Or so he said. It had taken ten minutes just to sort out the names of Michael's brothers and sisters. And that would be the easiest piece of personal information for the NCAA investigator to extract from Michael Oher.

"How did it come to be that—uh—you began living with the Tuohys?" she now asked.

"Uh—" said Michael. "When I came to Briarcrest my tenth-grade year. Uh. Coach Tuohy was—uh—a volunteer coach. . . . And, uh, I met him there. I decided to live with him summer after my junior year. He talked to me all the time. He was in my situation."

"Okay," said the lady, dubiously.

"He didn't have much growing up and I didn't have much growing up," said Michael.

"Okay," said the lady, even more dubiously.

"It wasn't the summer," said Sean. "It was before your birthday. It was about March of 2004. . . . But he lived here off and on all the way to then."

"Describe your living situation at the time," said the lady. "Because when you say that, you know, that Mr. Tuohy was in your same situation, I don't necessarily know what that means. So can you describe a little more about your situation?"

"How he didn't have a lot coming up," said Michael. To which he added nothing.

Her boss back in Indianapolis was an NCAA lifer named Dave Didion. Didion oversaw the investigations of the nation's top football prospects, and said he very much enjoyed the work because "it's like a jigsaw puzzle that comes in a box with no pictures on it." This jigsaw puzzle was even more perplexing: the box came locked. When the NCAA investigator asked Michael when he had last seen his father, he said, "When I was about ten," and left it at that. When she asked him why he didn't live with his mother, he didn't say anything at all. When she asked him who had paid his tuition at Briarcrest, he said he had no idea. When she asked him what he had done for food and clothing, his answer suggested he didn't really need food or clothing. Exasperated, she asked Sean if perhaps he had bought clothes for Michael. To which Sean replied he'd bought him "maybe a T-shirt"—which might have been strictly true, as Leigh Anne did the shopping.

Sean didn't trust these people. They didn't think in terms of right and wrong. All they cared about was keeping up appearances. The NCAA rules existed, in theory, to maintain the integrity of college athletics. These investigators were meant to act as a police department. In practice, they were more like the public relations wing of an inept fire department. They might not be the last people on earth to learn that some booster or coach had bribed some high school jock, but they weren't usually the first either. Some scandal would be exposed in a local newspaper and they would go chasing after it, in an attempt to minimize the embarrassment to the system. They didn't care how things were, only how they could be made to seem. A poor black football star inside the home of this rich white booster could be made to seem scandalous, and so here they were, bothering Michael. The lady said she was just trying to establish the facts of the case, but the facts didn't describe the case. If the Tuohys were Ole Miss boosters—and they most certainly were—they had violated the letter of every NCAA rule ever written. They'd given Michael more than food, clothing, and shelter. They'd given him a life.

It didn't help that his new market value had already led Michael to become more cynical of the people around him. The point the NCAA lady was driving toward was now never very far from his mind: maybe these rich white folks had been so helpful to him the past two and a half years only because they had identified him as this precious asset. Case in point: his own high school coach. The Snake, who had been in quiet negotiations with Tennessee for a coaching job, had tried to talk him into going to Tennessee. Then right after Michael announced he was going to Ole Miss—and not Tennessee—The Snake announced that he, too, was going to Ole Miss. Coach O had offered him a job.

Sean tried to explain to Michael that that was just how the world worked—that Hugh Freeze was born to coach football and Ole Miss was lucky to have him—but Michael reserved the right to dwell on the selfish motives of others. For his senior yearbook, he'd selected his quote, from a rap song, which he'd expurgated for Briarcrest Christian School consumption: "People ask me if I ever reach the top will I forget about them? So I ask people if I don't reach the top will y'all forget about me?"* He didn't go so far as to treat Leigh Anne with suspicion but, as Leigh Anne put it, "with me and Sean I can see him thinking, 'If they found me lying in a gutter and I was going to be flipping burgers at McDonald's, would they really have had an interest in me?'"

The thing was, you never knew when these doubts would surface. When the NCAA lady finally quit bugging him about his clothes, she turned to the matter of his new pickup truck. (*Who had told her about the truck?*) She asked Michael if Sean had bought the truck for him as a reward for signing with Ole Miss. Sean had tried to cut her off at the pass, and treated the question as absurd. But Michael had just chuckled. "You mean, I'd a got a truck

---

* From Playa Fly, "Crownin' Me": "Nigga's ask me . . . / If I ever reach the top will I / forget about them . . . / So I ask nigga's if I don't reach the top, will yall forget / about me. . . ."

if I'd gone to Tennessee?" he asked Sean, right there in front of the NCAA investigator. He might have been joking. Then again, he might not have.

The woman let that one go, or seemed to. Putting food, clothing, and transportation to one side, she moved on to shelter. Where, she asked, had Michael slept at night, both immediately before he had come to the Briarcrest Christian School, and immediately after?

"At Tony Henderson's," said Michael. Big Tony. The man whose mother's dying wish had led him to cart his son, and Michael Oher, out of the hood. Now, when Michael thought at all about Tony, he wondered why he was working so hard to stay friends with him. Once a week, it seemed, Tony reminded him of all he had done for him.

"Did you live with Tony all the way from eighth-grade year to sophomore year—or were there stops in between?" she asked.

"Stops in between," he said.

"And so tell me . . ." she began.

"You ain't got enough paper for this," said Sean.

"You tell me where you lived," said the NCAA lady to Michael, ignoring Sean. "'Cause that's what I'm going to ask you. Was it just different stops per night? Who would you be living with?"

Michael began, haltingly, to list families, black and white, who had sheltered him during just the first year and a half at the Briarcrest Christian School. The lady took down the names, as she had taken down the names of his brothers and sisters, with growing incredulity. *In how many different homes could one sixteen-year-old boy sleep?*

"This is a *huge* undertaking," said Sean. "This is like an eighty-five-page document. This is a *monstrous* undertaking. It was a nomad existence."

"Okay," she said, but to Michael, not Sean. "And that's because of your limited resources growing up."

Michael didn't say anything, just nodded.

"That and because his mom was in and out of rehab centers constantly," said Sean.

"Is it safe to assume that you didn't have a permanent address with your mom?" asked the NCAA lady. Michael nodded. The woman became even

more curious: then where *on earth* had he lived before he stumbled so luckily into Big Tony's house? How had he survived? Had he been homeless as a
child? That's when Michael mumbled something about "foster homes."

Sean was aware that Michael had had some contact with the foster home
system but not because Michael had volunteered the information. Not long
before, the Briarcrest football team had thrown a party for itself at the Chicka-
saw Country Club. The busboy had come by their table, spotted Michael, and
nearly dropped his tray. Michael had jumped up and given the busboy a bear
hug. Then they both began to weep. When Michael sat back down he
explained, in a very few words, that they had been in a foster home together for
a year, when he was around eight years old. Further details he declined to offer.

The NCAA lady now wanted the answer to a question the Tuohys had
never asked: how many foster homes had Michael been in? Michael sat there
thinking to himself.

"How many?" asked Sean. "Two? Three?" He was beginning to wonder
why the NCAA needed to know all this stuff.

"Um," said Michael, finally. "Two, I think."

"And that's here in Memphis?" asked the lady.

Michael nodded.

"I'm saying," said Sean. "It's a book."

Not a good one. Michael's answers were as nourishing as a bag of stale
potato chips, and as vexing as a Rubik's Cube. The lady was now officially
frustrated. She'd come all the way from Indianapolis to interrogate Michael
Oher, but she was getting no answers from Michael Oher, and too many
from this rich white Ole Miss booster whose roof, for some reason, Michael
Oher lived under. She stared intently at Michael and said, "Michael, you
have to talk to me." It had no obvious effect. The most basic facts of his own
life he either didn't know or didn't recall. She must have decided that Sean
was the problem because when Sean tried to answer yet another question
she'd directed at Michael, she turned on him and said, "I'll interview you
later." She might as well have said, "Shut the hell up."

"I'm just concerned," said Sean. "With Michael, you got to pull it out of
him. And I'll help you pull it out of him."

If Michael disagreed with this assessment, he didn't let on.

"Okay," said the NCAA lady, wearily.

For the next five hours the two of them tried, each in their own way, to coax from Michael Oher his personal history. This investigation obviously turned on the Tuohys' motives, and his. To understand motives she needed to know, or thought she needed to know, the complete biography of Michael Oher. But the biography of Michael Oher was a slippery subject. Indeed, the more you questioned Michael, the more you understood that his answers depended on the way you'd phrased the question. Ask him how many foster homes he had lived in and he would say he wasn't sure. Ask him if he had lived in two or three different foster homes, he would treat it as a multiple choice test, with two options, and would answer "two" or "three." Ask him, instead, if he had lived in nine or ten different foster homes, and he would have said "nine" or "ten." He treated the NCAA investigator as he treated everyone who asked him about himself: as an intrusion. To his one-word answers he would add *nothing*—not a scintilla of color commentary or new information.

Five hours into the interrogation, at ten o'clock at night, Miss Sue arrived and announced that she and Michael needed to study for a test. At that moment, late in Michael's senior year, his grades fell so short of the NCAA's requirements that whatever crimes against college football recruiting this NCAA lady found him to have committed were irrelevant. He wouldn't be allowed to attend Ole Miss on academic grounds. "But I'm not finished," protested the NCAA lady. Sean asked how much more time she needed and she said, "At least five more hours." Five more hours, both Sean and Miss Sue said, was exactly what Michael didn't have, and wouldn't have for many weeks.

And with that, the NCAA investigator walked out the door and past the statue of Colonel Rebel in the Tuohys' front yard. She'd be running this information by her superiors at the NCAA, she said. If they shared her dissatisfaction, she'd be back for more. When she was gone, Michael shed his stone face for a quivering one and went and found Leigh Anne. "That lady upset me," he said, tears in his eyes. "I never want to talk to her again." Leigh

Anne's head swiveled angrily until her eyes found Sean. "Don't you let that lady back in this house," she said, as if he had any control over the NCAA. And Sean thought: *Chalk this down as another sleepless night.*

TO GET INTO THE NFL Michael Oher needed to first get into college, and to get into college he needed to meet the NCAA's academic standards. The NCAA had a sliding scale of ACT scores and grade point averages; the higher the ACT, the lower the required GPA. Given Michael's best ACT score (12), to play college football he would need a 2.65 overall GPA. He'd finished his sophomore year with a 0.9. A better performance the back end of his junior year, when he'd moved into the Tuohy home, had raised his cumulative average to 1.564. That's when Leigh Anne took over more completely. Before Michael's senior year, she called every teacher at Briarcrest and asked them to tell her exactly what Michael must do to earn at least a B in their class. She didn't expect them to just hand Michael a grade—though she wouldn't have complained if they did. But to her way of thinking a B was the fair minimum to give any normal person willing to take the simple steps. She would hound Michael until he took those steps. Just give me the list of things he needs to do, she told the teachers, and he will do them.

And he did. Two days into his senior year he had come home, dropped his massive North Face book bag onto the kitchen table, and said, "I can't do this." Leigh Anne thought he was about to cry. The next morning she told him to suck it up and pushed him right back out the door. But that's when Leigh Anne had brought in Sue Mitchell.

As a tool for overhauling the grade point average of Michael Oher, as well as for broadening his experience of white people, Sue Mitchell had a number of things to recommend her. In her thirty-five-year career she had taught at several of the toughest Memphis public schools. At Bartlett High School, her final stop, she had taken over the cheerleading squad and whipped them into five-time national champions. She had applied to work at the Briarcrest Christian School, but Briarcrest had rejected her out of hand because, though Miss Sue said she believed in God, she had trouble proving it. ("The application did not have *one* question about education," Miss Sue said. "It was all about religion, and what I thought about homosexuality and drinking and smoking.") She hadn't been Born Again, and she didn't often go to church. She also advertised herself as a liberal. When Sean heard that, he hooted at her, "We had a black son before we had a Democrat friend!"

Still, in spite of these presumed defects, Miss Sue was relentless and effusive—the sort of woman who wants everything to be just great between her and the rest of the world but, if it isn't, can adjust and go to war. And that's what she did. She worked five nights a week, four hours each night, for free, to help get Michael Oher into Ole Miss. The Tuohy family looked on with interest. "There were days when he was just overwhelmed," said Collins, who saw the academic drama unfold both at school and at home. "He'd just close his book and say, 'I'm done.' " When he did this, Miss Sue opened the book for him. She didn't care about football, but she cared about *Ole Miss* football, and it gave her pleasure to think she was contributing, in her way, to the Lost Cause. She also, fairly quickly, became attached to Michael. There was just something about him that made you want to help him. He tried so hard, and for so little return. "One night it wasn't going so well and I got frustrated," she said, "and he said to me, 'Miss Sue, you have to remember I've only been going to school for two years.' "

His senior year he made all A's and B's. It nearly killed him, but he did it. The Briarcrest academic marathon, in which Michael had started out a distant last and instantly fallen further behind, came to a surprising end: in a class of 157 students, he finished 154th. He'd caught up to and passed three of his classmates. When Sean saw the final report card, he turned to Michael with a straight face and said, "You didn't lose, you just ran out of time." Then they both fell about laughing.

He'd had a truly bizarre academic career: nothing but D's and F's until the end of his junior year, when all of a sudden he became a reliable member of Briarcrest's honor roll. He was going to finish with a grade point average of 2.05. Yet, amazing as that was, it wasn't enough to get him past the NCAA. He needed a 2.65. And with no more classes to take, he obviously would not get it.

Now it was Sean's turn to intervene. Watching him pore over the NCAA rule book searching for ways to raise Michael's grades after grades had ceased to be given out called to mind a rich man's accountants cracking the tax code. He approached American higher education with cold calculation and joyful cynicism. One of the lessons he had picked up from his own career as an NCAA student-athlete was that good enough grades were available to anyone who bothered to exploit the loopholes. When Sean first arrived at Ole Miss, he learned, just in time, that freshman English had flunked many a jock. He went looking for a loophole and quickly found one: Beginner's Spanish. For some reason he didn't care to know, Ole Miss allowed freshmen to substitute a foreign language for the serious English class. He'd had eight years of Spanish in school, so the returns were impressive: two A's in Spanish without lifting a finger instead of the two D's in English for which he'd have had actually to read books.

Now Sean had been out of school for twenty-two years and so his grade-rigging skills were a bit rusty, but the skill for avoiding books was among the last to abandon the aging athlete. Plus he had help. Coach O was on board. Having completed his move from USC to Ole Miss, Coach O was now giving speeches to auditoriums filled with Ole Miss boosters. They didn't understand a word he said, but he could still whip them up into a frenzy. At some point in every speech he'd say that every championship team had a rock on which it was built and the name of his rock was Michael Oher.

From Coach O, Sean learned about the Internet courses offered by Brigham Young University. The BYU courses had magical properties: a grade took a mere ten days to obtain and could be used to replace a grade *from an entire semester* on a high school transcript. Pick the courses shrewdly and work quickly and the most tawdry academic record could be renovated in a single summer. Sean scanned the BYU catalogue and his eyes lit upon a promising series. It was called "Character Education." All you had to do in one of these "Character Courses" was to read a few brief passages from famous works—a speech by Lou Gehrig here, a letter by Abraham Lincoln there—and then answer five questions about it. How hard could it be? The

A's earned from Character Courses could be used to replace F's earned in high school English classes. And Michael never needed to leave the house!

There was a hitch, of course; there was always a hitch. But like every great prestidigitator Sean knew that a hitch was also an opportunity. The BYU courses might be used to replace F's on Michael Oher's transcripts with A's, but only if they were taken during the school year—and the school year was almost over. That's when Sean discovered, deep in the recesses of the NCAA rules, yet another loophole: the student-athlete was allowed to generate fresh new grades for himself right up until August 1, so long as that student-athlete was "Learning Disabled."

Whatever that meant, thought Sean. He had no idea if Michael was actually learning-disabled, but now that it was important for him to be learning-disabled, Sean couldn't imagine any decent human being trying to argue that he wasn't. But just in case some dark soul wanted to make that case, Sean began to compose the rebuttal in his head. "He's just got to be LD," he said, as he flipped through the yellow pages of his mind looking for someone to provide him with the necessary paperwork. "It's some brain disorder in most people, but in his case it's 'cause he didn't sleep in a bed for the first fifteen years of his life."

Of course he couldn't just declare Michael learning-disabled himself: he needed a document signed by some pointy-headed shrink. Sean had no idea where to find such a person, and so he called the Briarcrest academic counselor, Linda Toombs, who came up with the name of a bona fide licensed psychological examiner—a woman named Jakatae Jessup. A few days later Sean wrote a big check to cover the cost of a battery of tests, and dropped both it and Michael at the front door of Jakatae Jessup's office in East Memphis.

Jakatae Jessup was white. She and her colleague, Julia Huckabee, also white, had no interest in God, or in football, or in the vast majority of East Memphis defined by both. They were, by Memphis standards, charming oddballs. "Krogerites," they called themselves—and defined the term as people who shopped at the Krogers grocery store on Sunday mornings, while the rest of Memphis went to church. Most of the children they tested came referred by public or private school administrators. These kids would be dropped off right after school and stay for several hours, with a break for dinner, which, as a part of the deal, the psychologists supplied. When Michael came through their door to have his brain examined, they were shocked by the implications. "My first thought," said Huckabee, "was that we're not going to have enough money to feed him."

They gave him the Wexler Intelligence Test, and then a series of achievement tests. They asked him what 1 plus 1 equaled. They showed him a picture of an apple and asked him what it was. They asked him to draw a picture of a house. (Michael later told Leigh Anne he thought they were testing him for insanity.) The holes in his mind were obvious enough. He was still working well below grade level. He would probably never read a book for pleasure. He'd never been taught phonics or, if he had, he'd been taught so badly that he might as well have not been taught at all. When a child knows the sound that goes with the letter, depending on its position in the word, and knows the sense of the word, depending on its position in the sentence, he can instinctively decode the language. A child who had been taught phonics can be given a nonsense word—"deprotonation," for example, or "mibgus"—and still be able to pronounce it. Michael had no idea. "I don't think he knows how to read yet," said Jessup. "I think he's just memorized a tremendous number of words." When he sat down with a reading assignment, he was like a man with a partial combination trying to open a locked safe.

Still, it didn't take his testers long to see that the new subject was highly unusual. They saw lots of children with glitches in their hard wiring, but they'd never seen anyone like Michael. He was eighteen years old, and he obviously hadn't learned very much—yet he had both the ability and the desire to learn. "You can watch somebody taking an IQ test and see how they learn from experience," said Jessup. "They get a problem, then a slightly harder version of the problem, and they can apply what they learned from the first problem to the second. Michael learned something from every single thing I put in front of him."

Reptile eggs look a lot like bird eggs. Some are —— while others are oblong.

Michael knew the answer—"round"—but he wanted them to confirm it for him. "You're not supposed to tell a kid whether he's right or not," said Jessup, "but it was life or death for Michael. And it was clear we weren't going to go on until I wrote it down. I've never seen kids this old still absorbing knowledge the way he is. You see it in seven-year-olds."

At the age of sixteen, when he arrived at Briarcrest, Michael could still have been taught phonics. He wasn't, the psychologists surmised, because he had worked very hard to disguise his grotesque deficiencies from his teachers. "He was not letting people at Briarcrest know what he could or couldn't do," said Jessup. "Only Michael knew that there was a big gap between where he was and where he was perceived to be." Fearing that he wouldn't be given the chance to catch up on the sly—that he'd be outed as stupid—he was faking it, and hoping no one noticed. But he wasn't stupid. Far from it. "He's great if there is any context at all," said Jessup. "He can figure it out. He just needs a basic literacy program to decode words."

But that's not what most interested his intelligence testers. Michael Oher had been tested, and more than once, as a child. Those tests had pegged his IQ at 80. Now the two psychological examiners established that his IQ was currently somewhere between 100 and 110—which is to say that he was no more or less innately intelligent than most of the kids in his class at Briarcrest. The mind described by the new IQ test was not recognizably the same mind that had been tested five years earlier. "I compare it to photographs," said Jessup. "If you put Michael then side by side with Michael now, you would not be able to recognize these two people as the same."

That wasn't supposed to happen: IQ was meant to be a given, like the size of one's feet. It wasn't as simple as that, of course, but Jessup had never seen such concrete evidence of the absurdity of treating intelligence as a fixed quantity. "We speak of fluid and crystallized intelligence," she said. "Fluid is your ability to respond on the spot to a situation. Crystallized is what you've picked up along the way. The two are obviously related—how can you respond if you have no experience? When they tested Michael in the Memphis City Schools he was probably already deficient—both of those things had become compromised. He had so little experience. Then he had this rich *drowning* in experience that fed both of those."

Neither she nor her partner had ever seen anything like it, and they'd both been administering these sort of tests for twenty years. She knew the literature and so she knew that studies of the effects of environment and nurture on mental development tend to create two study groups, the haves and the have-nots. "The have-nots learn whatever words they happen to hear on TV, the haves hear a million different words by the age of three," said Jessup. " But you only get to compare the two groups. You almost never see a case where the subject moves from one group to the other." Those low IQ scores Michael generated as a child, they guessed, were caused by his encountering, inside the problems, a hole in his experience, and then simply giving up. Problems on the page, he'd come to assume, were problems beyond his ability to solve. "What they [Briarcrest] taught Michael was not just reading and writing and math," said Jessup. "They taught him how to solve problems and how to learn. He stopped giving up."

When she'd finished the testing, Jessup called Sean Tuohy. She wanted to see him in person; what she had to say was too interesting to relate over the phone. She drove to the Tuohy home and delivered a fairly long lecture to which Sean listened politely. ("I understood about two words she said," he noted later.) When Jakatae Jessup was done, he had only one question for her.

"Is this going to get me by the NCAA, or not?" he asked.

It was. If Michael's IQ really was as low as advertised, Jessup explained, he wouldn't have been classified as learning-disabled: he was just learning as well as his brain would allow. Now that he was established to have greater capacities, his problems could only be interpreted as a disability. Michael, to everyone's delight, was certifiably LD.

THUS BEGAN THE great Mormon grade-grab. Mainly it involved Miss Sue grinding through the Character Courses with Michael. Every week or so they replaced a Memphis public school F with a BYU A. Every assignment needed to be read aloud, and decoded. Here he was, late in his senior year in high school, and he'd never heard of a right angle, or the Civil War, or *I Love Lucy*. But getting the grades was far easier than generating in Michael any sort of pleasure in learning. When Briarcrest had given him a list of choices of books to write a report on, Miss Sue, thinking it might spark Michael's interest, picked *Great Expectations*. "Because of the character of Pip," she said. "He was poor and an orphan. And someone sort of found him. I just thought Michael might be able to relate." He couldn't. *Pygmalion* came next. Again, he hadn't the faintest interest in the thing. They got through it by performing the work aloud, with Michael assigned to the role of Freddie. "He does wonderful memory work," said Miss Sue. "It's a survival technique. You can give him anything and he'll memorize it." But that's all he did. Engaging with the material in any deeper way seemed impossible. He was as isolated from the great works of Western literature as he was from other people. "If you asked him why we're doing all this," she said, "he'd say, 'I got to do it to get to the league.' "

It was always work, and so it was always tiring, and every now and again Miss Sue needed a break. One night the Detroit Pistons were playing the San Antonio Spurs in the NBA finals, and Michael insisted on watching the game out of one eye. With the other eye he watched Miss Sue, and some book. If he wasn't going to take any more interest than that, she thought, why should she?

That's when Sean came through the door. Miss Sue handed Sean the reading assignment—Character Education I, Lesson II—and went to stretch out on the Tuohys' sofa.

The text was "The Charge of the Light Brigade." That Sean Tuohy would know a poem was as likely as Sylvia Plath hitting a jump shot at the buzzer, but Sean knew "The Charge of the Light Brigade." He hadn't seen it in twenty years but he still could nearly recite it by heart. He grabbed the sheet, got between Michael and the NBA finals, and said, "You ready, Bubba?" Then he boomed:

Half a league, half a league,
Half a league onward,

All in the valley of Death
    Rode the six hundred.
"Forward the Light Brigade!"
"Charge for the guns!" he said:
Into the valley of Death
    Rode the six hundred.

Rather than stop to explain, he raced on to the next, his favorite verse:

"Forward, the Light Brigade!"
Was there a man dismay'd?
Not tho' the soldier knew
    Someone had blunder'd:
Their's not to make reply,
Their's not to reason why,
Their's but to do and die:
Into the valley of Death
    Rode the six hundred . . .

Now he realized he should give Michael a bit of help. "You know Death Valley at LSU?" he asked.

"Death Valley" is what LSU football fans had nicknamed the LSU football stadium. Michael had visited Death Valley. Now he was now planning to ride into it, on the opposing team's bus.

"Well, this is where it comes from," said Sean. "This guy," he said, waving the work of Alfred, Lord Tennyson, "is writing about Ole Miss–LSU."

"The Charge of the Light Brigade" was now a football story, and Sean read it all the way through. Performed it, really. Then he read it again, more slowly. In his crackly North Mississippi–West Tennessee baritone, its sounds couldn't have been much less stately than the sounds Tennyson heard as he wrote.

Cannon to right of them
Cannon to left of them,
Cannon in front of them
   Volley'd and thunder'd . . .

He stopped again and asked: "So where are they now?" He compelled Michael to imagine the valley, and the surrounding artillery. Prostrate in the adjoining room, Miss Sue saw Michael's body language change. He usually leaned away from the lesson; this time he was leaning toward it. "Michael holds back so many things," she said. "Even his interest." For the first time since she met him, she could sense that he was conceding an interest. In a poem! She knew that he absorbed only what he could visualize. She thought: *Sean is making him SEE the poem.*

Sean charged on. Toward the end, Michael tried to stop him. Twice he asked, "Did they all die?" "Did they all die?" But Sean kept booming on, right through to the final stanza:

When can their glory fade?
O the wild charge they made!
   All the world wondered.
Honor the charge they made!
Honor the Light Brigade,
   Noble six hundred!

"They're all going to die?" asked Michael, when it was over.

"They're all going to die," said Sean.

Michael leaned over and switched off the NBA finals. "What's a league?" he asked.

Sean actually didn't know. Obviously, though not to Michael, a league was a unit of distance. Fortunately, BYU kept a crib sheet on line and Sean went to the computer and pulled it up. They went through the poem and replaced several of what Sean conceded were "goofy words"—*league, blun-*

der'd, battery, shatter'd and sunder'd—with words Michael knew. "Saber" was the exception. Michael didn't know what a saber was but when Sean explained, "it's a big long-ass sword, bigger than the knives you used in the hood," they agreed to let Tennyson keep it. Then Sean read it again.

> *Half a mile, half a mile,*
> *Half a mile onward . . .*

After the second reading Michael said, "Why would anybody do that?"

"The point is that this is about courage," said Sean.

"But they're going to all get killed!" he said.

"And you honor that," said Sean, "because they used courage, even if it was dumb."

From the next room Miss Sue hollered, "Michael Oher, if there's a war broke out, you head straight to Canada! Do you hear me?"

If Michael heard her he didn't show it.

"And sometimes courage *is* dumb," said Sean. "What they are saying is not that it's right or wrong. What they are saying is that it's not for us to question the coach. If you're the left tackle and the coach tells you to block the whole other team, you do it first, and you ask questions later."

"Why didn't we read any great poems like that at Briarcrest?" asked Michael.

And Sean thought: *You did. But it didn't mean anything to you, because they took it for granted that you knew what a saber was.*

"Let's read it again," said Michael.

NEARLY A MONTH after her first visit, Miss Joyce Thompson from the NCAA returned. This time she arrived early and found Michael at home alone. They sat together uncomfortably. She started to explain all over again the purpose of her visit—there were these rules forbidding people affiliated with college football programs doing any favors for big-time high school football players, etc.—when Michael interjected.

"I *should* be paid," he said.

She laughed, but nervously.

"They're making all this money off football," he said. "Why shouldn't they pay the players?"

She treated it as a silly question. It wasn't. The reason the NCAA needed investigators roaming the country to ensure that college football teams, and their boosters, weren't giving money or food or clothing or shelter or succor of any sort to the nation's best high school football players is that the nation's best high school football players were worth a lot more to the colleges than the tuition, room, and board they were allowed to pay them. The NCAA rules had created a black market—and done for high school football players what the Soviet police had once done for Levi's blue jeans. A market doesn't simply shut down when its goods become contraband. It just becomes more profitable for the people willing to operate in it. There were a number of colleges—and Ole Miss was one of them—for which the expropriation of the market value of pre-professional football players was something very like a core business. Whether NCAA investigators impeded, or enabled, this state of affairs was an open question.

Michael, newly alert to his own market value, had wondered about that: if he was allowed to auction his services in the 2004 market for college football players, how much, exactly, would they have paid him? The going black market rate for a Memphis high school superstar five years earlier appeared to have been around $150,000. One hundred fifty grand is what the University of Alabama booster Logan Young paid to the high school coaches of Albert Means, in exchange for persuading him to play for the Crimson Tide. Who knows what the University of Alabama might have paid if it could have cut a deal with Means directly?

At any rate, in 2004, one hundred fifty grand sounded almost quaint.

But the NCAA lady didn't want to engage Michael on the subject. If there wasn't a principle to prevent rich college boosters from feeding, clothing, and educating black inner-city football players, the NCAA investigative unit would be out of business. She went back to trying to determine which rich white person had given what to Michael Oher. Before she got very far, one of those rich white people came through the side door. He wasn't happy to see her.

The first time the NCAA lady had walked into his living room, Sean Tuohy had been all false bonhomie. He'd held out his pleasantness the way a trainer, faced with an ill-tempered horse, might hold out a carrot, with the clear implication that it could always be withdrawn. Now it was. As Joyce Thompson, NCAA investigator, switched on her tape recorder and asked the very same questions he had already spent five hours answering, Sean began to redden.

"Michael," she asked. "Who took care of your basic needs?"

She went over the same questions: food, clothing, shelter, the truck. What about spending money? She had no more luck getting satisfying answers out of Michael this time than she had the last. But this time she had a Plan B. If he wasn't going to talk to her about who gave him what, she was going to press him about his grades. She'd seen his transcripts: how did he intend to get himself academically qualified? Michael didn't know, but Sean told her that they had just started the BYU program of correspondence courses.

"Can you tell me how you're doing it?" she asked.

Sean offered a basic summary, and then disclaimed any more detailed knowledge. The great Mormon grade-grab was being managed by Michael's tutor, Miss Sue.

"Do you take the test on the computer?" the lady asked Michael. "In a book?"

Once again Michael didn't answer. Sean did. And what followed sounded like a courtroom exchange.

Sean: I have no idea. You'd have to ask her [Miss Sue]. She's doing it.
NCAA Lady: But Michael's taking the class!
Sean: I have no idea, and I know he doesn't either. She's conducting it, so you'd have to ask her.
NCAA Lady: That wasn't explained? Or you don't know how that's

done? Whether or not you take a lesson, you grade it, you hand
it in?

Sean: No! I mean I think I was clear: I'm not being flippant. I don't
know. And neither does he. We'll find out for you. And you can
keep asking.

NCAA Lady: It just surprises me.

Sean (hollering): Well, it can surprise you. But we don't know.

NCAA Lady: You don't know what core subjects they are going to be
in?

Sean: There'll be an English and a math.

Michael: Depends on how the ACT turned out.

That was another loophole Sean had found. Now that Michael had been
certified as learning-disabled, he was allowed to retake the ACT tests as
many times as he wanted, with Miss Sue on hand to help him parse the questions. That'd be worth a few extra points, and a few extra points on the ACT
meant fewer needed on the GPA.

"Okay," said the NCAA lady, obviously hoping to encourage Michael, and
not Sean, to elaborate. He didn't.

"I figure when I get to the second course, I'll look for the third one," said
Sean. "And when I get to the third one, I'll look for the fourth one."

NCAA Lady: Okay.

Sean: What's wrong with that answer? You rolled your eyes. Let me
tell you now: that's really rude. To look at me and roll your eyes
like I don't know what I'm talking about. Or that I'm trying to
mislead you.

NCAA Lady: All right. Now may I answer you?

Sean: Absolutely.

NCAA Lady: It's not that—

Sean: And I won't roll my eyes and accuse you of anything!

NCAA Lady: First of all, I'm not accusing you of anything.

Sean: It's the body language I'm getting.

NCAA Lady: Can I finish my statement?

Sean: Sure!

She then explained how surprised she was that Sean didn't know the details of the BYU study program, given how he seemed to have calculated every other angle on the court. How could he not know, for example, even the subject matter of these courses?

"It could be one of *nine* different courses," shouted Sean, brandishing a copy of Michael's high school transcripts. "He's still got eight F's on here."

Which brought them to the nub of the NCAA lady's displeasure. She must have been feeling like a Keystone Kop. She didn't understand these BYU courses. She didn't know exactly what Michael was doing to get himself academically up to snuff. She remained unclear who had given what to Michael, and when, so she had no real idea exactly how many of their rules against booster graft had been violated. All that was bad enough. But what really bothered her was that *Michael wasn't talking.* "This is the interview for Michael," she said to Sean. "And like last time you're doing most of the talking. And I need to hear from Michael."

"Well," said Sean, as if she'd just made the world's most preposterous demand. "*He* doesn't know."

NCAA Lady: Well, if that's the case, say, "I don't know."

Sean: He said he didn't know.

NCAA Lady: But you're still answering all his questions!

Sean: He said he didn't know. And so I did my best to answer it for you and you just didn't like the answer.

NCAA Lady (now staring straight through Michael): Well . . . I'm just trying to make sure that *you* don't know.

Sean: What part of "I don't know" fooled you?

NCAA Lady: That you're his legal guardian and you don't know if he's supposed to take English or math or science. That's the part that still baffles me.

Sean: Ma'am, I hate that it baffles you. But all you asked me to be is
truthful. You didn't ask me to be smart.

It was then that Michael's face broke into a smile. More than a smile.
When he registered what Pops had just said, he let loose this wheezing
laugh . . . *heh* . . . *heh* . . . *heh* . . . *heh*. He sounded just like Muttley, the
cartoon character, sidekick to Dick Dastardly. Michael Oher might never
be sure of Sean Tuohy's deeper motives. But he could be sure of this: Pops
was funny!

Michael watched with something like amusement as Sean and the NCAA
lady sparred for the next few hours. The NCAA lady did what she could to
remain calm and polite and retain the high ground while Sean yelled at her
and turned red in the face and hurled abuse from the ground below. (He kept
calling the NCAA "The Evil Empire.") The NCAA lady asked some detailed
question, and one of two things followed. Either Michael supplied an unsat-
isfying answer or Sean hollered at her. Finally, the NCAA lady gave up, and
let Michael go off to get another A in some course he couldn't even describe.

Once Michael was gone, the blood drained out of Sean's face. Out came
the carrot. He apologized for being so upset, but said she had to understand
that Michael had found the first round of questioning very disturbing. He
felt he had failed Michael, he said, by letting her grill him like that. As he
spoke, the NCAA lady studied him.

"Nothing was promised to you or your family?" she asked.

"*Me?*" said Sean. "I don't need anything."

His arms were extended in a way that said—*Behold! Do you not see the
million-dollar house gorgeously appointed with hundreds of thousands of dollars in furnishings? Did you somehow miss the five cars in the driveway? The
BMW? Do I need to call my pilots and order* Air Taco *to buzz NCAA headquar-
ters?* Sean made this one point—that both he and Michael were too rich to
be bought—several times. Once, after the NCAA lady had asked Michael if
any Ole Miss boosters had given him any money to go to Ole Miss, Sean had
said, "Ma'am, he's *richer* than any Ole Miss boosters." Sean Tuohy was up
from nothing and now he had done so well for himself and his family that

no one could give him anything he couldn't buy. He'd lived his life to be able to say that.

"Well, I know *that*," the NCAA lady said. Then she laughed, and relaxed. "But I just have to ask the question."

For the first time, she seemed human. Girlish, even. She ceased to be an investigator from the NCAA and became a woman named Joyce Thompson. And Joyce Thompson was genuinely curious about this domestic situation. A poor black giant monosyllab of the Memphis ghetto comes to live with, and apparently be loved by, a rich white right-wing family on the other side of town: how did that happen? She offered to turn off her tape recorder—Sean told her he didn't care if she left it on—and then set about satisfying her honest curiosity.

Joyce: Is he normally quiet like that?
Sean: When I met him that was *talkative*.
Joyce: How many times would you say he was here?
Sean: Hundreds. It was an open door to him.
Joyce: Did he just show up?
Sean: A lot of times he'd just show up.

She took that in.

Joyce: How did you two ever meet?
Sean: I told him I was Collins's daddy. That's how I introduced myself to him.
Joyce: Did he open up to you?
Sean: No. Gosh no. I barely got his name out of him.
Joyce: And so at some point he came over here and he spent the night. When's the first time he spent the night?
Sean: I don't know. Sometime during that basketball season. . . . This sounds bad but he was probably left at school one day, and I happened to be there.

She asked about Michael's childhood, and he told her how little they still knew of it. They talked about the problems of parenting. She confessed that she didn't know them firsthand. But she wondered how any mother could let her child wander the world looking for a bed without caring to know where he wound up. She wondered why on earth a rich white happy family in East Memphis would go to all this trouble for some poor black kid. And, finally, she wondered how Sean now felt about the experience. That final piece of curiosity led Sean to think aloud about the implications for his family of Michael Oher. "It's ruined us," he said. "Because so far as I can see, there's no downside. We can't look at a kid who's in trouble now without asking, 'If we had him, could we turn him around?' So what do we do when he leaves? Do we do it again?"

It was then that Joyce Thompson vanished and out came the NCAA investigator, with barely disguised shock. "Have you thought about doing this *again*?" she asked.

THERE WAS ONE final piece of unfinished business in Michael Oher's Briarcrest career. The senior yearbook picture was due, and Michael didn't have one. It was a Briarcrest tradition for every senior to have his baby picture in the annual. Her lack of a baby picture for Michael drove Leigh Anne to distraction. "You don't want to be the only senior who doesn't have a baby picture in the annual!" she said. She had made Michael give her the name of the foster home he admitted to having lived in when he was eight years old. She called the foster mother, who sounded vague; at any rate, she had nothing on him. She went down to his biological mother's apartment and harassed her for pictures. Finally, she had come upon a single shot, taken by an employee of Memphis Children's Services, when Michael was about ten years old. She had come home with it and given it to Michael.

Michael had looked at it and exclaimed, "Mama, that's me!"

"That sure is you!" she said.

Then he'd taken it into the den and stared at it for fifteen minutes.

But the picture didn't solve the problem. It wasn't a *baby* picture. One night Leigh Anne had an idea. She flipped on her computer and went online and found, as she put it, "the cutest picture of a little black baby I could find." She downloaded the stranger's photo, and sent it in to Briarcrest.

Briarcrest held its graduation ceremony in a church. The Tuohys were all in the audience, of course, and they had brought Miss Sue with them. Steve Simpson was there and so was Jennifer Graves, who said she'd never seen anyone work so hard for a piece of paper as Big Mike had worked to get his Briarcrest diploma. Big Tony was on hand—even though his son, Steven, wouldn't graduate until the following year. In spite of Big Tony's efforts to coax her out of her apartment, Michael's mother didn't make it. Dee Dee had told Big Tony that she wanted to see her son graduate from high school, as no one in her entire family ever had gotten past the tenth grade. Big Tony had arranged to pick her up that morning. But when he got to Dee Dee's apartment he found the lights out and the door locked. He thought he heard someone inside, but whoever it was refused to answer.

The Briarcrest president gave a long speech filled with many words of warning to the graduating class. He explained that when they left Briarcrest and went out into the world, they would encounter "all kinds of groups that claim some kind of privilege based on their lifestyles or perversions." (There was no need to say "gay"; they knew all about sodomy.) He spoke sternly about the danger of "seeking false happiness in a variety of narcissistic pleasures." After that final jolt of fear from God, the graduates were called down from their tiered seats at the back of the stage to collect their reward. Steve Simpson called their names, one by one; one by one they filed down. Michael wasn't called down until nearly the end. He sat waiting on the top tier, upper lip tucked beneath lower, either choking back his emotion or settling his nerves.

"Michael Jerome Oher," said Steve Simpson, and smiled.

The crowd had been told not to cheer for individuals, but a few people just had to break the rules. Miss Sue cried. Leigh Anne hooted and laughed and clapped. Collins was graduating too, but there was never any doubt Collins would graduate. It was Michael that was the news on this day. "He's so fired up," she said, as she watched him amble down, trying to keep his little scholar's cap from falling off. Sean smiled too, but Sean was paying closer attention to the small group of underclassmen in formal wear gathering on the side of the stage. The Briarcrest Choir. One of the kids, a whey-faced doughboy, was twice as large as the others.

"You see that big guy in the middle," said Sean. "That might be Michael's replacement at left tackle. That's not comforting, that he sings in the choir."

The NCAA needed its proof of Michael's new and improved grade point average by August 1. On July 29 Michael took his final BYU test—another Character Course. Sean sent the test to Utah by Federal Express, and the BYU people promised to have the grade ready by two o'clock the following afternoon. "The Mormons may be going to hell," said Sean. "But they really are nice people." With Michael's final A in hand, Sean rushed the full package to the NCAA's offices in Indianapolis. The NCAA promptly lost it. Sean threatened to fly up on his plane with another copy and sit in the lobby until they processed it—which led the NCAA to find Michael's file. On August 1, 2005, the NCAA informed Michael Oher that he was going to be allowed to go to college, and play football.

Now came the time to figure out what that meant for his football career. In big-time college football it was highly unusual for a freshman to walk onto campus and start playing. And, when the freshman was an offensive lineman, it was almost unheard of. The offensive line had the most intellectually demanding jobs on the field, apart from the quarterback. Even the best ones expected to spend a season practicing with the team, learning the plays, but not actually playing in the games. In return, they were granted by the NCAA an extra year of eligibility.

But Coach O wasn't having any of this. He called Sean and told him (a) that Michael was already his best lineman, and (b) that Michael was such a high-profile recruit he needed to become a kind of shop window for future high-profile recruits. Michael would have to start for the Ole Miss Rebels his freshman year.

Sean drove down to Ole Miss to have a word with Coach O. He didn't think he could talk him out of sticking Michael in the starting lineup, and he wasn't sure he wanted to anyway. He thought it would be good for Michael to see right away what he was up against—to learn that natural ability might not be enough to "get to the league." But he worried that Coach O might not fully understand what a challenge big-time football would be for Michael. Michael had just turned nineteen. He'd never lifted weights or trained for football in the way that serious football players usually do. He hadn't had the time. He had played fifteen games in high school on the offensive line. In less than a month, he'd be starting in the SEC, across the line of scrimmage from grown men of twenty-two who had spent the past four years majoring in football, and were just six months away from being drafted to play in the NFL. As these beasts came after him, he'd need to think on his feet.

Coach O wasn't one for sitting behind a desk. When he had people into his office at Ole Miss, he'd install them on his long black leather sofa while he marched back and forth, giving pep talks. The subject of Michael Oher brought out the student in him; when Sean came, he sat behind a desk. Coach O actually had a yellow pad to write on. He didn't get up. He didn't answer the phone. He took three pages of notes.

The two of them talked about many aspects of Michael Oher, but eventually Sean got around to his mental development. Michael's mind, Sean said, "is like a house built on sand. He doesn't know what 'agenda' means, but he knows eight thousand more complicated words." Sean didn't worry all that much about Michael's schoolwork, as he planned to ship Miss Sue down to Oxford with him; Miss Sue could take care of Michael's grades. What he was worried about was Michael's ability to understand football plays. "Michael can read," he said, "but it just doesn't register very well. If you give him a play book filled with X's and O's, he'll say, 'Yeah, I get it.' Then he'll run on the field and won't have any idea what he's supposed to do. If you think you can just put it on a chalkboard and he's going to know the play, it's not going to happen. But if you take him aside and explain it to him using mustard bottles and ketchup bottles—some visual aide that enables him to *see* it—not only will he remember it, he'll remember it for the rest of his life."

"This is very important," said Coach O, scribbling notes.

"Coach," said Sean. "My faith believes that the Lord sends down gifts for everyone and our job is to find those gifts. Michael's gift is the gift of memory. When he knows it, he knows it."

Coach O stopped scribbling and looked up. "I'm going to tell you one thing, Sean," he bellowed. "He's got some pretty good fucking feet, too. You seen them feet? Now them feet: *that's* a fucking gift!"

—

CHAPTER NINE

BIRTH OF A STAR

T HE REDBRICK MONSTROSITY RISES FROM A HOLLOW BESIDE A quiet road in the Buckhead section of Atlanta. To call it a home would be to give the wrong impression. It's less a shelter than a statement: the long sweeping driveway, the lawn that could double as a putting green, the giant white columns, the smooth stone porch inscribed with greetings in Latin. Through the leaded glass windows can be glimpsed sleek marble floors leading to a grand staircase lit by chandeliers with enough wattage to illuminate an opera house. It's the sort of place where the door really should be answered by an English butler, but Steve Wallace answers his own door. He wears shorts, T-shirt, and sandals, and has the pleasantly surprised air of a man who has just woken up from a dream that he is rich only to discover that he's actually rich. The only thing that the home and its owner have in common is that they are both huge. He walks across his great stone porch and onto his lawn to adjust the sprinkler. He limps; but they all limp. One nasty scar runs down his right knee and another lines his left ankle. Former NFL linemen age painfully and die young. No life insurance salesman in his right mind sells them coverage at the usual rates.

Hard as it is to believe now—as he returns to his mansion and passes through its stone halls toward the magnificent den with its elaborate audiovisual system—there was a time when Steve Wallace worried about such financial trivia as life insurance. He worried about making a living. He wasn't born with money; all he knew how to do was block, and in 1986, when he started his NFL career, blockers didn't get paid much. His first contract guaranteed him $90,000 a year, which was pretty good, but he wasn't sure how long it would last. He sat on the bench, and waited, without knowing exactly what he was waiting for. It turned out he was waiting for Bubba Paris to eat himself out of a job.

After the 49ers won their first Super Bowl, in 1981, Bill Walsh had used his first draft choice to select Paris. Bubba was meant to be the final solution to Walsh's biggest problem, the need to protect Joe Montana's blind side. "At three hundred pounds or less," said Walsh, "Bubba would have been a Hall of Fame left tackle. He was quick, active, bright, and he had a mean streak." Bubba also had a history of putting on weight, but, as Walsh said, "we felt we could deal with that. And we did. Briefly." Walsh fined Bubba for being overweight. He inserted clauses in Bubba's contracts that paid him bonuses for showing up for work under 300 pounds. He sent Bubba to Santa Monica to live at the Pritikin Diet Center. He even hired a fitness instructor to drive over to Bubba's house every morning and feed him less than Bubba fed himself. Walsh did everything he could think of to keep Bubba from expanding. And then one day the fitness instructor showed up at Bubba's house and, as Walsh put it, "The car was in the driveway, the drapes were closed, and nobody answered the door."

In his first four seasons Bubba's weight jumped around, but the trend line pointed up. Offered many choices between carrots and sticks, Bubba reached every time for another jelly doughnut. The 49ers won the Super Bowl again, after the 1984 season. But the next three seasons they went into the playoffs with high hopes and were bounced in the first round. In 1985 and 1986, they were beaten badly by the New York Giants, and in both games Lawrence Taylor wreaked havoc. He'd been too quick for Bubba. The 49er offense, usually so reliable, had scored only three points in each of those games. Joe Montana had been knocked out of the 1986 game with a concussion. The hits didn't always come from the blind side but the blind side was the sore spot. As 49er center Randy Cross said, "Increasingly, we game-planned specifically for that rush guy on the right side." The right side of the defense, the left side of the offense, was the turf Bubba Paris was meant to secure. "There's that old Roberto Duran idea from boxing," said Cross. "Get the head and the body dies. More and more teams were coming for our head."

It was at the end of the 1987 season that Bill Walsh's frustrations with his promising left tackle peaked. That left side of the line was now, obviously, the pressure point that a very good pass rusher could use to shut down the 49er passing game. And Bubba Paris just kept getting fatter, and slower, and less able to keep up with the ever-faster pass rush. During the regular season Bubba's weight hadn't mattered very much. He was waddling onto the field at well over 300 pounds, and the 49ers still cruised through the season. They'd finished with a record of 14–2. Amazingly, they had the number one offense *and* the number one defense in the NFL. Going into the playoffs, they were viewed as such an unstoppable force that the bookies had them as 14-point favorites to win the Super Bowl, no matter who they played.

They appeared to be a team without a weakness; but then, the regular season is not as effective as the playoffs at exposing a team's weakness. The stakes are lower, the opponents generally less able, their knowledge of your team less complete. It's when a team hits the playoffs that its weaknesses are most highly magnified; and in the 1987 playoffs, Walsh discovered that his seemingly perfect team had a flaw.

The first game was against the Minnesota Vikings, and it was supposed to be a cakewalk. But the Vikings had a sensational six five, 270-pound young pass rusher named Chris Doleman, and he came off the blind side like a bat out of hell. He was fast, he was strong, he was crafty, he was mean. He wore Lawrence Taylor's number, 56, and when he was asked who in football he most admired, Doleman said, "The one guy who has the desire to be the best, and the tenacity, is Lawrence Taylor. I'm not saying I want to be exactly like Lawrence . . ." Every blind side rusher knew about the anxiety of influence. Doleman wasn't exactly Lawrence Taylor but he was exactly in the tradition of Lawrence Taylor. He'd been drafted as an outside linebacker, but in the 4-3 defense, which the Vikings played, the outside linebacker wasn't chiefly a pass rusher. Finally it occurred to the Vikings coaches to try him as a right defensive end—that is, to make him a pass rusher. To give him the role in the 4-3 that Taylor played in the 3-4. He was an instant success.

Fearing that Doleman might shut down his passing game, Bill Walsh considered his trick of pulling a guard to deal with him. John Ayers had moved on, and the 49ers had no one quite so well designed to the job. Anyway, the trick was old: the Vikings would see it for what it was and quickly move to exploit the hole left in the middle of the 49er line. They had a weapon to serve just this purpose: right tackle Keith Millard. He lined up beside Doleman, and was himself—oddly, for a tackle—a speedy pass rusher. Send the guard to help with Doleman and you left Millard to run free. Walsh couldn't do that.

Thus Bill Walsh received another lesson about the cost of not having a left tackle capable of protecting his quarterback's blind side. This time the lesson was far more painful than the last. This time he had *expected* to win the Super Bowl. He had built the niftiest little passing machine in the history of the NFL, manned with talented players, and this one guy on the other team had his finger on the switch that shut it down. Chris Doleman hit Joe Montana early and often, but even when he didn't hit Montana he came so close that Montana couldn't step into his throws. Backup left tackle Steve Wallace watched from the sidelines. "He never let Joe get his feet set," he said later. What Doleman did to Joe Montana's feet was minor compared to what he did to his mind. "Every time Joe went back, he was peeping out of the corner of his eye first," said Wallace, "then looking at his receivers." The pass rush rendered Joe Montana so inept that in the second half Walsh benched him and inserted his backup, Steve Young. Young was left-handed, which enabled him to see Doleman coming. Young was also fast enough to flee—which he did, often. Against a team they were meant to beat by three touchdowns on their way to an inevitable Super Bowl victory, the 49ers lost 36–24. Afterwards, Vikings coach Jerry Burns told reporters that "the way to stop [the 49ers] is to pressure the quarterback. Our whole approach was to pressure Montana."

A football game is too complicated to be reduced to a single encounter. Lots of other things happened that afternoon in Candlestick Park. But the inability of his left tackle to handle the Vikings' right end was, in Walsh's view, a difference maker: it created fantastically disproportionate distortions in the game. "Bubba got beat," he said. "Doleman and Millard just *dominated* the game." After the game, Walsh was so shattered he walked right out of Candlestick Park without pausing to speak to his players. Always a bit leery of the way Walsh viewed them—as cogs in his intricate machine—the players would later point to that playoff loss as the beginning of the end of their feeling for their ingenious coach. "Walsh couldn't talk to us the day after," defensive back Eric Wright later told the *San Francisco Chronicle*. "He lost a lot of respect with the players. When it was going well, he was there. When the ship was shaky, he couldn't face us."

Walsh coached football just one more season, and he decided to hang his fortunes on something more dependable than the Bubba Paris Diet. But Bubba had no obvious replacement. His backup was Steve Wallace, and Wallace hadn't been trained as a left tackle. He'd been drafted by the 49ers in the fourth round in 1986, and was known chiefly for having blocked for running back Bo Jackson at Auburn. The joke was that Auburn had only three plays: Bo left, Bo right, and Bo up the middle. Having spent most of his college career run blocking, Wallace had to teach himself how to pass-block; but Wallace was a student of the game, willing to pay a steep price to play it, and the recipient of Walsh's highest compliment: nasty. As in: "Steve Wallace was a *nasty* football player."

A year after their loss to the Vikings, the 49ers found themselves in exactly the same place: in the playoffs, facing the Minnesota Vikings. The 49ers weren't as good as they had been the year before, and the Vikings were better. They, not the 49ers, now had the NFL's number one defense. It was led by Chris Doleman who was, if anything, even better at sacking quarterbacks.

The night before the game, Steve Wallace didn't sleep. "I'd just try to go to bed early and hope somewhere along the way I fell asleep," he said. The inability to fall asleep on the night before the game had already become a

pattern for him. Apparently, it came with the left tackle position. Will Wolford, who protected Jim Kelly's blind side for the Buffalo Bills, had exactly
the same experience. He started out his career as a guard—and slept—then
moved to left tackle—and didn't. Late in his career, he moved back to guard,
and, presto, he could sleep again. The left tackle position, as it had been
reconceived by the modern pass-oriented offense, presented a new psychological challenge for the offensive lineman. In the old days, no one could
really see what you were doing, and you usually had help from the lineman
on the other side of you. That was still true at the other line positions. A mistake at guard cost a running back a few yards; a mistake at left tackle usually
cost a sack, occasionally cost the team the ball, and sometimes cost the team
the quarterback.

And—here was the main thing—you only needed to make one mistake
at left tackle to have a bad game. The left tackle was defined by his weakest
moment. He wasn't measured by the body of his work but by the outliers.
"You have this tremendous ability to be embarrassed," said Wallace. "You
know you can't afford three bad games in a row. They gonna say, 'Nice knowing you.' And it only takes *one* play—if he has one sack, then he's interviewed after the game. And you're the guy who gave up the sack. I could be
good on thirty-four out of thirty-five pass plays, and all anyone would
remember was that one sack."

This point was driven home to him the Saturday before the Vikings
game, when Bill Walsh called the team into the auditorium for the pleasura-
ble viewing of its past highlights. Walsh did this before every game. He
thought it helped his players to see themselves at their best before they went
out to play. The players watched Jerry Rice dash into the end zone, Ronnie
Lott intercept a pass, and Joe Montana thread the ball between defenders.
They whooped and hollered and cheered for each other. It was all good fun,
all positive. But at the very end of the highlight reel, Walsh, perversely, had
inserted a single negative play: the Doleman sack.

The sack came during the regular season in a game the 49ers won,
24–21. Doleman had got by Wallace just that once, but he had crushed Joe
Montana. Wallace didn't need to be reminded of the play. That one sack was

all he had thought about for days. Doleman had beaten him to the outside. Wallace had reached out to punch him but he, not Doleman, had lost his footing. Doleman rose up off Montana, jumped around celebrating, and then found Wallace, to editorialize.

"You got this *all day*," he'd said.

Wallace responded as he had done thirteen other times that season, by starting a fight. "I remember thinking: if I don't do something, he may get *ten* sacks," he said. "So I decided to mix it up." The NFL hadn't yet begun to levy big fines for fights, and Wallace had taken full advantage of the freebies. He now had a reputation as one of the league's dirtiest linemen—because he started so many fights. "I thought that's how it had to be," he said. "I had to fight if I was going to make it. And I had some folks to feed. And when you have some folks to feed you have a whole different mentality."

That really was how Wallace thought about these beasts bent on killing Joe Montana: *you go by me and my family goes hungry.* And it wasn't all that far from the truth. His first paychecks would be so thoroughly consumed by the $1,426 monthly note on the new house his parents had bought for themselves that he'd finally summoned the nerve to tell them to sell the house. He was deeply insecure. People were saying that he wasn't a good pass blocker, and he wasn't all that sure they were wrong. Just that morning—the morning Walsh played the tape of the Doleman sack—Doleman was quoted in the paper saying "the reason Wallace fights so much is to cover up his lack of ability."

Now he had to face Doleman again. Doleman was about to go to the Pro Bowl for the second straight year. No one on the team had forgotten what Doleman and Millard had done to them in the playoffs the year before. And yet Bill Walsh felt the need to replay that one sack. Over and over again Wallace watched Doleman beat him and crunch Joe Montana. He didn't understand why Walsh needed to humiliate him. He said nothing, of course, but was at once livid and ashamed. He wasn't going to sleep tonight anyway; now he wasn't going to sleep with a vengeance. "All night long I'm laying there thinking: *why did he show that one play?* A lot of times you can't understand what Walsh was doing until he's done it." At some point that night he decided "the lesson for me was to concentrate one play longer. As hard as you can possibly work, you can do it for one more play."

The next day, after he'd suited up, Wallace received another explanation for Walsh's perverse behavior. John McVay, the team's director of football operations, pulled him aside in the hallway and said, "You are going to be the key to this game. The game is going to turn on your performance." This wasn't the front office pep-talking. McVay was a former NFL head coach—and he was completely serious.

This was new. Until this season, his first as a starting NFL left tackle, Steve Wallace had never experienced line play as an individualistic event. But that is what the left tackle position had become: a one-on-one encounter, a boxing match. The passing game, increasingly, was built around the idea of getting as many receivers out into patterns as quickly as possible. More receivers meant fewer pass blockers. Fewer pass blockers meant the left tackle had to deal with whatever was coming at him all by himself. Every now and then a running back might nip at Doleman's heels on his way out to catch a pass. On very rare occasions a tight end might line up beside Wallace and lend a shoulder. But mostly it would be just him and Doleman, one on one. And the importance of the private battle was now clear to him. "No one had ever said anything like that to me before," said Wallace. "No one had ever said, 'The game depends on you.' I never thought a lineman could be that important. I started thinking, 'Oh my goodness . . .'"

NUMBER 74 TROTS to the edge of the tunnel leading from the locker room to the field. He loves this moment. This moment is the offensive lineman's one shot at positive recognition. Later in his career he'll milk it for drama. He'd sprint so fast from the tunnel that the other players wouldn't put a hand out to slap his "because they were afraid I'd break it off." When he'd started playing football as a kid, he wanted to play tight end; even then, he preferred basketball. He enjoyed attention. It's still not natural to him to play a game in front of millions of people and go completely unnoticed. It's like playing the cantaloupe in the school play.

"At left tackle, Number Seventy-four, Steve Wallace!"

His name is announced to the packed stadium and he runs out. He's still so nervous and new that he concentrates on not stumbling. The day is sunny and bright but the turf, he notices, is slick and muddy. That's a break. Opposing teams who came to Candlestick Park were deceived by the sunshine. They'd think: on such a nice day the ground just must be firm. The ground was seldom firm. By the second quarter they'd be slipping and sliding, yet they wouldn't think to change their cleats. A pass rusher like Doleman counted on traction to turn the corner. If he forced Doleman to carve especially tight turns, Wallace knew, the turf might do the rest.

When he reaches the 49ers' sideline he looks across the field, to find Doleman. "I'm looking to see if he's all cocky, like, 'I'm gonna kick your butt,' you know." Back when Bubba was starting, he'd engaged in this tribal chest-pounding ritual with certain opponents. Before the game he'd look across the field, find the guy he was going up against, and literally start howling and beating his chest. Wallace is too worried about the task at hand to pound his chest. In any case, he doesn't catch Doleman's eye; but as he looks around, he notices another piece of luck: Jerry Markbreit. Markbreit will referee the game. He's Wallace's favorite ref. Jerry let left tackles get away with a lot, like where they'd line up. On passing plays he'd want to line up a few inches further back from the line of scrimmage than was strictly legal. If it became a race to cut off Doleman on a wide loop, those few inches might make all the difference. A lot of other refs would just flag you for not being exactly on the line. Jerry at least warned you before he flagged you.

The Vikings got the ball first. Steve Wallace thinks: *just get to halftime. Worry about the rest of the game then.* He couldn't even think about an entire game. Before he mucked out the Augean stables, Hercules probably carved them in half in his mind, too. Wallace thinks in terms of getting through the half without humiliation. He thinks: *make it to halftime without a sack, you got a chance.*

He watches the 49er defense try to stop the Vikings offense and prays they don't leave the 49er offense with their backs to their own goal line. *If we get the ball in a bad place,* he thinks, *Doleman's gonna be even harder to handle.*

They give up a field goal: 3–0 Vikings. The offense takes over on its own twenty-yard line. That was fine.

Wallace had made up his mind before the game that he would take a different approach. He'd play within himself. Doleman's words in the paper had stung: *the reason Wallace fights so much is to cover up his lack of ability.* "I said to myself: no matter what happens, I'm not going to fight him today. And it helped me to become a true left tackle."

When he looks back over his career from the end of it, he will say that this was the day he embraced his position. He is focused on his technique—on where his feet are, where his hands are, the timing of his contact. He adjusts according to the tiny hints that Doleman gave him of what he plans to do next. Wallace keeps a mental list of the different moves of pass rushers. He has names for them: the spin, the swim, the power, the shoulder grab, the arm drag, the hand slap, the hip toss, the dead leg ("they fake as if they're stopping just to make you freeze your feet"). Each guy was a little different; each guy had his own moves. Doleman hasn't yet learned to spin. He'd develop a spin move later and it would make him so good at getting to quarterbacks that he'd break the NFL's single-season sack record. But he has a swim move, where he brings his arms crashing down on top of the left tackle's arms, to break his hold. He also has a speed move—which is what he'd used to beat Wallace during the regular season.

Wallace worries about Doleman's initial move. He worries even more about the move Doleman will make in response to whatever Wallace has done to defend himself against the initial move. "It's *all* feet and hands," said Wallace. "Once your body gets engaged with a guy, he can very easily use a counter—once you've stopped his initial move, he pushes off. That's why you can't stop moving your feet."

The first series is a bust in which he plays no role. Bill Walsh decided, uncharacteristically, to open the game running the ball. He achieved nothing but predictability. After two runs for losses, on third and very long, everyone in the stadium knows that Montana will pass. The Vikings blitz with what appears to be their entire team and sack Montana. Three plays, minus nine yards, and punt.

But the defense quickly gets back the ball. It's during this second series that the heavyweight bout between Chris Doleman and Steve Wallace really begins. On the first play, Montana takes a five-step drop and Doleman comes with the same speed rush that he used to beat Wallace the first time they met. Wallace now understands that he'd gotten beat that one time because he'd been too jumpy, too eager to make contact. He prides himself on playing offense with the aggression of a defensive player, but that aggression is now counterproductive. The left tackle position is all about control—of self, and of the man coming at you. "Control the number," Wallace tells himself. "Control that inside number. As long as I can control that inside number, I can push through him." He fixates on the "6" on Doleman's jersey, the way a basketball defender stares at the midsection of the dribbling opponent.

Doleman lines up far outside and, at the snap of the ball, sprints straight upfield. He's quicker than Wallace, and has the distinct advantage of running straight ahead while Wallace backpeddles. Wallace can't get a purchase on him; his only hope is to give him a single hard push at exactly the right moment. If he hits Doleman the moment after the snap, he will achieve nothing. He'll throw himself off balance, just as he did before, and speed Doleman on his journey upfield, en route to Joe Montana's back.

What happens on this first serious encounter between these two huge men happens so fast it's nearly impossible to comprehend with the naked eye in real time. Doleman sprints upfield, probably expecting to collide with Wallace on his first or second step—but he doesn't. Wallace has taken a new angle. "I had to make sure that his body was completely by me . . . Wait . . . Wait . . . Wait . . . Then I hit him."

He'd met Doleman as deep in the backfield as he possibly could without missing him altogether. They collided, briefly, at the spot where Doleman wanted to be making a sharp left to get at Montana. The hit kept Doleman from turning, and drove him further upfield. Steve Wallace had traded the pleasure of violence for the comfort of real estate.

Nobody notices, of course. His contribution was the opposite of drama. He'd removed the antagonist from the play entirely. What the fans and the television cameras see is 49er wide receiver John Taylor come wide open in the middle of the field. Joe Montana hits him with a pass, and Taylor races for a gain of twenty yards.

Doleman must have thought that first play was a fluke, because on the next one he tries exactly the same move. Upfield he comes, at speed, and once again Wallace takes him right on past the action. What the fans see is Jerry Rice catching a touchdown pass. What Chris Doleman sees, from a distance, is Joe Montana throwing a touchdown pass. What the fans at home hear is the announcer, John Madden, saying, "The 49ers need production out of three key people. Two of them just produced." The three key people to whom Madden refers are Montana, Rice, and running back Roger Craig. They are stars; they accumulated the important statistics: yards, touchdowns, receptions, completions. Wallace is not considered a producer. He has no statistics.

The next time the 49ers get the ball, Steve Wallace suspects that Doleman might adjust. Doleman now knows that Wallace is quick enough and agile enough and intelligent enough to deal with his speed rush. He'll come with his bull rush.

In the playoff game the year before—which Wallace had watched from the sidelines—Doleman had opened the game with a bull rush and knocked Bubba Paris flat on his back. ("When you knock a three-hundred-thirty-pound guy on his ass," Wallace observed, "that's a very serious thing.") He expected the bull rush early. If Doleman established his ability to knock Wallace flat on his back—to run right over him—he'd force Wallace to plant his feet early, to brace himself. Planted feet doom a left tackle. Planted feet are slow feet. If he plants his feet, Wallace knows, Doleman will see that his feet are planted—and then he'll go right back to his speed rush. When a left tackle plants his feet, he gives the pass rusher a half step head start in his race to the quarterback. That half step might be the difference between a productive Joe Montana and a Joe Montana being carried off the field on a stretcher.

As in sumo wrestling, the awesome crudeness on the surface of the battle disguised the finesse underneath. Keeping Doleman off Montana's back is less a matter of brute force than leverage, angles, and anticipation. The outcome of the struggle turns on half steps and milliseconds. "I know early there are maybe three plays where he is going to try to bull-rush me," says Wallace. "And you know that if you're not ready, he's going to beat you like a dog for the rest of the day, because then you are setting with slow, controlled feet rather than happy feet. The trick is to see that bull rush coming early, and go out and pop him. You deliver a quick karate blow—*Pow!*—like a real quick punch, to stun him. But your feet never stop. If your feet ever stop, you're beat."

Here comes the payoff for all those hours he spent studying game tape. He's watched many hours of Chris Doleman rushing passers. He's learned that Doleman tips his bull rush—and how can he not?—by the set of his stance, the tilt of his body, his attitude. Now Doleman comes with the bull rush. And he's ready for it.

What the fan sees is . . . nothing. Doleman is 270 pounds of raw, explosive muscle. There is probably not a human being among the 62,457 present who could withstand the force of his furious charge. To the naked eye, however, it looks like he's not even trying. He's just stuck on the line of scrimmage, leaning against Steve Wallace. Why watch that? Watch, instead, the real action: Jerry Rice catches another touchdown pass!

The next time the 49ers have the ball (they now lead 14–3), Wallace looks up to find Doleman gone. Doleman has moved to the other side of the field, in search of a better venue to practice his black art. On the other side of the field, however, he's in Montana's line of vision. He also must deal with two blockers, the right tackle plus the tight end. Two plays into the experiment he returns to his natural point of attack. For him it's the blind side, or nothing.

Today, it's nothing. Not one sack. A single tackle, and that comes on a rare play when Wallace isn't assigned to block him. "When you're locked in," says Wallace, "you can't explain it. You just feel it." Today, he was locked in.

At halftime the score is 21–3. Joe Montana has thrown three touchdown passes. Just as Montana received more than his share of the credit when things went well, he received more than his share of the blame when things went badly. Before the game, a lot of people were saying and writing that Joe

Montana was washed up. Finished. Over the hill. Montana was only thirty-two years old. But the 49ers had lost their previous three playoff games. In those three games Montana had thrown four interceptions, zero touchdown passes, and for a grand total of 529 yards. This one half he'd thrown three touchdown passes and had been, as John Madden put it, "about as efficient as a quarterback can be." All talk of Joe Montana being finished, said the announcers, was obviously silly. Joe Montana was going to keep on playing, and become maybe the greatest quarterback ever to play the game.

No one ever mentions Steve Wallace's name. The cameras never once find him. His work is evidently too boring to watch for long without being distracted by whatever's happening to the football. Worse, the better he does his job, the more boring to watch he becomes. His job is to eliminate what people pay to see—the sight of Chris Doleman crushing Joe Montana.

In *Instant Replay*, a diary of a year playing on the offensive line for Vince Lombardi's Green Bay Packers, Jerry Kramer points out that without instant replay technology no one would ever notice line play. As Steve Wallace arrives in his magnificent rec room, and begins to fiddle with the remote control to his VCR, he suggests that there are limits to what instant replay will do for a lineman. He finds the old tape of the 1988 Vikings–49ers play-off game. He fast-forwards through the first three quarters of the game, pausing the tape only three times, after each of Jerry Rice's touchdowns. Each time Rice arrives in the end zone and turns, he is lifted high in the air by . . . Steve Wallace. Wallace made a habit of sprinting at full tilt downfield after a touchdown. The main side effect of this behavior was for a picture of Steve Wallace to appear, briefly, in the middle of the television screen. The blocks that made the touchdowns possible, he assumed, weren't worth watching.

Midway through the fourth quarter, the former left tackle locates a final moment of interest. The 49ers lead 28–9, and have the ball. The game is all but over. Just then, Roger Craig takes a handoff and sprints through the left side of the line for an 80-yard touchdown, the longest in 49er playoff history. Craig has sprinter speed but he barely has time to turn and raise his arms over his head before he collides with . . . Steve Wallace. Craig ran a forty-yard dash in about 4.5 seconds, and Wallace ran it in about 5.5 seconds, so, in theory, it should have taken at least 2 seconds for Steve Wallace to reach Roger Craig. If so, they were the briefest 2 seconds in the history of time.

"Did you see who the first guy down there with him was?!" shouts John Madden, who alone among the announcers paid some attention to offensive linemen. "The first guy in the end zone with Roger Craig is Steve Wallace! Steve Wallace was the guy who made the first block to break him loose!"

Wallace smiles and rewinds the tape—the game ended with the 49ers on top 34–9. Doleman had more or less given up trying to get to Montana by the middle of the third quarter. None of it matters. Steve Wallace wants to see this one play again. This business of All-for-one-and-one-for-all-and-who-cares-if-I-get-any-attention-or-credit-for-myself-so-long-as-the-team-wins was nice as far as it went. But it didn't go down to the bottom of Steve Wallace. "As long as you'd play hard and get a little grimy and dirty, Madden would take care of you," said Wallace. But even Madden needed a little help: that's why you chased the running back 80 yards to the end zone.

"The first guy in the end zone with Roger Craig is Steve Wallace! Steve Wallace was the guy who made the first block to break him loose!"

Having reviewed his one moment of glory a second time, the former left tackle clicks off his big-screen television, settles back into his fine leather sofa, and smiles. "It's all part of it," he says.

THAT SEASON THE 49ERS won the Super Bowl. After the game, Bill Walsh retired, but his innovation continued to sweep the league in various forms. The passing game grew ever more important, the quarterbacks ever more valuable. Yet there was still little change in the value of the people who protected the quarterback. Steve Wallace had no sense that he would one day be rich, and neither did any other lineman. The purest case study was Anthony Muñoz. By the late 1980s, Muñoz was regarded as the finest left tackle ever to play the game. He was quick, huge, versatile, and athletic—in addition to playing football at USC, he'd played third base for the baseball team. He came into the league in 1980 and became a fixture at the Pro Bowl. Even he

was constrained in his financial demands by the conceit that one good lineman was no different from any other. All for one and one for all. "They
would actually say that linemen are interchangeable and can be replaced at
any time," Muñoz recalled. "They'd actually say we can just take another guy
and toss him in there. But you were aware that the left tackle was especially
important. He just wasn't paid as if he was especially important."

In 1987, after he had been to six straight Pro Bowls, a lot of people were
saying Anthony Muñoz might just be the greatest offensive lineman in the
history of the game. With his contract about to expire, Muñoz and his agent
walked into the Cincinnati Bengals' front office and asked for a raise. The
best NFL quarterbacks were now making more than $2 million dollars a
year and the best pass rushers were making $1 million. "We were asking for
half a million a year," recalled Muñoz, "and we were told that there was no
lineman alive who was worth that much."

The people who evaluated football players and football strategies understood that the parts were inextricable from the whole, of course. You didn't
get Joe Montana and Jerry Rice's "production" without production of some
sort from Steve Wallace. Bill Walsh and John McVay obviously understood
that if Wallace didn't do his job, then Montana couldn't do his. Take a half
second away from Joe Montana's pocket time, and all those people saying
Montana was washed up might have been right. But there was a difference
between saying that Steve Wallace was necessary and acknowledging that
what Steve Wallace did was extremely difficult—that it wasn't a job for just
any old lineman.

The market for football players was rooted in subjective judgments and
ancient prejudices. "Before free agency, they just paid you whatever they felt
like paying you, and your only recourse was to withhold services," said Tom
Condon, an offensive lineman for the Kansas City Chiefs in the 1980s who
went on to become a leading players' agent. But there were hints of how a
free market in football players might differ from a shackled one. The amateur draft, for example, which had aspects of an open market. College players had no say in which NFL team they played for, but the NFL teams were
free to choose among the college players, and the order of their choices

revealed their preferences. And in 1988 the preferences of the Tampa Bay Buccaneers shocked a lot of football people. Ray Perkins was the Buccaneers' head coach at the time, and Perkins had been the head coach of the New York Giants when they'd drafted Lawrence Taylor. Perkins had the fourth pick of the first round and was expected to take one of the two available star wide receivers, Sterling Sharpe or Tim Brown. Instead, he took a left tackle named Paul Gruber. "We had Gruber rated the highest player on the board," Perkins told a *New York Times* reporter. "We would have taken him if we had the first pick of the draft. I've changed my mind about the left-tackle position. It's now a skill position because he lines up against more and more teams' best athlete, their right defensive end or linebacker, the Lawrence Taylor types. That's why I feel good about Gruber. He is one of the best athletes I've ever seen."

Whatever had caused Ray Perkins to change his mind about the left tackle was causing a lot of other people to change their minds, too. That became clear after the 1992 season when, to put an end to labor strife, NFL players and owners agreed to a new labor deal. The players accepted salary caps tied to leaguewide revenues, so that salaries would rise with revenues. In addition, players were granted the right of free agency. The new deal had a number of immediate effects. One was to make it possible for teams to go out and buy the players they thought they needed on the newly open market. Another was to focus NFL front office minds on how to allocate their dollars. Every team now had more or less the same number of dollars to spend on players—the number dictated by the cap—and so the team that spent the dollars most efficiently should win. What was the best way to spend those dollars? On a quarterback? On defense?

The new market officially opened on February 1, 1993, the day after the Super Bowl. Two months later, Peter King of *Sports Illustrated* reported its shocking early verdicts. More than any other football writer, King had earned the trust of NFL's front offices, and so was able to channel their thoughts. All the players lucky enough to be entering free agency were cutting sweet deals for themselves, he reported. But the real shock was the dollar value the new market assigned to offensive linemen. Just a few years earlier, the Bengals had told Anthony Muñoz that no offensive lineman on earth was worth half a million dollars a year. The Denver Broncos quickly signed a couple of free agent linemen, Brian Habib and Don Maggs, for three times that amount. A few days later, Vikings center Kirk Lowdermilk moved to the Indianapolis Colts for $2 million a year, then groped for the adjective to describe his feelings. "Stunned is not the word," he told King. "There is no word in the English language to describe it." A few days after Lowdermilk grappled with his new dollar value, the Green Bay Packers paid $1.52 million a year over three years to buy a guard named Harry Galbraith away from the Miami Dolphins.

The strange bidding frenzy for offensive linemen no one had ever heard of persisted. After the Los Angeles Rams offered $1 million a year to bid away a guard named Leo Goeas from the San Diego Chargers, the *San Diego Union-Tribune* ran an article under the headline: "Farewell, Leo Goeas, Whoever You Were." The newspaper sought comments from the Chargers' old left tackle Billy Shields, who had retired in 1983. "I played eleven years," said Shields, "and I didn't make a million dollars over my *entire career*."

That was the general drift of public commentary from NFL insiders: bafflement. The Bengals' offensive line coach Jim McNally called the explosion in pay for linemen "a fast rush to get players who probably aren't worth it." One AFC coach called the Habib deal "the worst contract I've ever seen in this league." Another skeptic pointed out that Don Maggs was a B-list left tackle and certainly not the guy to be guarding John Elway's blind side. Just the past season Maggs had been badly beaten by . . . Chris Doleman. Retired NFL linemen were the most disturbed; when Friedrich Engels coined the term "false consciousness" to describe the inability of the working class to understand the nature of its oppression, he might just as well have been writing about NFL linemen. The offensive linemen had swallowed hook, line, and sinker other people's opinion of their worth. They accepted as plain truth the widely held view that they were the team's most fungible members. You didn't see a lot of former quarterbacks wondering why current NFL quarterbacks were being paid millions of dollars; but these old linemen couldn't understand the new value placed on linemen. "There's a lot going on in football right now that makes no sense," said old Chicago Bears center Mike Pyle, who made fourteen grand a year back in the 1960s. "And this tops the list."

Of course the people shelling out the millions tried to explain themselves. They argued that the numbers spoke for themselves: just the previous season, nineteen out of the twenty-eight starting NFL quarterbacks had been knocked out of games with injuries *by mid-November*. The Broncos' director of football operations, Bob Ferguson, pointed out that his team's star quarterback John Elway had been sacked *fifty-two* times: Maggs and Habib were being paid to stop that kind of thing from happening. Ferguson actually went so far as to thank Broncos' owner Pat Bowlen for his willingness to spend football money in ways football money had never been spent. "You have to give credit here to Pat," he said, "because these were not famous guys. When I talked to him about Habib, he kept calling him 'Rashid.' "

In the midst of this upheaval, the only free agent A-list left tackle, Will Wolford of the Buffalo Bills, announced his new deal: he'd be leaving the Bills for the Indianapolis Colts, who had agreed to pay him $7.65 million over three years. That was more than any lineman had ever been paid, of course, but the money wasn't what was most astonishing. Wolford's agent, Ralph Cindrich, later said that at least four other teams had been willing to match the Colts' offer. What had set the Colts apart from the other bidders was a clause they agreed to insert into Wolford's new contract. It guaranteed that Will Wolford, left tackle, would remain the highest paid player on the Colts' offense for as long as he played on it. Better paid than the Colts' running backs, the Colts' wide receivers, or any of the other acknowledged stars. Even if the Colts went out and got themselves the NFL's most expensive quarterback, Wolford's salary would rise to eclipse his, too. "I thought linemen would get a little more money from free agency," said Wolford later. "But I didn't think *that* would happen. I was numb."

He wasn't the only one. The Bills were furious: how could any lineman demand a clause that guaranteed him he would be paid more than star quarterback Jim Kelly, or star running back Thurman Thomas? The NFL didn't like the idea of any player having a clause in his contract guaranteeing him more money than his teammates, and it made noises about voiding the deal. That's when Ralph Cindrich went on the warpath. He asked, pointedly, if the league would have the same reservations if the clause had been in some quarterback's contract. He accused the league, in the pages of the *New York Times*, of "discrimination against offensive linemen." And the NFL let the deal slide, but only after saying no such deal would be permitted in the future. "There's a mentality about linemen that goes back to high school," said Cindrich. "When you picked your football team, these were the last guys picked."

There wasn't a left tackle in the game who imagined himself to be as valuable as the star running back, much less the quarterback. How could this happen? How could the people paying these vast sums assign a value to a player that he wouldn't dare assign to himself? How could they justify it, when the left tackle had no statistics to measure his value—no "production"? Bill Polian was the general manager of the Bills in 1986, when the team used its first-round pick to take Will Wolford of Vanderbilt University. When Wolford jumped to the Colts, Polian was working in the league office and found himself embroiled in the discussions over the disturbing new contract. Then in 1997 he left—to become the GM of the Colts. "You want to know why this organization gave Will that contract?" he asked. "He got it for the simple reason that he shut down Lawrence Taylor in the Super Bowl."

Left tackles everywhere failed to sleep the night before they faced Lawrence Taylor. What they didn't appreciate was that there was gold in their anxiety. Their fear was a measure of their value. A year earlier, the Bills had lost to the New York Giants in Super Bowl XXV, 20–19. Yet Lawrence Taylor hadn't been a factor—and a lot of front office executives apparently noticed the relative tranquillity on the blind side of Bills quarterback Jim Kelly. In effect, they had asked themselves a question: if we were to play the Giants, how much would I pay to have Lawrence Taylor erased from the field of play? The number was higher than they ever imagined. Until the next year—because the number kept rising. And in 1995, Steve Wallace of the San Francisco 49ers became the first offensive lineman to sign a contract worth $10 million. The quarterback might still get all the glory. But the guy who watched his back would be moving into a bigger house.

That was the beginning of what became a massive revaluation of the left tackle position. The NFL had a new designation: the "franchise player." A team could claim one player as its franchise player, and thus prevent him from becoming a free agent. In exchange, the team had to pay him the greater of 120 percent of his old salary or the average of the league's top five salaries at his position. Of the twenty-eight franchise players named in 1993, nine were left tackles, the most at any one position. (Steve Wallace was one of them.) These moves simply reflected the left tackle's rapidly rising cost. NFL teams saw, instantly, that a left tackle even after he'd been designated a franchise player was cheaper than a left tackle purchased on the open market.

All through the 1980s and into the 1990s, offensive linemen had competed with tight ends and kickers for the title of lowest paid players on the football field. In 1990, for instance, the average starting offensive lineman was paid $398,000 a year, while the average wide receiver made $504,000 a year, the average defensive end made $551,000 a year, the average running back made $620,000 a year, and the average quarterback made $1.25 million a year. The left tackle, Anthony Muñoz pointed out, made his living trying to prevent a guy making twice as much as he did from killing a guy who made three times more.* By the 2005 season, the left tackle would be paid more than anyone on the field except the quarterback, and the percentage difference between the two of them had shrunk dramatically. The average pay of the top five starting left tackles was $7.25 million a year, compared to $11.9 million for the quarterbacks.

The curious thing about this market revaluation is that nothing had changed in the game to make the left tackle position more valuable. Lawrence Taylor had been around since 1981. Bill Walsh's passing game had long since swept across the league. Passing attempts per game reached a new peak and remained there. There had been no meaningful change in strategy,

---

* The data for defensive end pay, because it includes the salaries of both ends, underestimates what was paid to the ends, like Chris Doleman, coming off the blind side, who tended to be paid a lot more than their counterparts on the other side. For salary data, the author would like to thank the front office of the San Francisco 49ers and the NFLPA.

or rules, or the threat posed by the defense to quarterbacks' health in ten years. There was no new data to enable NFL front offices to value left tackles—or any offensive linemen—more precisely. The only thing that happened is that the market was allowed to function. And the market assigned a radically higher value to the left tackle than had the old pre-market football culture.

And still no one really knew who he was. If he was never distinguished from his fellow linemen, it was because his contribution had always been indistinguishable from theirs. His exact value had always been a mystery, in part, because he never did anything by himself. To say that one lineman was more important than the others was as preposterous as arguing for the special value of a single synchronized swimmer. That was about to change: football strategy had broken up the collective. Or, rather, it had yanked this one member of the collective out into his own private business. Hardly anyone knew who he was—yet. But they knew the guy he was paid to stop! And two days after the game it would occur to them that Chris Doleman or Lawrence Taylor or Bruce Smith hadn't factored into the game. It was as if the star hadn't played.

That was the great left tackle's shot at recognition. He wasn't himself in the spotlight. No one was taking his picture. But he reflected the light of the star across from him. He was a kind of photographic negative.

UNTIL THEY STARTED paying left tackles huge sums of money, the NFL talent evaluators didn't really have a rigorous idea of what one looked like. There was no prototype. And for a brief period, right after the birth of free agency, all sorts of unlikely characters who would soon be dismissed as physically ill-equipped for the position made a fortune playing left tackle. Steve Wallace knew he could have used another 50 pounds. "I'd have given myself a big wide ass," he said. "I didn't have that girth in the butt." Will Wolford wasn't the prototype, either. In college he'd played right tackle; his first year with the Bills he'd played right guard. Like Wallace, he had been thrust into this strange new role on the offensive line—head to head with this wildly dangerous beast bent on killing the quarterback—and figured it out. He got by on guile rather than sheer physical ability. Like Wallace, he could have used a few more pounds. Plus his arms were too short. Judged physically not up to the task, he was moved back to guard in 1996 and retired after the 1998 season. As late as 2006 he said, "If I had long arms I'd still be playing."

Once the money started to fly, the talent evaluators became connoisseurs of left tackle flesh. The Wallaces and Wolfords were exposed as physically inadequate; the left tackle now had to meet a list of physical specifications rarely found in a human being. "I can sit in the draft room today and tell you the most likely things the scouts will say, when they talk about a college lineman," said Ernie Accorsi, the general manager of the New York Giants. "The first is, 'He's a tackle, but he'll have to be a guard in the pros.' The second is, 'He played left tackle in college, but he'll have to play right tackle in the pros.' " The left tackle was now meant to be the 300-plus-pound guy who was also among the best athletes on the field. Now that he was making rarefied sums of money, he was expected to be, by definition, rare. "It's tough to find three-hundred-fifty-pound guys who can move their feet," said Accorsi. "They are either six two, or their arms are too short or their hands are too small or their feet are too slow or they simply aren't athletic enough. You can coach a lot of things but you can't coach quick feet. You can't make a guy's arms longer, or his hands bigger. And you can't make them taller."

Accorsi inadvertently made an interesting point. It was probably true that the NFL couldn't lengthen the arms or stretch the torsos of fully grown men. On the other hand, they could wave millions of dollars in the air and let the American population know that the incentives had changed. Boys who thought they might make careers as power forwards, or shot putters, might now think twice before quitting the high school football team. Huge sums of money were there for the taking, so long as you met certain physical specifications.

Case in point: Jonathan Ogden. At the dawn of free agency, Ogden, the son of a Washington, DC, investment banker, had just graduated from the St. Albans School. He was six nine and weighed nearly 350 pounds, but his weren't the right sort of pounds, at least to begin with. When he arrived at

UCLA, to play football and put the shot, Ogden's nickname was "Fat Albert." He liked football but he loved the shot put—and had a legitimate chance to make the U.S. Olympic team. At St. Albans he had played right tackle and enjoyed it, because teams typically ran the football behind the right tackle and run blocking was fun. At UCLA, his new coach told him he was moving to left tackle and becoming, chiefly, a pass blocker. Ogden bridled. "I called my father," he said, "and I told him, 'They're trying to make me play left tackle!' My dad told me just to do it—because if I was going to play football, left tackle was the position to play." For a few years after the birth of free agency it helped a young man suited to play left tackle to have an investment banker for a father. After that the finances became so obvious that no one needed an investment banker to interpret them.

Jonathan Ogden remained unsure of his future in football. His freshman year at UCLA wasn't especially encouraging. The leap from high school to college was giant, much bigger, in his view, than the leap from college to the pros. "My entire freshman year," he said, "was a blur." His high school team had about ten plays; his college team ran, more or less, a pro offense. Pass blocking—which struck him as an almost passive activity—was a lot less interesting to him than run blocking. But by his sophomore year he had figured out where he was meant to go, and what he was meant to do, and it came naturally to him. After that season—the 1994 season—*four* of the defensive ends he'd faced were taken in the first round of the NFL draft. He'd gone head to head with four extremely good blind side pass rushers—Willie McGinest, Shante Carver, Trev Alberts, Jamir Miller—and hadn't allowed a single sack. "It was then I thought, 'If they can be first-round picks, why can't I be a first-round pick?' "

Good question! Nobody called him Fat Albert anymore. Ogden had slimmed from 350 to 310 pounds and then built himself back up in the UCLA weight room to 345 pounds. Muscle had replaced fat. He was faster and quicker and stronger and altogether terrifying. Six foot nine inches and 345 very mobile pounds. "I had some weeks in college where I could have had a cup of coffee in one hand and blocked the guy with the other," said Ogden—and when this elicits a laugh, he raises his hand and says, "No. Seriously." There were games when they'd just give up, and he'd look around and say, "They're not rushing!" His junior year was when he first heard himself described with a term he'd hear ad nauseam for the rest of his football career: *freak of nature.* He heard scouts say, also, that he was a "finesse" player. He reckoned that scouts always had to have one critical reservation, and so they'd dreamed that one up for him, as he had no flaw. "Coming out of college I was the best pass blocker in the country," he said. "It wasn't even close. They had to have one 'but.' "

But . . . to accuse him of being a "finesse" player? "Who the hell were they looking at?" he asked. The *job* might not call for aggression. But the *player* was ferocious. At the end of Ogden's junior season, UCLA was getting creamed by Kansas in the Aloha Bowl. They were down by 31 points going into the fourth quarter, the game was clearly over, and yet the defensive end he'd been manhandling all day just kept coming hard. Ogden thought he could see what he was up to: he thought he might beat Jonathan Ogden and make a name for himself. Maybe the guy had been reading the stuff the NFL scouts were saying about him in the newspapers—that deep down Jonathan Ogden was soft. "He kept coming," said Ogden. "So I picked him up, slammed him to the ground, and drove him into the dirt. When I was on top of him, I said, 'Look, man, it can either be like this for the rest of the quarter or we can relax and finish the game.' And he actually slowed down!"

The Baltimore Ravens selected him with the fourth pick in the 1996 draft—and handed him the largest signing bonus of his year: $6.8 million. He celebrated with a trip to Las Vegas. He was sitting at the blackjack table when someone tapped him on the shoulder and said, "Hey, aren't you Jonathan Ogden?" He turned around: it was Charles Barkley, the basketball legend. Here he was, a supposedly obscure offensive lineman, and Charles Barkley knew who he was. And he hadn't played a down in the NFL. After that, Ogden put aside his ambition to put the shot for the U.S. Olympic team.

As a boy, Ogden had been terribly shy. When he'd been required to compete in a spelling bee he had turned his back on the audience, as he couldn't face them and spell at the same time. A few years into his sensational NFL career you couldn't find a soul who would describe Jonathan Ogden as shy. He was bright and chatty and funny—and about as sure of himself and his abilities as a human being can be. And why shouldn't he be? He did what he did alone, and he did it as well as anyone ever did it. He had the proof: his quarterbacks never got sacked. When they went back to pass, they knew that what was behind them didn't matter. Opposing players weren't pleased to see him. "It can be intimidating if you allow it to be," legendary pass rusher Bruce Smith told the *Washington Post* when the reporter asked him what it was like to go head to head with Jonathan Ogden. "I know when I walk up to the line of scrimmage and I have to look up, I only think to myself: 'What in the world did his parents feed him?' "

Before the 2000 season the Baltimore Ravens re-signed Ogden to a six-year deal worth $44 million. That was what one prominent agent referred to as "one of the great what-the-fuck moments in the history of pro football negotiations." At that moment Jonathan Ogden was being paid more money than any quarterback in the NFL—and eight times more than Trent Dilfer, the quarterback he'd be protecting.

Now the highest paid player on the field, Ogden was doing his job so well and so effortlessly that he had time to wonder how hard it would be for him to do some of the other less highly paid jobs. At the end of that 2000 season, en route to their Super Bowl victory, the Ravens played in the AFC Championship game. Ogden watched the Ravens' tight end, Shannon Sharpe, catch a pass and run 96 yards for a touchdown. Ravens center Jeff Mitchell told *The Sporting News* that as Sharpe raced into the end zone, Ogden had turned to him and said, "I could have made that play. If they had thrown that ball to me, I would have done the same thing."

Having sized up the star receivers, Ogden looked around and noticed that these quarterbacks he was protecting were . . . rather ordinary. Here he was, leaving them all the time in the world to throw the ball, and they still weren't doing it very well. They kept getting fired! Even after they'd won the Super Bowl, the Ravens got rid of their quarterback, Trent Dilfer, and gone looking for a better one. What was wrong with these people? Ogden didn't go so far as to suggest that *he* should play quarterback, but he came as close as any lineman ever had to the heretical thought. "If you're going to throw the ball," he said, "just make it work. Nothing against all the quarterbacks we've had since I've been here—all twenty of them, it seems. But if we're going to complete ten of thirty passes, no TDs and two picks, then let's just run the ball. At least I can have some fun."

The left tackle had become a star, but of a curious kind. He knew he was a star, and his teammates and coaches knew it, too. But to the general fan he remained obscure. The TV cameras still weren't on Ogden, and their indifference to his work hadn't escaped him. "There's a little bit of satisfaction in playing well, but not that much," he said. "Nobody pays any attention to what I do as a lineman. All those offensive linemen in the Hall of Fame. I mean, they all deserve to be there. But who knows who they are? The first one you can think of is Anthony Muñoz. The only one you can think of is Anthony Muñoz." Generally overlooked, Ogden offered conspicuous displays of his athletic ability, just for the hell of it. It was as if he wanted the coaches who sat down and studied the game film to know how he measured up against the people getting all the attention.

That game against the Tampa Bay Buccaneers, for example. The Ravens quarterback throws an interception. The cornerback who has picked off the pass flies down the sideline—it's 60 yards to the end zone and there's nothing between him and it. Most of the Ravens just watch: there's no chance they'll catch the speedster, so why bother? A couple give it the old college try and lumber after him for twenty yards or so, with no real intention of catching him, like old dogs chasing after a new sports car. Jonathan Ogden, however, actually tries. He doesn't have an angle, and, really, how is a six nine, 350-pound man going to catch a five eleven, 185-pound man employed specifically for his foot speed? The angle is all wrong, and yet . . . he seems to be catching up. As Ogden runs, you can't see his facial expressions or read his mind, but his body language is eloquent: *you little supposedly fleet-footed sonofabitch. Me and you. One on one. Twenty-yard dash. I'll leave you in the dust.*

There's no way that Jonathan Ogden, NFL left tackle, can be faster than an NFL cornerback, but don't tell him that. He knows that he's special—one of a kind. Or, perhaps, first of a breed. "To be the next me, it's really not easy," he said. "'Cause you really can't teach some of the things I've been able to do. You can't teach someone to be six nine. You can't teach someone how, when they are off balance, to recover. To be good, you almost have to be born to play left tackle." To be born to play left tackle you must be born to do a great deal more than play left tackle. With the cornerback 15 yards from the end zone, Ogden still trails him by 10 yards. Between the monster and the midget is a single player, another Tampa Bay defensive back serving, unnecessarily, as an escort. Realizing, finally, that he won't catch the cornerback, Ogden decides to use this poor unsuspecting fellow as a human missile. Still running at full tilt, he grabs this 200-pound man and launches him at his teammate—and just misses. The cornerback who picked off the pass and ran it back for a touchdown has no idea what nearly hit him. He races into the end zone and celebrates his wonderful self. The crowd cooperates, and gives him all their attention. But they shouldn't have.

—

CHAPTER TEN

THE EGG BOWL

I N 1958, WHEN A BLACK TEACHER FROM GULFPORT, MISSISSIPPI, named Clennon King tried to enroll in Ole Miss, and was instead carted away by Mississippi state troopers to an insane asylum, the football coach couldn't have imagined it had anything to do with him. When, in 1962, James Meredith came and stayed, the campus was engulfed in riots, and the football coach watched as his practice field became a staging area for army helicopters—but his team still went 10–0 and ended the season as national champions. But not long after that Ole Miss coaches set out to recruit the black athlete and found that history interfered. "There just aren't that many white guys in Mississippi who can play," said one of the Ole Miss football coaches. "The game is so much about speed now. The defense is so much about speed now. We need the best black kids if we're going to have a chance." But they seldom attracted the best black players; and since the early 1970s the Ole Miss football team has had about it a delicious fatalism. The civil rights movement achieved many things, and one of them was to create a plausible analogy between Ole Miss football and the Confederate army.

In part because of the needs of their local football team, there wasn't a town in America more concerned than Oxford, Mississippi, with seeming to have dispensed with race as an issue. The effort the locals put into avoiding obvious racism rendered the near-total lack of interaction between black people and white people in Oxford, Mississippi, almost as invisible as it was in the rest of the country. The history of the place was inescapable, however, if for no other reason than all these extremely annoying outsiders kept dragging it into otherwise pleasant conversations. As late as the fall of 2004 coaches from other SEC schools—including the University of Alabama—were phoning up Michael Oher and telling him that he shouldn't go to Ole Miss because black people weren't welcome there. And if Michael Oher hadn't put down the phone and found himself staring at his very own white Ole Miss family, he might have taken an interest in the subject. Mississippi's past had created the climate for Mississippi's present, and it would continue to do so until the present was otherwise notified. Bobby Nix, a white Ole Miss graduate from the early 1980s who now tutored football players, made this point routinely. To help the black kids feel as if they belonged at Ole Miss, Nix often took them into the places frequented by the old white affluent Ole Miss crowd. The Grove, say, or the Square. Usually he would end up feeling awkward and self-conscious. "When you show up with them," he said, "you'll get this look. It's like you have the crying baby on the airplane."

That look could have meant any number of things. The color of their skin was just the beginning of what set the Ole Miss football players apart. They had gold caps on their teeth and blue tattoos on their skins. They wore different clothes: oversized ersatz sports apparel so loose fitting that every stiff breeze threatened to leave them naked in the streets. They drove different cars—these jalopies outfitted with hubcaps worth twice the market value of the entire vehicle. You'd see them driving around in these bizarre-looking rigs with the front seats tilted so far back that the driver appeared to be an astrologist hard at work in a fully reclined Barcalounger. Many of them didn't speak or write standard English; to all but the most attentive white Ole Miss football fan, the black football players were barely comprehensible. Many of them, according to their tutors, were *less* well prepared for college than Michael Oher. The typical incoming player in Michael's class had third-grade level reading skills. Several had never taken math. *Ever.*

But if they wanted to play college football—if they wanted a shot at "the league"—they had to go through the tedious charade of pretending to be ordinary college students. Of the seventy players who survived Coach O's first grueling spring practice, more than forty were classified as "academically at risk," which meant, among other things, that they spent a great deal of their time inside a redbrick building with dark windows on the fringes of the Ole Miss campus, being spoon-fed books by an army of tutors. "We tell them that they are employees of a corporation," said Nix, one of the more experienced of those tutors. "And that they might be dropped at any time for lack of performance." A big part of the tutor's job was to steer the players away from the professors and courses most likely to lead to lack of performance. The majority of the football team wound up majoring in "Criminal Justice." What Criminal Justice had going for it was that it didn't require any math or language skills. Criminal Justice classes were also almost always filled with other football players. Of course, football players weren't the only Ole Miss students majoring in Criminal Justice. But when the Criminal Justice program took the field trip to Parchman Farm—aka the Mississippi State Penitentiary—the football players were the only students with friends on the *inside*.

When people on the streets looked at the black football players, and made Bobby Nix feel as if he was holding the crying baby on the airplane, they might have had other things in mind but the color of their skin. And in other places, Nix might have discounted those looks. Here in Oxford he couldn't. Here every look was filtered by the past.

The perception that Ole Miss's treatment of black people might not be up to the high standards of, say, the University of Alabama was just one of the many problems Coach O faced when he set out to convince the region's top high school football players to come play for him—but he couldn't ignore it. Coach O had been hired by Ole Miss in large part because he had proven himself to be a gifted recruiter of black football players. He'd never been a head coach, or run a football offense. And while he had an obvious knack for firing up a football defense, his single most important career achievement was to have recruited a pair of national championship football teams for the University of Southern California. When Coach O had arrived in the late 1990s the

USC football team was faring poorly, and losing the best Los Angeles inner-city athletes to other schools. Coach O decided that what he needed was an example. Talk just one great inner-city high school player into committing to USC, prove that he can have a great experience, and others would follow. His opinion leader had been a defensive lineman named Shuan Cody—a *USA Today* High School All-American who, after three years at USC, went on to become a second-round draft pick of the Detroit Lions. When Coach O looked at Michael Oher, he saw Shuan Cody. But he was more than that. Not only was Michael Oher black, famous, and the best offensive lineman anywhere near Oxford, Mississippi. Michael Oher had a white sister who was an Ole Miss cheerleader and belonged to one of the snootiest white sororities on campus. The possibilities were endless.

IT DIDN'T TAKE LONG for word to arrive back at Ole Miss that the new head coach was out there saying he planned to build his football team on the back of Michael Oher. Ole Miss's two starting tackles, Bobby Harris and Tre Stallings, dug out Michael Oher's high school recruiting tape just to have a look at this new guy everyone was talking about. Stallings and Harris both were entering their senior seasons with at least a shot at playing in the NFL—Stallings would be taken in the sixth round by the Kansas City Chiefs, and Harris would sign a free agent contract with the San Francisco 49ers. Stallings, especially, expected to be the center of attention when people paid attention to Ole Miss offensive linemen. Then he rolled the tape of Michael Oher playing left tackle for the Briarcrest Christian School. "We both just laughed," said Harris. "I'd have to say he was the best lineman I'd ever seen with my own eyes—Terrence Metcalf [of the Chicago Bears] would be second. He was just maulin' people. Tre and me just looked at each other and said, 'He a beast!' "

Coach O handed the same tape to George DeLeone. DeLeone, in his thirty-sixth year of coaching offensive linemen, in college and the pros, had just arrived at Ole Miss from Syracuse University. He popped in Michael's tape, and as he watched he thought, *Oh my God.* "The flexibility in those hips! The arch in that back! That mass! Those feet!" he exclaimed, as he rewatched. DeLeone had seen plenty of future star NFL linemen back as college prospects. "Orlando Pace," he said, "or Andre Gurode with the Cowboys. In my judgment Michael Oher looks just like those guys did at this stage. It's a kinesthetic sense. You can't teach it."

In modern times Ole Miss's football team had enjoyed only the briefest and most fleeting moments of glory but had always been good at sending offensive linemen to the NFL. In the most recent NFL draft—the draft of 2005—their center Chris Spencer was picked in the first round by the Seattle Seahawks, and one of their guards, Marcus Johnson, was taken in the second round by the Minnesota Vikings. Before that, Terrence Metcalf had gone to the Bears, Todd Wade to the Texans, Stacey Andrews to the Bengals, Ben Claxton to the Falcons, Tutan Reyes to the Panthers, and Keydrick Vincent to the Steelers. None of those players had been in the starting lineup his freshman year. George DeLeone assumed Michael Oher would be treated like any other great offensive line prospect. He'd be red-shirted, sit out a year, and learn the system. In his thirty-six years of college coaching DeLeone had inserted a freshman into his starting lineup just once. And that had been back in 1986, on a losing Syracuse team, in a far weaker college conference than the one Ole Miss played in. Even then, Blake Bednarz—that was the kid's name—had started several years in high school, weight trained seriously, and arrived at Syracuse with a good understanding of his position. And he'd stunk! "Blake ended up being a great player for us," said DeLeone, "but he wasn't one that year."

Now Coach O was insisting that Michael Oher start for Ole Miss . . . immediately! The kid had played a grand total of fifteen high school games on the offensive line. "He's a kid who has never really been in a weight program," said DeLeone. "And he'll be going up against grown men who have been in the weight room for five years. And he's doing it in the best league in the country for defensive linemen." To make matters worse, the college game had grown a lot more complicated in the past twenty years. The Ole Miss offense would be a combination of the Atlanta Falcons' running game and the Tampa Bay Buccaneers' passing game. DeLeone assumed that no how matter how quickly the kid took to the game he'd need a full season to learn whom to block, and how to block him—and now he was being told by Coach O that Michael had some kind of learning disability, and that he'd have to teach him the plays using ketchup and mustard bottles. "A visual learner," Coach O had called him. Whatever that meant.

With the first game of the season less than two months away, DeLeone hopped in his car and drove the hour and a half from Oxford, Mississippi, to the Tuohy home in Memphis. Ditching the Ole Miss playbook with its X's and O's, he gamely set out to teach Michael Oher what was essentially an NFL offense. The kitchen chairs stood in for linebackers. The fancy dining room chairs—the Tuohy lady had just enough of them, luckily—served as the defensive and offensive lines. Coach O had told him to get the kid out on the field as quickly as possible, so DeLeone turned him into a right guard. It wasn't the kid's natural position. His natural position was left tackle. But the right guard had physical help on either side of him, and verbal instructions, from both the center and the tackle. It was the easiest position to learn, but, even so, DeLeone did not believe any true freshman could learn it. "Michael Oher is without question one of the greatest athletes I have ever seen for a guy his size," said DeLeone. "But what we're asking him to do is impossible to do."

In the safety of the Tuohys' kitchen they made progress—the kid was driving the fancy dining room chairs off the line nicely—when Leigh Anne came through the door. When she saw Michael firing off the line and getting fit with her furniture she took control of the defense. "The linebackers can stay," she said, tensely. "But you put my two thousand dollar dining room chairs back! Right now!" She then proceeded to tell him that she had examined his playbook with its X's and its O's and that it was "never going to work."

Coach DeLeone had a better idea than changing the playbook: keep Michael on the bench. How could an offensive line coach in good conscience stick any freshman into an SEC football game, much less a lineman who did-n't know the plays? The first few games he actually tried this ploy. Coach O had made him start Michael Oher; but in the middle of the second quarter, when Coach O's attention was diverted, he'd have an upperclassman tap Michael on the shoulder and quietly inform him he was being replaced. Michael would go sit on the bench until Coach O noticed he was there, and flip out.

Leigh Anne he assumed he could ignore; Coach O he assumed he could not. "Everyone who coaches college football is intense," said DeLeone. "But O's intensity is at another level."

ALRIGHTEERIGHTEERIGHTEE *righteeerighteeeee!! Hooo! . . . Hooo! . . . Hooo! . . . Hooo! LessgoooooLessgoooooLesssgooooo!"*

It was seven o'clock in the morning, and already Coach O was out roaming the halls of the practice facility, hollering at the top of his lungs.

The players filed past him, wearily. The linemen came as a group, a study in ectomorphism. Fourteen 300-pound men lumbering down a narrow hallway was a sight worth seeing. Their movements were regular, synchronized, and slow. Each step was a discrete event, requiring conscious effort. They transferred all their weight onto one leg, paused in preparation for the next three-foot-long journey, and then shoved off. They looked like a herd of circus elephants. All but one, the biggest of them all, who skipped along lightly on the balls of his feet.

Michael Oher now had a swagger about him. A lot of people he didn't know were talking about him. Before the season *Sports Illustrated* had named him one of the five freshman football players in the country to watch. At one of his first practices, newly installed at right guard, Michael could only shake his head as a defensive end bull rushed the left tackle and sacked the quarterback. But after the play he walked over to the defensive end and said, "If I was left tackle you wouldn't know what our backfield *looked like*. You'd need a road map." But he wasn't the left tackle; Bobby Harris was.

"Hoo! Hoo! Hoo! Bobbah Harris YouWAKEyet????!!!! C'mon Bobbah Bobbahbobbahbobbah! . . . WhatyouthinkBobbyHarris??"

"Aw-rye coach," said Bobby Harris.

"Mikka Oh! Mikka Oh! Howdooosaaaaaa!"

(Michael Oher! Michael Oher! How you doin' son?)

"*ReddostahCOMpeet'n?*"

(Ready to start competing?)

"*Lessturnbackdaclock. Two a days all over again! Hoo! Hoo! Hoo! Hoo!*"
His voice broke and became a piercing, dog-whistle-like shriek, and then he
vanished around a corner.

A human geyser of adrenaline and testosterone, he had maintained this
pitch from the first day of spring practice until this morning, the day before
the team was scheduled to play its final game of the season. He'd done it in
spite of presiding over what had to be one of America's most dysfunctional
football teams. He'd been handed a weak and dispirited group of players and
instantly set about trying to determine who among them met his standards.
After three grueling weeks of spring practice, seventeen of Ole Miss's eighty-
five football players quit. Some decamped for other colleges; some just went
home. Coach O immediately went looking for their replacements. Now, as
the season entered its final week, his nose for available football carrion
would be the envy of any vulture. He knew by heart the rosters of many junior college teams. He knew where to post ads on the Internet to solicit college football players. When Hurricane Katrina drove the Tulane University
football team out of New Orleans, there, at the city limits, stood Coach O,
hoping to lure away Tulane's finest—prompting the Tulane head coach to
call him, publicly, "lower than dirt."

Coach O wasn't lower than dirt. He was a desperate man in a dire situation. Here he was in his first, and possibly only, shot at making it as a head
coach in big-time college football. And he had no players! His defense was
actually very good—and Coach O, who ran the defense, ran it well. But
Coach O had no real experience with a football offense, and his offensive
coaches weren't giving him a lot of help. Each week they trotted out plays
that might be run with success only by physically superior football players.
And each week the Ole Miss offense ran onto the field without the faintest
hope of success. Going into the final game of the season the Rebels were 3–7,
but their record did not capture the flavor of their despair. In seven SEC
games they were 1–6 and their lone win came against Kentucky, which was

seldom a thing to be proud of. Their offense had scored the grand total of 77 points. Of the 117 Division I-A football teams Ole Miss ranked 115th in points scored. "We must have the worst offense in college football," said Michael, and he wasn't far wrong.

The coaching staff had passed through all the stages of grief—denial, shock, anger, sadness, resignation—and entered a stage overlooked by the psychology textbooks: the terror of total humiliation. They were about to travel to Starkville, Mississippi, to face the Mississippi State Bulldogs. The Ole Miss–Mississippi State game was called the Egg Bowl, in honor of the egg-shaped trophy passed back and forth for the previous twelve or thirteen centuries between the two schools. It had been several years since Ole Miss had lost the egg; no senior on the Ole Miss football team had suffered the indignity of surrendering the egg. It had been several years, for that matter, since Mississippi State had beaten any other team in the SEC. As Hugh Freeze, who was now Coach O's closest confidante and chief aide de camp, put it, "This is a game we don't need to be losing. You don't lose to Mississippi State."

A football game between Ole Miss and Mississippi State was more than just a football game—but then that was thought to be true of many Ole Miss football games. Before the previous game, against LSU, the second-to-last game of the season, Ole Miss's dean of students, Sparky Reardon, tried to explain the extreme emotions associated with the event. "It's kind of like the situation in the Middle East," he told the Ole Miss student newspaper. "Fans of one grow up hating the other and really don't know why." The twist to the Mississippi State rivalry was that the fans knew exactly why they hated each other. The game served as a proxy for the hoary Mississippi class struggle, between the white folks who wore shirts with collars on them and the white folks who did not. Mississippi State was a land grant college, originally called Mississippi A&M. The desperate contempt Ole Miss football fans felt for Mississippi State was echoed in the feelings of fans of the University of Texas for Texas A&M and fans of the University of Oklahoma for Oklahoma State—formerly known as Oklahoma A&M. These schools were not rivals; they were subordinates. Theirs was not a football team to be beaten but an insurrection to be put down. This notion was most vivid in the Ole Miss imagination: that the state of Mississippi, with the sole exception of the town of Oxford, was once a Great Lake of Rednecks. In recent decades the earth had warmed, and the shores of Great Lake Redneck had receded, so that, strictly speaking, perhaps it should not be described as a lake. But still, the residue was a very large puddle. And the one place in the puddle deep enough to ruin a shiny new pair of tassel loafers was Starkville, Mississippi.

And now the only thing between the players and the game was this final morning of preparation. The players stumbled in and parsed themselves into small groups according to their positions. The running backs went off into a room with their fellow running backs, the linebackers disappeared with line-backers. The fourteen offensive linemen herded themselves into what instantly appeared to be an inadequate room, and settled behind desks that seemed designed for midgets. Michael took his usual seat, in the back of the room.

If Michael Oher felt any social anxiety leaving Memphis for Oxford he hadn't shown it. Once or twice he'd asked questions of Miss Sue about Ole Miss that suggested a certain vague apprehension. "Is it true they got frater-nities that won't let in black guys?" (It was true.) "Will I be the only person at Ole Miss who doesn't drink?" (The small club of teetotalers was accept-ing all applicants.) But his wasn't the ordinary story of the boy going away to college. He'd left home, but home had come along for the ride. Miss Sue was still his private tutor. Hugh Freeze was still his football coach. Sean and Leigh Anne were, on many nights, in the house they'd built a couple of hun-dred yards off the Ole Miss campus. Before the first home game of the sea-son Sean Junior had walked just ahead of him through the Grove, hand in hand with Coach O. And when they'd gotten to the stadium Collins was right there on the sidelines, leading cheers.

He felt right at home, in his own way. He didn't run with a crowd but he had many friends. He floated back and forth between white Ole Miss and black Ole Miss. He enjoyed his own company and kept much of himself to himself. When the other linemen chattered he just sat and watched them.

"There was a *transvestite* in Chevron this morning," said one of the other linemen. "It was scary."

Several of them started, at the horror of it. The circus elephants had stumbled upon their mouse.

"And it wasn't buying anything either," said the 300-pound lineman. "It was just standing there. *Staring.*"

"Aw, man!" said another gargantuan fellow.

"Jesus," said a third.

Michael just shook his head and said nothing. When the digital clock turned from 7:29 to 7:30 Coach DeLeone came into the room, hunched and limping and deeply weary. T-shirt, sweat pants, reading glasses, gray hair cut in the style of a marine sergeant: if you had to guess what he did for a living you would guess George DeLeone was a retired military man, with a string of Purple Hearts. In fact he was a former undersized college lineman whose knee injuries still plagued him. He didn't look happy, but then he had no reason to be happy. The offense had been abysmal, and the Internet pundits and the newspaper columnists were pointing to his offensive line as the problem. His situation was grim: he was on the verge of losing his job. Now he hoped to persuade his linemen to join him in grimness and to see the gravity of their predicament.

"All right, men," he said, as he fiddled with the overhead projector. "I want to thank you for everything you've done for me this year."

No one said a word. Then one of them realized: "Coach, was that a joke?"

They all laughed, even Michael.

"We all set, ready to go, or we gonna laugh?" barked DeLeone, wrong-footing them utterly. "Guys! Can we just have one game where we come in on Sunday, look at the tape, and say, 'This is how we can play as an offensive line'? Let's play this game with some frickin' pride on the offensive line. That means something to me, and I hope it means something to you. We can laugh next week. Laugh Sunday night. Now . . ."

He calmed down, without any help from his players, and pulled out his plastic sheets—the sheets with the X's and O's on them. Then he switched on the overhead projector and assumed his usual position beside it.

Bobby Harris gave a huge yawn.

"Sit up please, Bobby," said Coach DeLeone.

Bobby sat up.

"Thank you."

The final lesson of their miserable season took the form of a pop quiz: Coach DeLeone called the name of a lineman and a play. The lineman was meant to respond with his assignment on that play. The air was soon thick with jargon and code. "Rip" and "Liz" and "Willie" and "Philly" and "Rum" and "Pookie" and "Trios" and "A-Gaps" and "3-Techniques." A gifted student of language would require a month to grasp it all. Throughout DeLeone kept one eye on his most troubling pupil, Michael Oher. Michael was now Ole Miss's starting right guard. A third of the time he had no idea where he was meant to go, or whom he was meant to block. The other two thirds, when he knew what he was supposed to do, and was sure of himself, he'd beaten up on much older opposing players. He'd pancaked a linebacker at Tennessee, and another at Alabama, both future NFL draft picks. After he'd crushed the Tennessee kid, and as he sat on top of him, he'd gotten into his face and said, "You lucky, if I'd come here to school, you'd be getting this every day." You had to like the kid's confidence—taking it that way to a senior all-conference linebacker. And, as confused as he was at times, he'd had games after which the film revealed him as the best performing lineman on the team. "He's getting by on his raw athletic ability," said Matt Luke, a former college lineman himself turned Ole Miss assistant coach. "It's the best I've ever seen. And my entire college line except me is in the NFL."

The games in which Michael had excelled also happened to be the games before which Sean Tuohy had sat down with him for six hours or so and reviewed the plays. Now he sat rubbing his knees, pushing down so hard on them with his hands he seemed to be trying to rip off a layer of his own skin. ("That's a nervous reaction he has," said Leigh Anne.)

He'd put fifty hours into this course for every hour he had put into math or English. But of all the courses he had taken, the course in playing offensive line had proved the most difficult. It *was* the most difficult. The plays were all new to him, and in a code foreign to him, and on each play there were a mind-numbing number of variations. On a football team, only the quarterback experienced the same level of complexity as the offensive line. As Michael struggled to organize inside his mind the blizzard of new material, this sixty-something-year-old coach with his funny East Coast accent kept hollering in his ear. Coach DeLeone prided himself on his rigor and the high expectations he had for his players. "One of my players misses a class I'm here at six in the morning running him," he said. "I know this: I don't see a lot of history professors out there running people around the building."

Today—the last day of preparation for the Mississippi State Bulldogs—is in theory a review. In fact, the coaches, grasping at straws, have put in new plays, with new terminology. Michael Oher isn't the only lineman who has no clue what's going on.

"Michael Oher!"

Michael stirred, uneasily.

"Twenty-eight Gem," barked his coach. "Gem tells the right guard to do what?"

"Go get the Mac," Michael said. The Mac is the middle linebacker. Unless he's the Mike. The main thing is he's not the Willie or the Sam—the nicknames for the other linebackers.

"Go get the Mac," said DeLeone, approvingly.

Michael knew that much. But—he was thinking, as he sat there—the Mac moved around. So did every other player on a college defense. What if the Mac wasn't where he was supposed to be? "The problem is," he said later, "I got eight guys running in front of me two seconds before the ball's snapped." Back at Briarcrest they had three basic running plays, and Michael had been assigned to block the same man no matter what the defense. Ole Miss had dozens of running plays, with half a dozen different blocking assignments on each of them. Whom he blocked, and how he blocked them, depended on where the defenders stood at the snap of the ball. There was a good reason for the new complexity. In high school if some defender came free and went unblocked—well, the team would take that risk for the sake of keeping things simple. In college the coaches couldn't risk a defender going completely unblocked, because the defenders were so routinely dangerous. A defender who went completely unblocked in the SEC could end the quarterback's season.

"This is the last time to talk about these assignments," DeLeone shouted. "We got to nail this, men!"

It was as if Coach DeLeone had read his thoughts. Even though he'd given him the right answer, the coach seemed upset. He was getting himself all worked up again.

"You must step up!" shouted Coach DeLeone.

He'd changed gears. He meant this literally—that when the ball was snapped the linemen needed to step forward, not backward. "Both guards last week stepped on the quarterback," the line coach continued. "This *cannot* happen this week." Last week they'd played LSU and lost 40–7. Against LSU the Ole Miss quarterback had gone down several times, in the most embarrassing way possible, with his foot pinned to the ground by one of his own linemen. At least one of those feet had been Michael's.

"You must step up!!" He was screaming again. "You must step up!! We got that, Michael Oher??"

Coach DeLeone's face was red, but his toenail was still black and blue from having been stepped on during practice, two months before, by Michael Oher.

"Yes, sir," said Michael. He thought: *If this old guy doesn't calm down, he's gonna have a heart attack right here and die.* But, once again, the coach calmed himself. "What's the deal with Mississippi State?" he asked, innocently.

The linemen searched in each other's blank faces for the right answer, but failed to locate it. It was Bobby Harris who finally ventured a guess.

"That we hate them?" he said.

"Someone is saying that the Mississippi State coach is guaranteeing a win," said DeLeone, incredulously. "They think that much of us that they're *guaranteeing* a win?"

Ah—that was it. A faint stab at a motivational speech. But that wasn't Coach DeLeone's job. Which was just as well, as it was time to go listen to Coach O.

TEN MINUTES LATER Coach O had his football team arranged before him. One final pre-game speech to deliver before he could put this dreadful season behind him. He waited for them to quit horsing around, which they always seemed to need to do for at least ninety seconds, and then strolled with authority to the podium.

"Let me say this about Mississippi State," he began.

He paused for dramatic effect.

"They hate you, we hate them."

He paused again. No one could disagree.

"I purposefully have not had much for the other team. 'Cause I don't respect them much. I say I respect them in the paper. I don't respect 'em. I don't have *nuthin'* for them. The other guy has been putting up the scores of last year."

He hardly needed to explain himself because everyone in the room already understood. They might not have read the papers but they had at least heard the rumor that Sylvester Croom, Mississippi State's head coach, has been riling up his players by posting the scores from past defeats at the hands of Ole Miss. Croom also stood accused of trash-talking. He'd gone in front of a group of Mississippi State boosters, spoken about Ole Miss, and gotten himself quoted in the papers. All he'd actually said was "I don't ever think about Ole Miss. If our kids play as well as they can, we're going to beat their butt." But every right-thinking Ole Miss football fan and player must agree that Croom has violated football decorum—which is of course only what you'd expect from a Mississippi State football coach. "This is totally wrong," Coach O now says. "Let's put these guys *way* below our program. Think about class and Ole Miss. Think about how we are, think about how they are."

A Great Lake of Rednecks!

"Understand that their team is going to come out fired up," he continues. "He [Coach Croom] didn't even let 'em go home for Thanksgiving. Wanted 'em all living in a hotel in Starkville. *Dumpy ass* hotel in Starkville. I can just about imagine it."

Coach O actually didn't share the social pretensions of his employer. He was just a good ol' boy who didn't present himself as anything but a good ol' boy—he said his boyhood idea of going out to a fancy restaurant was driving thirty miles to Kentucky Fried Chicken. He'd have been perfectly content in a dumpy ass hotel in Starkville. He was just speaking from the Ole Miss script—and doing it well, in view of the circumstances.

The circumstances were that the Ole Miss football team, like the Mississippi State football team, consisted mostly of poor black kids from Mississippi. When the Ole Miss defense gathered in a single room, the only white people were coaches. On the football field the players became honorary white people, but off it they were still black, and unnatural combatants in Mississippi's white internecine war. Even as Coach O worked to fire them up for the game, many of the seniors had their bags packed and their cars running. After the game they'd vanish, en masse, from the Ole Miss campus. They'd just walk right out of the locker room and get in their cars and drive away. Several who might have stayed and picked up their degrees will decide it wasn't worth hanging around five months to do it. They'll have spent four years shuttling between their off-campus apartments, their Criminal Justice classes, and football practice on the off chance of making it to the NFL.

Coach O was finished imagining the dumpy ass hotel in Starkville. It clearly pained him to dwell on the negative qualities of their opponents; he was by nature a positive man. He wanted to end on a positive note. "You come to school here," he said, seriously. "You graduate. You go to the NFL. That's what I want our program to be." And then he began to ramble, sounding like a man talking in his sleep.

"Just gonna win tomorrow," he said. "Focus. Details. Let's focus."

THE NEXT MORNING the Ole Miss Rebels' buses rolled into Starkville. At Ole Miss there was money in the air; here there was just hostility, and the sights and sounds of resentment. Every State fan carried a cowbell, and rang it incessantly, as they hurled insults at the Ole Miss players. The players changed into their uniforms on cold concrete floors, and hung their street clothes in old wooden cubbyholes. Once dressed, they crowded into the foyer outside the locker room, like soldiers on a troop carrier about to storm a beach. That's when one spotted, beneath a pile of cardboard boxes, empty Gatorade bottles, and surgical tape, an oddly shaped trophy badly in need of polishing.

"*Dat* da egg?" he asked, incredulously.

Another player looked over, then another. The Ole Miss staff had brought the old trophy along with them, in case they lost and had to hand it over.

"Dat is da egg," said someone else.

With that, they raced out onto the field, to the clanging of cowbells and hoots of derision. Never mind the barnlike quality of the locker room; never mind the rickety old stadium itself: the football field was a work of art. There was no substance on earth more lush or thick or green or beautiful. Turfology, as it happened, was Mississippi's State great academic strength. At the mention of State's turf-tending skills, the Ole Miss snob would become serious and acknowledge that, whatever you might want to say about State, they knew how to grow golf courses. "Don't forget to look down and check out the grass!" had been one of two pieces of advice Sean had given Michael before he left for the game. The other was, "Never take your helmet off in Starkville."

And Michael didn't, but more out of shame than fear of being brained by a beer bottle. The game took the Ole Miss team through a speeded-up version of the emotions of their season. First came hope: five plays into the game the Ole Miss quarterback, Ethan Flatt, hit his fastest receiver, Taye Biddle, for a 41-yard touchdown pass. But Biddle, one of the seniors who would quit school immediately after the game, might as well have kept on running out the back of the end zone and into his car. Ole Miss never called that play again. Instead, their offensive brain trust decided to use their unbelievably slow, fifth-string running back to test the strong interior of the Mississippi State defense. In the press box before the game, the Ole Miss offensive coordinator, Noel Mazzone, happened to walk past a TV on which was playing a North Carolina State football game. Six months earlier, Mazzone had left his job running the North Carolina State offense to take the job of running the

Ole Miss offense. Seeing his former team on TV he snorted and said, loudly enough for journalists to overhear, "Should have stayed there, at least they had some players."

Bill Walsh had shown how much an imaginative coach might achieve even with mediocre talent; Noel Mazzone was demonstrating how little could be achieved by a coach who did not admit any role for the imagination. The next five times Ole Miss had the ball Mazzone used the opportunity to prove that his slow, fifth-string running back couldn't run through a giant pile of bodies in the middle of the field. Once the Ole Miss offense faced third and long, as it invariably did, everyone in the stadium knew a pass was coming. There was nothing for the Ole Miss quarterback to do but drop back and wait to be buried under the Mississippi State blitz. Most of the time, just before he was crushed, he managed to throw an incomplete pass or an interception.

Three punts and two interceptions later Mississippi State led 21–7. Rather than try a different strategy—say, the surprising pass play that had worked the first time they had the ball—the Ole Miss coaches tried different players. First they switched their fifth-string running back out for their sixth-string running back. (Between them they ran the ball twenty-five times for 31 yards.) Then they switched their first-string quarterback out for their second-string quarterback—the fellow who had started the season as the first-string quarterback. (Between them they threw four interceptions.) The frantic search for the right combination of players reflected their more general football worldview: they believed in talent rather than strategy. They placed less emphasis on how players were used than who they were. Whoever had the best players won: it was as simple as that.

It was a bleak and deterministic worldview, implying, as it did, that there was little a strategist could do to raise the value of his players. More to the point, it was a false view, at least for running a football offense. The beauty of the football offense was that it allowed for a smart strategist to compensate for his players' limitations. He might find better ways to use players, to maximize their strengths and minimize their weaknesses. He might even change the players' sense of themselves. But Ole Miss not only lacked a smart strategist: it lacked a coach who understood the importance of strategy. The genius of Bill Walsh was missing; so, for that matter, was the genius of Leigh Anne Tuohy. There wasn't a soul on the Ole Miss sidelines thinking seriously how to make the most of what another person could do. They were all stuck dwelling on what other people couldn't do.

After each failed series the linemen trotted to the bench and plunked themselves down for a chalk talk delivered by assistant line coach Matt Luke. This served mainly to highlight their near-total confusion. After one series the right tackle, Tre Stallings, confessed he had gone the wrong way because he thought the center, Daryl Harris, had shouted "Philly," when he had in fact shouted "Willie." After another series there ensued a long argument—for them—about the difference between "G" and Gem." After a third series three of the linemen got screamed at for firing out and blocking linebackers instead of blocking the linemen right in front of them. After a fourth series a coach thrust a headset at Michael Oher so that Michael could listen to Coach DeLeone, up in the press box, holler at him to try harder. After a fifth series the left guard, Andrew Wicker, hurled his helmet on the ground and shouted, "We're getting our ass kicked by *State*." And they were—largely because none of them had any clear idea what he was meant to do on any given play.

By halftime hope was rapidly giving way to denial. At the start of the third quarter denial gave way to depression, with hardly a pause for the intermediate stages of bargaining and anger. The change came on a single play. With Ole Miss down 21–14, the team had the ball and began, slowly, to move it. It was, as always, third and long, and the Ole Miss quarterback, Michael Spurlock, called for a pass. That in itself posed a problem, as he was only about five nine, and unable to see over the linemen. To compensate for his stature, Spurlock had the habit of just taking off toward the sideline the minute he received the ball. The price he paid for his new view of the field was to render himself nearly useless as a passer—he was running too fast to throw the ball with accuracy—and to confuse the linemen assigned to protect him, as they had no idea where he was.

On this play it hardly mattered. Ole Miss had lined up with two tight ends: both ran the wrong way and missed their blocks. Ole Miss had a tail-back: he, too, ran the wrong way and failed to block the defender he was meant to block. Three of the five Ole Miss linemen—Michael plus the center plus the left guard—all blocked a single Mississippi State defensive tackle. With most of Ole Miss's blockers ungainfully employed, a Bulldog linebacker shot through a gap and sacked the Rebel quarterback for a 20-yard loss, almost killing him in the bargain. After that Coach DeLeone, watching from the press box, yanked Michael Oher from the game. Michael ended his season on the bench, a simmering symbol of his coach's frustration.

From his seat beside his wife, high in the stands, Sean Tuohy watched the loss take shape with the calm of an asset manager who long ago banked his annual returns. In the grand scheme of Michael's career this one game—this entire season—didn't matter. Just by taking the field as a freshman, Michael's stock remained high. Sean's main goal had been to make sure that Michael didn't have the same experience of college sports that he had had, and that Michael didn't wind up depending on the mercy or the intel-ligence of his coaches. Now Sean understood that the Ole Miss coaches needed Michael far more than he needed them. Their careers were at stake; Michael could always transfer—a fact Leigh Anne had brought to the atten-tion of the Ole Miss coaches more than once. Leigh Anne had already told Coach O that if Noel Mazzone and George DeLeone returned to run the Ole Miss offense for one more year, Michael would not—and the two coaches were almost sure to be gone after this game. Michael didn't need to worry about the bigger picture; the bigger picture was arranging itself to maximize his value. "See how his face looks right now," said Sean, his binoculars trained on Michael. Michael's upper lip was tucked under his lower, and his eyes stared straight ahead at nothing. "That's how he looks when he's plan-ning on not talking to anyone for a while." He could afford to pout.

THE DAY AFTER his team's embarrassing 35–14 loss to Mississippi State, Coach O fired his offensive coordinator and began to look for a new offensive line coach. Then he sat down and wrote out his depth chart for the 2006 football season. The first name he moved around was Michael Oher's. Michael became Ole Miss's starting left tackle. "If I could do it over," said the head coach, "I'd have just put him there to begin with and let him figure it out."

The plan started with Michael Oher but didn't end there. Coach O might not have Bill Walsh's gift for taking average talent and tricking it into being better, but he knew how to find and attract great talent. Over the next few months he set out to pluck the finest football talent from the junior colleges and high schools of America—and, to judge from the high marks he received from the recruiting services, he appeared to have succeeded. At the center of this effort, oddly enough, was Michael Oher. "In every conversation Michael's name came up," he said. "He was my tool. And when we had the top guys on campus, I had him show them around."

Michael walked away from his freshman season wondering what that had all been about. And then, strangely, the honors began to roll in. He was named a First Team Freshman All-American, and First Team Freshman All-SEC. He was named pre-season All-SEC by magazines and also by the SEC's coaches. *College Football Weekly* listed him the best player on the Ole Miss offense. His value, once perceived, was indestructible. He could play on one of the worst football offenses in the nation and nobody would hold it against him. The experience had been a blur. But all anyone seemed to care about was that (a) he was still the biggest guy on the field and a freakishly gifted athlete, (b) he'd picked up the college game faster than anyone had the right to expect, and (c) when he knew what he was supposed to do, he'd knocked some folks around. And while that wasn't as often as anyone would have liked, it had been often enough that players and coaches now knew he'd eventually figure it out.

So often given the benefit of doubts, Michael Oher now set out to confirm the wisdom of the people who showed such faith in him. After the season, for the first time in his life, he hit the weight room. Six months later he emerged a different shape; he went in a square and came out an inverted triangle. He went in being able to bench-press 225 pounds and came out bench-pressing nearly 400 pounds. He went in weighing 345 pounds and came out weighing 320—without, it seemed, an ounce of fat on him.

But there still lingered this ominous feeling about him. He might be injured at any time, of course, but that wasn't the source of the feeling. There was another, more disturbing risk, because it was harder to pin down. He could never shake entirely the place he had come from, and he could never change entirely who he was born. Every now and then, for instance, he'd go back to his old neighborhood and when he did bad things often happened. At Leigh Anne's urging he had gone to see his mother—and the next thing Leigh Anne knew she was getting a call from a clearly flustered Big Tony, and the only words she could understand were "truck" and "dead" and that Michael was in the custody of the Memphis police. When Michael had arrived at his mother's house he'd found the police there, arresting her. For some reason she'd been driving around in a truck that belonged to a man the police had just found, murdered. The police had asked Michael why he was there, he'd told them, and they'd put him in handcuffs and taken him to central lockup. Sean had sprung him, then given Michael a little speech about black people and the police and the unlikelihood of the former being treated graciously or even fairly by the latter. When a police officer told Michael to do something, no matter how rudely he put it, Michael was to say "yes, sir" and do it. And his first telephone call should be to Sean Tuohy.

In theory, when Michael went away to Ole Miss, he put some distance between himself and the hand reaching out from his past. But Michael had left behind inner-city social risks only to find that inner-city social risks had followed him to Oxford, Mississippi. One friend and teammate, having failed his Ole Miss classes, left school and went right back to his old neigborhood to peddle drugs—because it was the only way he knew how to make money. His three closest friends on the Ole Miss team all had children. One, Jamarca Stanford, had become a father at fifteen. Another friend was a tough defensive end named Peria (he pronounced it Pur-*Ray*) Jerry. Peria had so little knowledge of math or English he might as well never have been to school. Miss Sue not only tutored him, and got him reading and adding fractions, she mothered him incessantly. Michael didn't fully approve—he thought Miss Sue was *his*. One day he blurted out to Miss Sue, "You love Peria more than you love me." "I'll never love any of them more than I love you," said Miss Sue. "But he's catching up!" said Michael, outraged.

And he was: one day Peria looked at Miss Sue with tears in his eyes and said, "Nobody ever loved me till you," and it was all Miss Sue could do not to break down right there. Peria was so big that you forgot he was still, in most ways, just another needy child.

There were at least a dozen black football players from impoverished backgrounds auditioning for the role of Eliza Doolittle. ("I wish I could get me an adopted family," said Peria.) No one asked Leigh Anne for a shirt with a little alligator on it. But they all longed for some connection and the sense of being taken care of. Michael brought them home to Memphis, and so Leigh Anne got some idea of the risks to keeping Michael on the straight and narrow. To Thanksgiving dinner, for instance, Michael had invited a freshman linebacker named Quentin Taylor, who had no place else to go. At the start of the meal Michael leaned over and whispered, sternly, "Quentin, you're supposed to put your napkin in your lap." Right after that, Quentin let it drop that he had fathered three children by two different mothers. Leigh Anne pulled the carving knife from the turkey and said, "Quentin, you can do what you want and it's your own business. But if Michael Oher does that I'm cutting his penis off." From the look on Quentin's face Michael could see he didn't think she was joking. "She would, too," said Michael, without breaking a smile.

All these surprisingly good things were happening to Michael Oher. Still there was a sense that something surprisingly bad could happen at any time. And it did.

ONE AFTERNOON, long after their miserable season was over, Michael sat on the front steps of his dormitory with a couple of teammates. Up walked another teammate, a freshman linebacker named Antonio Turner. Antonio had visited the Tuohy home in Memphis, and apparently he didn't like what he had seen. Now he made a number of unflattering remarks about white people generally and about Michael's "cracker family" specifically. When he called Michael a "cracker," Michael gave him a shove, and Antonio punched him in the face—then ran. Michael gave chase, and the two of them raced in circles around a parked car like a couple of cartoon characters. Finally, Antonio said something about Collins and Leigh Anne Tuohy. What exactly he said no one ever exactly learned—and Michael refused to repeat it. But it had something to do with Antonio's intention to have sex with Michael's white sister, but only after he'd had sex with Michael's white mother. Whereupon Michael said he was going to his dorm room to change his clothes, because he didn't want to get Antonio's blood on his nice shirt.

When Michael walked back into the dorm to find a shirt he didn't mind spoiling with Antonio's blood, Antonio took off at a sprint. He ran to the redbrick study hall with the darkened windows used by the football players and monitored by tutors. Surrounded by teammates and white tutors, he figured he'd be safe. He figured wrong.

Michael knew he didn't need to run. He knew where Antonio had gone—there was no place else to go where Antonio would think he was safe. Michael walked across campus, calmly stalking his prey. Finally, he came to the study hall. There, in a small room filled with half a dozen players and tutors, he found Antonio, and charged.

Force equals mass times acceleration, as Hugh Freeze said, and when Michael's mass comes at you at Michael's speed, it's just an incredible force. With that incredible force he drove Antonio into the ground. Then he picked him up with one hand by the throat and lifted him straight off the ground. Antonio weighed 230 pounds but in Michael's big hand he looked, as one player later put it, "like a rag doll." Michael beat Antonio around the face and threw him across the room as, around the room, huge football players took cover beneath small desks.

That's when a lot of people at once began to scream hysterically—and Michael noticed the little white boy on the floor, in a pool of blood. He hadn't seen the little white boy—the three-year-old son of one of the tutors. Who had put the little white boy there? When he'd charged Antonio, the boy somehow had been hit and thrown up against the wall. His head was now bleeding badly. Seeing the body lying in his own blood, Michael ran.

Antonio, a sobbing wreck, was taken to the home of running back coach Frank Wilson, for his own protection. He was still alive, and the Ole Miss coaches planned to keep him that way. Back in the study hall Miss Sue sat listening to another football player, a linebacker named Robert Russell. She told him she didn't understand why these disputes must be resolved with violence. "Miss Sue," he said, "Michael and I weren't raised that way. No matter how much you try to wash us up behind the ears, we're going to go back to what we know."

Hugh Freeze called Leigh Anne, who was up in Memphis. Like a zoo director discussing a crazed rhinoceros with its trainer, he said, "You got to get down here and find him. You're the only one who can control him." Leigh Anne jumped in her car, took off for Oxford—and then stopped. Michael was gone, no one knew where he was, and she didn't actually believe she could find him. She pulled over to the side of the road and called Sean, who was somewhere on the West Coast with the Memphis Grizzlies. It was Sean who said, "He's running because that's all he knows how to do." He wasn't out looking for someone to kill. He was just trying to escape his predicament. Just a few months earlier Sean would have been shocked. But now he knew that when Michael got into trouble, he ran. He knew it because not long after Michael had left for Ole Miss he'd had an argument with Miss Sue and vanished for two days. He wouldn't return phone calls—nothing. Late one night, Sean and Leigh Anne had turned to each other in bed and considered the possibility that Michael Oher might never come back. That he'd just used them to get what he'd wanted and that he actually had no real feelings for them. "You think this is it?" Leigh Anne had asked. And the truth was, Sean didn't know. "Your mind does funny things when it's idle," said Sean. "But that's when I decided that the downside was that we'd helped some kid—so even if he'd been playing us all along there really was no downside."

But he knew something else, too. He knew that Michael had spent his life running. Not long before, he'd been in his Memphis office when a woman named Bobby Spivey, who worked for the Tennessee Department of Children's Services, finally returned his call. Spivey was the officer who had handled Michael's case. Sean had phoned her three times to see what he could learn about the missing years in Michael's life, and each time he found himself in conversation with Spivey's voice mail box.* Now, finally, Spivey herself was on his speaker phone, and embarrassed to say that most of the details of Michael's case were unavailable. The Department of Children's Services had lost his file. She remembered very clearly some things about Michael Oher, however. She recalled, for instance, the night that Children's Services had sent the police to remove seven-year-old Michael Oher from his mother's care.

"It was raining that night," said Bobby Spivey. "She was homeless. She was on drugs. Someone called the police and said she was walking around in the rain with her kids."

She recalled that Michael Oher had been taken away and put into a foster home—but that he hadn't stayed. "He was a runaway a majority of the time," she said, laconically. "He was real quiet. He wasn't disrespectful. He just ran." Eventually, the Memphis branch of the Tennessee Department of Children's Services had given up looking for Michael Oher. "He ran so much that we stopped trying to stop him," said this woman who had handled his case. The government had officially taken charge of Michael at the age of seven, she said, but lost track of him around his tenth birthday. She was curious to know what had become of him.

---

* He called only after I'd found Bobby Spivey's name and pestered him to use his status as legal guardian to learn what he could about Michael's early childhood.

CHAPTER ELEVEN

FREAK OF NURTURE

NCAA Lady: Can I ask you this—

Sean: He has no hate. No animosity. His memories are all good.

NCAA Lady: To be quite honest with you—do you fully know his childhood?

Sean: Oh, absolutely not. First of all he doesn't have a great relationship with *me*. Because he never had a daddy. I'm more of just an older man. He'll talk to my daughter or my wife. But we don't ask questions like that. Because a lot of times we don't want the answers.

NCAA Lady: You don't care.

Sean: I only care about what he cares about.

NCAA Lady: You don't ask, I should say.

Sean: We're trying to take care of geometry class tomorrow. What happened when he was four years old—if he's okay by it, we're okay by it. The timeline to us, we figure it'll come one day. We're in no hurry. We got a long time.

DENISE OHER COULDN'T SAY who murdered her father—just that he had been shot several times in his bed when she was a little girl. She couldn't tell you exactly when she had been removed from her mother's custody. She knew her mother was an alcoholic and totally incapable of taking care of her and her half-brother, Robert Faulkner. Her mother never cooked her a meal, read her a book, or took her to school—at least, not that she could recall. One day the police came for them, and took her and Robert away to an orphanage. She still didn't feel especially cared for—she never felt loved or anything like that. She skipped plenty of school, and even more when, at the age of fifteen, her mother somehow sprung her from the institution. Once out she fell in with the wrong crowd. It led her to drugs and other things and, at twenty, she gave birth to a baby boy. Four more babies soon followed. Around the neighborhood people would say, "Dee Dee is a breeder." And she was: inside of six years she had five little boys. Their father, she felt sure, was a man named Odell Watkins, but he declined the offer from the Department of Children's Services to acknowledge his paternity. Instead he took a DNA test. The test proved, just as she'd said all along, that Odell Watkins was the father.

By the late summer of 1985 Dee Dee was twenty-seven years old, and finished with Odell Watkins. She wasn't even half-finished having babies, however, and the father of her next child had just arrived on her front porch. He came directly to her from Robert, her brother.

Since they'd left the orphanage Robert had gotten the nickname "Skillet." Oddly enough, it was a skillet, and then a horseshoe, that Robert later used to crush his wife's skull after she told him she wanted a divorce. His wife's brutal murder landed Robert on Death Row at River Bend over in Nashville; but that all came later. The first time Robert had been thrown in jail for murder he'd been sent away for just a few years. Denise couldn't tell you who Robert had killed, or why. She just knew that her brother had been convicted for murder and sent away to Fort Pillow prison, where he'd met a man named Michael Jerome Williams. Why Michael Jerome Williams had been in jail Dee Dee either didn't know or would soon forget. All she knew was that Robert had wanted to send word to her of his well-being and that Michael Jerome Williams, on his way out of jail, had been kind enough to serve as messenger. "When I met him I wasn't with nobody," said Dee Dee.

"We got to talking and we wound up together. But he was a little bitty fellow. Five foot six, maybe."

Soon after Michael Williams visited her, Dee Dee discovered she was pregnant again. She had no money, no job, and was now flirting with a serious drug problem—but still she didn't worry about the welfare of this new baby. "God put it there," she said, "and He ain't going to put no mouth on this earth he can't feed." Unlike Odell Watkins, Michael Williams didn't dispute his paternity, and she named the baby after him: Michael Jerome Williams.

But right around the time the child was born, Michael Jerome Williams vanished. The Department of Children's Services went looking for him, and it was a full year before they found him—back in prison. By then Dee Dee had decided she didn't want her baby named for Michael Jerome Williams. Though she made no effort to change the baby's legal name, she began to call him "Michael Oher." Oher was her family name, which she had taken from her mother.

In the next four years Denise bore four more children, by several different fathers, none of whom stuck around. By the time Michael was five years old, and his memory kicked in to record events for posterity, Dee Dee was caring for seven boys and three girls, all under the age of fifteen. Only she wasn't really caring for anyone, as she'd become addicted to crack cocaine. "On the first of the month she'd get a check," recalled Marcus, Michael's eldest brother, "and she'd leave and we wouldn't see her until the tenth. . . . Them drugs tear everything up." As Dee Dee had no income except for whatever the government sent her on the first of each month, the children had no money for provisions. They had no food or clothing, except what they could scrounge from churches and the street. Surprisingly often, given the abundance of public housing in Memphis, they had no shelter. When asked what he recalls of his first six years, Michael said, "Going for days having to drink water to get full. Going to other people's houses and asking for something to eat. Sleeping outside. The mosquitoes." The winter was cold, but the summer was worse because the heat was so oppressive and the mosquitoes bit all night long.

Yet, by the time Michael turned seven his greatest fear was that some man in a uniform would come and take him away from his mother. His mother had her problems but she was never overtly cruel: she never hit them, for instance, and she often said she loved them. She just wasn't around that much and, when she was around, had nothing to give them. Marcus, now sixteen years old, knew that the police sometimes broke up families such as theirs. They'd heard snippets about foster homes, and the snippets hadn't been reassuring. The police just took you away and dumped you with people whose only interest in you was the cash they received for your presence. Michael's brothers spoke of the possibility that the police might take them away, and decided that, whatever happened, they would try to stick together.

On April 14, 1994, the Memphis courts, for the first time, registered Michael's existence. Listing Michael's name, as well as the names of his siblings, it rendered the following verdict: "It appears to this Court that said children are in need of immediate protection of this Court and that said children are subject to an immediate threat of said children's health to the extent that delay for a hearing would be likely to result in severe or irreparable harm."

A month before Michael's eighth birthday, the police cars rolled up in front of the shed behind the cottage that Denise had told the children belonged to a cousin of hers. The three little girls were out in front. Andre and Rico were someplace else. The four other boys—Marcus, Deljuan, Carlos, and Michael—were inside the shed. "We seen them pull up and we already knew what they were coming for," said Marcus. "We done seen it happen before with other people. We really thought they were going to scatter us up." Seeing the police, Marcus turned to his brothers and said, "Run!"

Michael prided himself on his foot speed. "I can fly," he liked to say. Speed was essential to the new plans he had for himself—plans he would cling to, with an amazing tenacity, for the next ten years. On June 20, 1993, he had been inside someone else's house and seen a basketball game on television. On that night Michael Jordan was using the Phoenix Suns as his foil for the public display of his greatness. The moment he saw Michael Jordan play basketball, Michael Oher knew who he was meant to be: the next Michael Jordan. Because he was seven, he thought it was an original idea. Because he was quiet, the idea went unexpressed, and so undisturbed.

But Michael Oher now had a secret ambition, and it would define much of what he did with himself for the next ten years. The ambition stood in defiance of a world that had assigned him no value. His father hadn't valued him enough to meet him. His mother hadn't valued him enough to feed him. He'd never been to a doctor, or been given medicine of any sort. He'd missed nearly as much school as he'd made. His older brothers cared for him and were good at finding food. But they had their own problems; they had no real ability to nurture. No one invested in Michael Oher, and so he yielded no visible returns. Michael did not consider himself without value, however. From the moment he laid eyes on Michael Jordan, he was, himself, destined to become the richest and most famous black athlete on earth.

When the police cars came and his brother screamed at him to run, Michael didn't really know what was going on. He just saw Marcus (sixteen), Deljuan (thirteen), and Carlos (eleven) sprinting out the back door. He flew after them. To be the next Michael Jordan, Michael Oher needed to be quick and agile—and he was. His older brothers were still faster than he was, but Michael pumped his little legs as fast as they'd go, and he finally caught up to them. When they'd finished running they stood on the second floor of an abandoned auto repair shop down the street, huffing and puffing. From a broken window they watched their mother scream as the police took away her three baby girls—Denise, Tara, and Depthia—and put them in the back of the squad car. Marcus told his brothers that they'd probably never see those little girls again, and he was right.

Dee Dee wasn't capable of caring for her children, and she knew it, but she didn't want anyone taking them away from her. The boys wanted to stay together; they felt safe together; together they at least had each other. They all knew that the police would be back for the boys, and so they left the shed. Dee Dee got her hands—she wouldn't say how—on an old beat-up Monte

Carlo. For weeks she and the seven boys slept in the car. "Bodies on top of each other," is how Deljuan, who was now thirteen, recalled it. "We'd get up in the morning and go wash ourselves in the bathroom of a service station."

Unwilling to leave the small area on the west side of Memphis where she'd been born and raised, Dee Dee found herself at a disadvantage. A few weeks after the police nabbed her daughters, they caught up to Carlos and Michael on a day they attended school. The police took them from school to the home of a woman they'd never met, named Velma Jones. "Velma was a big lady," said Carlos, "about three hundred seventy-five pounds, and she got angry when you made her move." The children found her terrifying—and their fear was only heightened when she showed them what she did to children who misbehaved: sat on them. That was Michael's most vivid memory of the first few days, being sat on by Velma Jones. Carlos recalled being taken, with Michael, to the home of Velma's equally gargantuan twin sister, Thelma, who made them mop out the raw sewage that had spilled into her basement from a burst pipe. It was the first of a long series of unpleasant chores the boys were expected to perform for the fat twins.

BUT THAT WAS JUST the beginning of their misery. The house teemed with other foster children, older and bigger than Michael and Carlos, who picked on them. (When asked how many foster children the State of Tennessee had deposited with her, Velma later said, "I really don't know. I just got so much love and patience and energies. They just brought 'em to me.") Velma had a single biological child whom, in Carlos's view, she spoiled. She sent Carlos and Michael out to sell newspapers on Sundays, and when they returned she took away the money they'd made and gave it to her child. "Living with The Twins wudn't no happy thing," said Carlos. "They just treated us like we weren't people. Every night Mike cried hisself to sleep." The two boys slept in their first bunk bed, only Michael's lower bunk couldn't be called a bed, as it had no mattress. "I was sleeping on wood," he said. Carlos remembers Michael saying, almost every night, 'Carlos, I just want to go home.' "

Two nights into their stay Michael ran away, all by himself. ("I can fly.")

He was just seven years old, but still he ran right across Memphis and found his mother. Dee Dee told him that she had to take him right back to the foster home or they would all get in trouble, and Michael cried all the way back. A few weeks later he ran again—with the same result. Once his mother came to visit him. "That was a happy day," he said. "Yes, that was my one happy day." He and Carlos stayed with Velma Jones for nearly two years. Then, one afternoon, Velma sat them down and told them they were going to be sent to Knoxville. She might as well have said they were being sent to the moon. Neither had ever left a tiny little area in western Memphis. She told them to go back to their room, pack their few things, and prepare to leave. They went back to their room, ignored their few things, and jumped out the window.

This time it took the police two days to track them down. The Department of Children's Services had noted by now that Michael was a runner, and they must have requested some sort of psychological evaluation. At any rate, instead of packing him straight back to foster care, they took him to St. Joseph's Hospital. There he was deposited on what he took to be "the floor for bad kids." They subjected him to tests that caused him to conclude later that they were seeing if he'd gone crazy. But it wasn't half-bad; and the living conditions were a vast improvement on the foster home. "We had good food," he said. "I had a bed with a mattress. They even had videos."

Michael had just turned ten years old. After two weeks in the hospital, he ached to go home. "It got old," he said. "You want to be free after a while." Incredible as it might seem to anyone who knew only the bare facts of his case rather than his emotional predisposition, he missed his mother. It was as if Dee Dee had been put on earth to answer a question: how little can a mother care for her children and still retain their affection? His mother hadn't cared for him, but still he loved her. "I guess you're just supposed to love your mom," he said later. "Just because she's your mom." That hard-to-shake feeling would explain why, much later, when he was asked for the first time about his mother and her problems with drugs, he would stare blankly and pretend the subject didn't bother him. But when asked a second time, his brown eyes filled with tears.

The doors on both ends of the floor were locked. The hospital was old—

it would soon be torn down—and Michael noticed that the big metal doors at one end of the hall rattled. "I remember it like it was yesterday, actually," he said later. "We'd play up and down the floor. And at the end of the floor was an exit. One of those two-door exits that closed together with a lock between 'em. I got a sheet of paper and folded it together and stuck it down there. And it opened." At his moment of discovery there were too many people wandering around for him to escape cleanly. He kept his secret, and his piece of paper, to himself the rest of the day. "That night when I went to bed I kissed the paper and put it under my little pillow," he said. Between his room and the locked door a nurse's station intervened. The nurse at the window could monitor the entire hall. Early the next morning, when the halls were clear, he crawled on his belly directly beneath the window of the nurse's station. He reached the door without being seen, jimmied it open with his paper tool, and fled.

Now he found himself in a dark, concrete stairwell. Downward he plunged. "Door here, door there, and I was out," he said. "Like a thief in the night." ("We never did figure how he got out of there," said Bobby Spivey, of the Memphis Department of Children's Services.)

When he reached the street Michael still had no idea where he was. He wound up wandering for hours to cover what he later realized had been no more than half a mile between the hospital and a housing project called Dixie Homes. He arrived to find that his mother had moved again, from Dixie Homes into one of the most depressing public housing projects in Memphis: Hurt Village. Hurt Village had been built for white people back in the 1950s. The opening of its 450 units spread over 29 acres had been hailed by the mayor as "a great day in the history of Memphis." By the late 1980s it was occupied only by blacks, who were fleeing the place as fast as they could. Hurt Village had become an inferno of gangs and drugs and crime. The city had decided to rip it down, but didn't have the money to do the job. To spare themselves the expense of relocating the residents, the Memphis Public Housing Authority simply stopped maintaining their apartments. Without functioning air-conditioning, stoves, or refrigerators, the units became so unlivable that anyone who could leave, did. Once they'd left, the city came in and boarded up the abandoned apartment.

It was in Hurt Village that Michael found his mother. He checked in, then ran back to Dixie Homes and hid inside the place she'd vacated. Carlos soon materialized, and together they went on the lam. During the day they remained hidden; at night they came out and foraged. "Every day you were scared that the police might get you," said Michael. "You see the police, you just duck and dive." Two weeks later, feeling pretty sure they were in the clear, they left the vacant apartment at Dixie Homes and rejoined their mother at Hurt Village. The Hurt Village apartment had only two bedrooms, and Dee Dee had borne still more children. She kept one bedroom for herself; the seven children now in her charge shared a bed in the other. "Lots of feet, lots of hands, lots of heads—but we managed," said Michael.

This place in which Michael would grow up over the next five years was, by 1996, a portrait of social dysfunction. Hurt Village still had roughly a thousand residents. There were no two-parent families: zero. Only a tiny handful of the residents held jobs. They had a mean education level between fourth and fifth grade. Seventy-five percent of the adult residents suffered from some form of mental illness. (Drug addiction counted as a mental illness.) Knowing that Hurt Village was soon to be torn down, and replaced with some other social experiment, a group of social scientists from the University of Memphis, funded by the U.S. Department of Housing and Urban Development, began to collect data on the place. "It was its own little community," said Cynthia Sadler, an anthropologist who worked on the project. "They did not associate with people outside of Hurt Village, and people outside of Hurt Village did not associate with them." The zip code for Hurt Village, 38105, was social poison outside of Hurt Village. Several residents told the researchers that they'd ceased looking for work because potential employers would see their zip code and reject them out of hand. "In all our travels," said another researcher, TK Buchanan, "we never came across a single Cadillac welfare queen."

By the time Michael arrived, Hurt Village was largely controlled by gangs. The Vice Lords were the biggest gang in Memphis, but the Gangster Disciples were the fastest growing and they ran Hurt Village. Delvin Lane ran the GDs, and he had an army of fifty-eight gang members in Hurt Village alone. In the early 1990s Delvin had been a dynamic quarterback for Booker T. Washington High School. He'd been set to go off to the University of Wyoming on a football scholarship. That opportunity vanished when he was sent off instead to jail, on an aggravated assault charge. He remained a natural leader, a quarterback, and, when he got out of jail, he used his talent to administer a huge and growing drug business. The GDs sold several different drugs but crack was most profitable, Delvin said, because it was the most portable and the most easily hidden. The first of the month, when the welfare checks rolled in, he made sure he had plenty of crack cocaine. Dee Dee would be waiting, cash in hand.

For Michael's first three years in Hurt Village, Delvin was the closest thing to the man in charge. Delvin didn't actually live in Hurt Village but he held meetings there, and when he and his army rolled in for these they were an impressive sight: a caravan of twenty to thirty fancy cars from which emerged these expensively dressed guys *completely unarmed*. Everyone knew they had no guns on them, in case the police showed up; everyone also knew that within yards they had stashed an arsenal of Uzis and 380s and sawed-off shotguns, in case the Vice Lords showed up. A twelve-man security squad armed with 17-shot 9mm pistols—two clips apiece—controlled key positions. Flanking Delvin were his two biggest bodyguards. One was called "Tombstone." Tombstone was six four, 310 pounds, and the most frightening human being anyone had ever seen—until they caught sight of Delvin's second bodyguard, Rico Harris. Rico was known as "Big Brim," and he stood six seven and weighed 450 pounds. Big Brim's official title was "Chief of Security," and his job, literally, was to watch Delvin's back. His blind side. "Big Brim was extremely valuable to me," said Delvin. "Especially in a club environment. Big Brim could hit one person and knock five of them down. If I'm in a club and Brim is there, I got no worries. But if it's a smaller guy there, I got to find other guys to help."

For the first eighteen months after he'd fled St. Joseph's, Michael stayed away from school, for fear of being taken by the authorities. For that year and a half he played what he thought of as a game of hide and seek with the Department of Children's Services. In retrospect, it was never clear that the State of Tennessee knew the game was on. The amazing thing, thought Michael, was that no grown-up ever turned him in, or even questioned his status. Hundreds of adults saw him on the streets day and night—people from Hurt Village, people who knew his mother—and no one ever wondered what he was doing running around in the middle of a weekday. "No one ever said, 'What are you doing out of school?' he recalled. "No one made me do anything." He guessed that if he hid out for long enough, the bad people at the Department of Children's Services would give up looking and forget about him. And they did.

By the time he turned twelve years old Michael Oher was completely free of social obligations. He might as well have been alone on a raft floating down the Mississippi River—which flowed, unnoticed, less than a mile from Hurt Village. He stole a bike and rode it wherever he wanted to. He played games from morning until late at night. Every now and then the older guys started shooting their guns at each other—but that was just pure entertainment. "We'd sit on the hill and watch them shoot it out," Michael recalled. "It was like being in the Wild West." He didn't feel himself unsafe; the older guys with the guns left him and the other little kids alone. He played basketball ten and twelve hours a day, and grew ever more certain that he was destined to be the next Michael Jordan. Hurt Village had long since come to epitomize the despair of inner-city life, but it didn't occur for a minute to Michael to leave. "It was fun," he said. "Everything was fun. Nobody stopped me from doing anything."

He still had the old problems: where to find food and clothing. But now that he was older he was more capable of caring for himself. He got better at foraging for food, from neighbors and churches and the street. "I knew that on the first of the month you were supposed to have money to eat," he said. "Everyone else got food and you got nothing." He was growing so fast in every direction. Often he'd fall, and sometimes when he'd fall he'd hurt himself. Once he went over the front of his bike and opened a great gash on his elbow. He never went to the hospital; he didn't even know what stitches were. Instead, he assumed that there was no injury, left untreated, that would not heal. The insight extended into his internal well-being. He must have calculated that emotional connections with other people were more trouble than they were worth, for, with one exception, he stopped making them. The exception came when his basketball got away from him and broke a neighbor's flower pot. The lady was nice about it; it turned out she was new to Hurt Village and had a son named Craig. Craig Vail was a shy, quiet, small boy, who also loved to play basketball. He and Craig soon became inseparable; and Michael would later say that Craig was the one person in the whole world he fully trusted.

He also now had a kind of shadow brother: Big Zach. Zachary Bright lived a few doors down from Michael in Hurt Village. Big Zach was ten years older than Michael, but their resemblance was a constant source of wonder to the neighbors. "Everybody used to say, 'Zach, you got a brother!' " recalled Zachary Bright. " 'Guy down the sidewalk looks just like you!' " Zach went and had a look at Michael Oher for himself and couldn't deny the family resemblance. Their skin color was an identical dark chocolate. Their features, in the context of their huge selves, seemed small and delicate. They both had ears designed for men half their size, and narrow eyes that closed almost shut when they laughed or became angry.

They shared a similar athletic ability, too. In 1994, two years before Michael turned up in Hurt Village, Zachary Bright had graduated from Kingsbury High School. After his junior year he'd been one of the most highly sought after college football prospects in Tennessee. He'd had scholarship offers from nearly every major football school in the country. In a high school all-star game Big Zach's *backup* was Cletidus Hunt—who eventually went on to play for the Green Bay Packers. And in that game Big Zach had played defensive tackle, which wasn't his natural position. His natural position was left tackle on offense. He was six six and, while he weighed only 265 pounds, he had a frame that would support a lot more, once he received proper nutrition. He had great long arms and the grace and agility of a star basketball player. "Zachary Bright has the potential to be a big-time offensive tackle," Tom Lemming had written in his annual review of high school football stars.

Coach Bobby Bowden of Florida State had the same thought. Bowden had flown Big Zach down to Tallahassee, where he'd spent two days and nights being wined and dined by Heisman Trophy winner and future NBA guard Charlie Ward and future NFL superstar Derrick Brooks. Florida State had his locker ready and a jersey (No. 71) with BRIGHT stenciled on the back. But Big Zach's girlfriend had already given birth to their first child. She didn't want to go to Florida State, and the truth was he didn't really feel like doing his schoolwork or making his grades. Surrounded by friends who told him that he'd be wasting his time to even try college, he quit. He never even finished high school. When the next school year started, and Big Zach didn't show up for it, Bobby Bowden himself came up from Florida State to Hurt Village, in search of his prized recruit. Big Zach hid out with his girl-friend and their new baby until Bowden was gone.

Big Zach would one day reflect upon that strange and wasteful period in his life. "Guys who were around said, 'Everyone can't make it to the NFL,' " he said. "Telling me I wasn't really gonna make it. Years passed by. I was still thinking I was at the top of my game. But my time was passing me on by. After a while I decided I was too old for it." He'd shake his head in wonder at all he had thrown away and say, "I feel like I could a did something, if I were to start over and do it again. I didn't know how close I was. All I had to do was knock on the NFL door."

But the wisdom, and the sadness, came much later; in 1996 he was just two years out of high school and still having fun. And suddenly all these peo-ple started coming up to him to ask if that kid now living a few doors down the block was his little brother. He grabbed the kid and took him out on the basketball court to see how he handled himself.

Well, as it turned out. ("But it was more like football than basketball," said Zach.) Michael Oher was no longer Michael Oher: he was "Big Mike." Michael loathed that nickname; it was the enemy of what he hoped to become. "I didn't want to be big," said Michael. He wanted to be lithe and fast; he wanted to be Michael Jordan. The wider he became the more preposterous was that ambition, but it proved easier to ignore his width than to abandon his dream. Everyone might be calling him "Big Mike," but no one ever took a picture of him. There weren't many mirrors around, either. He seldom was faced with his own reflection. He fiddled with optical illusions, and took to wearing his shoes too small and his clothes too big. He did push-ups and sit-ups, thinking they kept him thin. He developed the odd habit—for a boy his size—of always looking for something high over his head to jump up and hit, or tap, or jump up on. Every game they played he arranged it so that his role in it stressed, and trained, his quickness and his agility. Craig was his only real friend, and Craig reassured him that no matter what anybody called him he was still, like Jordan, a born outside threat. He just had to keep working on his quick first step and his crossover dribble.

Of course, Michael could sense his own swelling mass, but only by its effects. He was pleasantly shocked when one day, while wrestling, he just picked up a kid as if he weighed nothing and hurled him across the yard. On the other hand, he was no longer winning the foot races against the other kids—but at least he was still running them. They'd go out into the turning lane on Danny Thomas Boulevard like they always did, but now he'd be given a head start. He devoted so much time and energy to defying his own size that it couldn't help but yield results. Even as he became one of the biggest human beings in Hurt Village, he remained quick and agile. He willed himself to be graceful—to remain a little man, inside a big man's body. Later, college coaches who came to watch him would see a freak of nature. But where had nature left off, and nurture taken over? It was, as always, hard to say.

Between the ages of ten and fifteen Michael Oher was left alone with his fantasy. He learned nothing in school, confined himself to the incredibly narrow life available inside Hurt Village, and developed nothing in himself apart from his athletic ability. No one told him he should be doing anything other than what he was doing. If Hurt Village was an island in the Memphis economy, Michael's home was a hidden cave on that island. It probably helped that Delvin Lane's Gangster Disciples discouraged its members from messing with little kids. At any rate, Michael didn't have anything to do with the gangs or anyone else but Craig. He dipped in and out of school, and was moved along from one grade to the next, meaninglessly. He watched every one of his older brothers drop out. Marcus quit after the ninth grade, Andre and Deljuan and Rico after the eleventh, and Carlos after the tenth. Each had fathered at least one child, and among them they had fathered ten. But Michael remained happy and free, without the faintest premonition that anything would ever change, or needed to.

Then, just before his fifteenth birthday, he met Tony Henderson. Big Tony had grown up in Hurt Village, too. He came back often in search of kids to play for the football and basketball teams he coached. If you had the skills and the size, it was hard to hide from Big Tony. Big Zach had played for Big Tony; so had Tombstone and Big Brim.

Big Tony's first impression of Big Mike was that his family life was unusually troubled, even by the standards of Hurt Village. His second impression was that Big Mike had no friends. "I never saw him hanging around nobody," said Tony. "He was real quiet." He quickly figured out that Big Mike, like half the other kids he knew, was living to be the next Michael Jordan, and Tony did what he could to help him realize the dream. The summer before Michael's freshman year in high school Tony, through a friend, sneaked Michael into the basketball camp run by Carver High School. The first day Tony's friend called him to say that Big Mike had fled the camp. Big Tony hustled on over and found Big Mike walking the streets, a mile away, with tears streaming down his face. He was fifteen miles from Hurt Village and he didn't have a dime in his pockets. He was walking home, he said. The coaches had taken one look at him and told him he wasn't a perimeter player—that he wasn't Michael Jordan. And once he'd taken his newly assigned position in the low post, the bigger older kids alongside him had started shoving and hitting him. "Mike was a big ol' kid," said Tony, "but he didn't want to be touched. They got mad at him because he wouldn't knock the other kids down. The coach told him he'd never be nothing, and Mike started crying."

Big Tony was friends with Harold Johnson, the basketball coach at Westwood High. Westwood was a long way from Hurt Village, but Tony figured if he was driving his son Steven to Westwood he might as well drive Big

Mike, too. At Westwood Big Mike played football, too, but his heart wasn't in it. The coach just threw out the balls and went and sat in the shade, and Big Mike coasted through the year as a defensive tackle on a bad team.

That was a shame, thought Big Tony, because Big Mike was getting seriously big. He reminded Tony of Big Zach: his size alone meant he'd attract the attention of college football coaches. For that to happen, however, he needed to get through high school, and that didn't seem even remotely possible. He was failing his freshman classes and, on many days, didn't even bother to show up for them. Other days Big Tony would drop Steven and Big Mike at school, and return that afternoon to find only Steven waiting. "He wasn't going back," said Big Tony. "Big Mike was going to drop out." The only reason Big Mike hadn't already gotten himself into a world of trouble, Big Tony thought, was that he was so loosely connected to the people around him. He wasn't at the same risk as Big Zach for the simple reason that he didn't have a crowd of friends tempting him with the fast life.

Still, there was only so much distance any young man who dropped out of high school could put between himself and the 'hood. "He didn't have nothing to turn to," said Big Tony. "What chance did he have to go straight? He had *no* chance." As Michael neared the end of his freshman year in high school, he had before him one obvious career path. Once he quit school he would have waiting for him a single, well-paying, high-status job: bodyguard to Delvin Lane. Or rather, since Delvin had moved on, to Delvin's successor. The job was to watch the back of the guy who ran the only real business in the neighborhood. Left tackle of the ghetto.

That's when Betty Boo died, and stated as her dying wish that her grandson receive a Christian education. And as odd as it felt to Big Tony to put Steven in his car and drive him into the heart of rich, white Memphis, it felt odder still to ignore his mother's dying wish. And Big Tony thought, *if I'm taking Steven I might as well take Big Mike, too.*

ONE OF THE TACTICAL disadvantages of being a six five, 350-pound black kid in a school built for white kids is that other people tend to recall their encounters with you in far more vivid detail than you do. The main thing Michael Oher would remember of his first few weeks at the Briarcrest Christian School was his own terror and confusion. All white kids looked alike; and they were all bizarrely enthusiastic and friendly. "Everyone was exactly the same," he said. "For three or four weeks, every time I turned the corner I'd see some white kid shouting hello to me and I'd think: *I just saw you!*" His senior year he'd figure out that, while he hated to read, he liked to write. Assigned to write a personal essay, he chose as his subject his first days at Briarcrest. "White Walls," he titled his piece. It began:

> I look and I see white everywhere: white walls, white floors, and a lot
> of white people. . . . The teachers are not aware that I have no idea of
> anything they are talking about. I do not want to listen to anyone,
> especially the teachers. They are giving homework and expecting me
> to do the problems on my own. I've never done homework in my life.
> I go to the bathroom, look in the mirror, and say, "This is not Mike
> Oher. I want to get out of this place."

The other thing he remembered about those first frightful days was his hunger. The free food had been the main reason he bothered to go to public school as often as he had. These Christians didn't give you lunch, and that shocked him.

Hunger and confusion did not prevent him from noting significant details about white people. He'd had no interaction with them before this. Now as he studied them he judged them ill-designed for survival. Astonishingly prone to exaggerating the severity of the most trivial illness or injury, they were forever racing off to doctors and hospitals, as if they were about to die. "They'd get a twisted ankle or something and they're walking around school with a *boot!*" Michael said. "I was like, 'What are y'all doing? You got to just walk it off!'"

In addition to their pathological friendliness, and their constant need for medical attention, they exhibited a bizarre tendency to leave their most valuable possessions unattended. Steven was in the grade below him, and so they didn't cross paths very often, but when they did they shared their incredulity: *these white kids left gold watches, hand TVs, name brand shoes, and wallets just lying around.* It was as if the doors to Ali Baba's cave had sprung open. The boys' locker room alone was a cornucopia; all you had to do was swoop your hand through once and you'd come away with fistfuls of cash. "A burglar's dream." Michael called it. One night they came home with money that wasn't theirs, and Big Tony found out and tried to explain to them a little bit about white people and how, lacking street smarts, they had established some rules to preserve their species and that, odd as those rules might seem, Steven and Michael needed to obey them. Rule number one was that a kid did not steal, or fight, or get into trouble of any sort; and what was a rule for white kids was an iron law for a black kid. Because a black kid who got into trouble in the white world was a black kid on his way out of that world.

CHAPTER TWELVE

AND MOSES STUTTERED

IN THE HOURS FOLLOWING MICHAEL OHER'S DISAPPEARANCE, hell broke loose. The Ole Miss study center for football players became a crime scene. The ambulance came for the little white boy, who continued to bleed from his head wound, and took him away. Campus police raced in, followed by the Oxford city police. Miss Sue screamed into the phone to Leigh Anne: "He's going to jail! They're going to put him in jail!" The teammate Michael had attacked, Antonio Turner, was hustled off, bruised and battered, to a coach's house, to be guarded like a witness in a protection program. The little boy's father—Bobby Nix, the tutor who had been at such pains to get the black players out into white Oxford—was understandably beside himself. He and his wife had already lost a child, and now he'd just seen his three-year-old son lying on the floor in a pool of blood, a victim of a black football player's rage. He said he was pressing charges.

Michael saw none of it: he was long gone. Ignoring the calls from Leigh Anne and the text messages from Sean, he drove around Oxford in a fog of anger and confusion. He was angry because Antonio had said what he'd said and then struck him; he was confused because he was newly vulnerable. He now had these people he loved, who loved him. Through them, other people could get to him. He was no longer just another poor black kid going

nowhere. He understood that most people, white and black, treated him
a lot differently than they would have if he wasn't a football star. But he
couldn't bring himself to be cynical about the Tuohy family. He knew other
people, white and black, were saying that these rich white Ole Miss boosters
had identified him early on as a future NFL lineman and bought him the
way you'd buy a cheap stock or a racehorse. That they might not need his
money but they liked his status, and had envisioned how he might serve the
Briarcrest and Ole Miss football teams. Michael didn't believe it. "I wasn't
anything when I first got to them, and they loved me anyway," he said.
"Nothing was in it for them."

A few hours after he'd fled the scene of the crime, he noticed that the
tone of Sean's text messages had changed. They started out urgent. Now
they were just funny.

Mike Tyson! U coming back into the ring for another round?

Michael began to compose himself. Three years ago he'd have just kept
on running and never looked back. He wouldn't admit that he was different,
but he couldn't deny that *things* were different. He was no longer a black
object skipping along the surface of a white background; he'd been woven
into the white fabric. So . . . why was he running? Who was he running from?
For that matter—where was he running *to*?

He opened his cell phone.

At that moment Sean was sitting on the floor of a movie theater's lobby in
Seattle, worrying that Michael might be looking for a bridge to throw himself
from. He'd been traveling with the Memphis Grizzlies, and the team had an
off day. Sean and his friend Brian Cardinal, the Grizzlies' forward, had gone
to see a movie, *16 Blocks* with Bruce Willis. The first call about Michael had
come as they walked into the theater. With his cell phone nearly out of juice,
Sean found the plug in the lobby and set about trying to fix things. First he
called Coach O, who, bless his heart, refused to be anything but calm. Then
he called Hugh Freeze, and learned that (a) the little boy needed stitches in his
head but was otherwise fine, and (b) the police, if and when they found
Michael, intended to take him to jail. That wasn't good. Jail meant, at the very
least, news stories. Jail meant the wrong kind of reputation.

Sean now considered how to play it. The poor white kid had been born with a talent for seeing the court, taking in every angle and every other player, and then attacking in the most efficient way possible. The talent translated beautifully from basketball into life. He knew that Leigh Anne had cheered for one of the senior officers of the Ole Miss campus police, Michael Harmon, back when he'd been a flanker on the Ole Miss football team, and considered him a friend. Bobby Nix, the father of the injured boy, had been Sean's fraternity brother at Ole Miss. Dr. Thomas Wallace, the vice chancellor of the university and an old friend of Sean's, was now serving as Michael's "mentor." Sean sat there on the theater floor, thinking how best to play this possession, while, every ten minutes, Brian Cardinal popped his head out of the theater door and said, "You haven't missed anything yet."

And he hadn't—the real action was right there on the lobby floor. After he'd left yet another text message for Michael—*make it funny*, he thought, *so he doesn't throw himself off a bridge*—Sean decided he needed a lawyer. The Ole Miss football team, and the school itself, he decided, should be allowed to handle matters as they saw fit. (Especially since he knew how they'd see fit.) And so he called his old friend Steve Farese.

Farese was the defense attorney then representing, among other clients, the nice lady in Selma, Tennessee, who had shot her Baptist preacher husband in the back and killed him. For Steve Farese, a single bullet fired into one's husband's back counted as a trivial offense: a human being could hardly think up a thing to do that Farese couldn't construe as innocent. The FedEx pilot accused of stuffing his wife in the trunk of his car and setting it on fire? Innocent! The rapper charged with rape? Innocent! The Ole Miss quarterback, Eli Manning, charged with peeing on the side of a campus building? Off and starting for the New York Giants! When Sean reached Farese, and explained that the police were about to take his son in and book him, Farese became excited. "Oh, no, no, no, no, no, they are not," he said. "Sean, this is just an *unfortunate accident.*"

That's when Michael called.

"Pops," he said, "you're my first call. Just like I promised."

"Michael," said Sean, "this isn't exactly what I had in mind."

Sean sorted it out; of course he sorted it out. He told Michael to turn himself in to campus police who, he felt sure, would keep him from the clutches of the Oxford police. He called Bobby Nix and anyone else whose opinion might matter. He explained the situation in a way that they'd completely understand and offered to pay for whatever needed paying for. And, after a long round of fulsome apologies and ten hours of community service, Michael was restored to his former status of model citizen—and the incident never even hit the campus newspaper. It just went away, the way it would have gone away for some well-to-do white kid. Of course, lessons were learned and points of view exchanged. Coach O, for instance, pulled Michael into his office to discuss The Responsibilities of Being Michael Oher. Rather dramatically, Coach O extracted from his desk a thick folder stuffed with newspaper clippings, and dropped it with a thud. *"Dajus da crap dey wrote bout me last sittee days!"* he boomed. (That's just the crap they wrote about me in the last sixty days!) He went on to lecture Michael on the burdens of conspicuous success. "Let me tell you something, son," he concluded (in translation). "It is lonely at the top. I hate you had to learn about this at such a young age, but there are going to be many Antonio Turners. This is the first of many incidents."

MICHAEL OHER'S CAREER as a football player wasn't a sure thing—there was no such thing in football as a sure thing. But his odds in life had changed, dramatically. In just the past three years he had encountered countless threats to his future that might have put an end to it had he remained socially unconnected to white people: illiteracy, bad grades, car crashes, a night with the Memphis police, an NCAA investigation, men in the street who offered to become his agent. Any one of these might have sent him right back to the prison of his past. It was part of being hopelessly poor that events conspired to keep you poor; if it wasn't one thing, it was another. That cycle, in Michael's case, had been broken. He was like a quarterback who had gone from playing in an unimaginative offense, incapable of making him look good, to playing in an offense designed by Bill Walsh.

There's an instant before it collapses into some generally agreed-upon fact when a life, like a football play, is all conjecture and fragments and partial views. Everyone wants to know the whole truth but no one possesses it. But Michael Oher already had collapsed into a generally agreed-upon fact: he was a success. The world that had once taken no notice of Michael Oher was now so invested in him that it couldn't afford to see him fail. Of course, he wasn't the first black kid to rise from poverty and make it in the white world. But Michael was different, because the white world had so unusually aided and abetted his rise. The white world had watched Michael Oher happen, or thought they had, and so could imagine how he might be replicated. He haunted that world.

The Briarcrest Christian School, for starters, wrestled internally with the implications of Michael Oher. Applications to the school from black inner-city kids shot through the roof—"They all saw what happened to Michael and they now want to go to Briarcrest, too," said Sean. The school's new president, Bill McGee, did not like the idea of throwing open the doors to poor black athletes who couldn't read or write, but the school's staff could see the benefits. "Yeah, we helped Michael Oher," said Carly Powers, the Briarcrest athletic director. "But I tell you something else. Michael Oher helped our school. He gave a lot of people here some hope that if you help some of these kids, it is possible that they'll come around and make something of their lives." Jennifer Graves, who oversaw students with special needs, and so supervised Michael's academic life, saw an even higher purpose in Michael. "Michael got saved when he was at Briarcrest," said Graves. "What better way to spread the word of Jesus than for Michael Oher to stand up and say it? What kid in the Memphis City Schools wouldn't listen?" She knew that Michael was still intensely private— and that his gift for avoiding social entanglements had probably made a lot of what had happened to him possible. But when it was pointed out to her that Michael didn't seem like the most obvious spokesman for any cause, she just smiled and said, "And Moses stuttered."*

---

* Exodus 6:12: "But Moses said to the Lord, 'If the Israelites will not listen to me, why would Pharaoh listen to me, since I speak with faltering lips?' "

The coaches who had come to Briarcrest to woo Michael Oher also had trouble banishing him from their thoughts. Nick Saban was now coaching the Miami Dolphins, but he sent the Tuohys a Christmas card. ("If I was still at LSU Michael would be playing for me!") And, every now and again, Saban mentioned to scouts and sports agents that he was waiting for this phenomenal left tackle at Ole Miss to age, so that he could draft him.

If Nick Saban was still interested, Phil Fulmer was obsessed. Fulmer's University of Tennessee, widely considered before the 2005 season to have a shot at the national championship, had finished a disastrous 5–6. But at the start of the season they scored a huge victory at home against the highly ranked LSU Tigers. After the game the euphoric Fulmer spoke to the television cameras on the field, then rumbled into the Tennessee locker room. He found his agent, Jimmy Sexton, waiting for him. "He'd just beaten LSU," recalled Sexton, "and the first thing he says to me is 'See if you can get Michael Oher to transfer.' "

Fulmer returned to the Briarcrest Christian School. With the departure of Hugh Freeze—and Michael Oher—the Briarcrest football program fell on hard times. But the team still had one big-time prospect, a pass rushing defensive end named Greg Hardy. "The Freak," as he was known, because he was six six and 245 pounds with lightning reflexes and sprinter speed. The Freak was a quarterback's worst nightmare. The Freak was also black and, right up to the moment Briarcrest let him in, the recipient of a Memphis public school education. He wasn't a great student, but his grades were good enough to qualify him to play college football. And Phil Fulmer was seriously interested in him.

But, as Fulmer stood on the sidelines of the Briarcrest practice field and watched, he couldn't help but notice, just down the sideline, a familiar figure: Sean Tuohy. The Tennessee football coach edged a little closer until at length he caught Sean's eye.

"You gonna adopt this one, too?" he asked.

"I don't know," said Sean. "I'm waiting to see how good he is."*

---

* In the end, the Freak accepted a football scholarship to Ole Miss, in part, he said, because he wanted to play with Michael Oher.

He was only half-joking. His experience with Michael Oher had left Sean alive to the possibilities. If these poor black kids were good enough at sports that the wider world had a natural interest in them, all they'd need was a little push, in the form of love and attention from someone like Leigh Anne, and they'd be on their way. "The problem isn't intelligence," he said. "It's access to the system." But Briarcrest had a new policy of shunning the inner-city black athlete, and it infuriated him. "They really aren't as obsessed as they should be with giving opportunities to academically challenged kids," he said. Sean was willing to provide the funds to pay for kids to go to Briarcrest, and yet Briarcrest was newly unwilling to take them.

SEAN JUNIOR MUST HAVE noticed his father's new interest in helping out, financially, every poor black boy who could hit a jump shot and every black girl who could pitch a softball. SJ was the only white player on his twelve-and-under AAU basketball team, and most of the black players were conspicuously poor. Just about every one of them had applied to Briarcrest, and if Briarcrest hadn't rejected them, his father was ready to bankroll them all. It got SJ to thinking about his own situation.

He now had a question he wanted to ask.

Three years earlier, Sean Junior, like his big sister Collins, had been more than happy to take Michael in. He didn't really view Michael as black or poor or a potential drain on the family's resources. He was more interested in Michael's capacity to serve as an entertaining big brother and wily co-conspirator. Still, now that Collins and Michael were off at Ole Miss, SJ couldn't help but feel left out. Collins was Miss Everything and dating Cannon Smith, the son of the billionaire founder of Federal Express. Michael was already being spoken of as a first-round NFL draft pick. Just the other day, a scout for the Chicago Bears had taken Michael aside and told him that he could be the best lineman ever to come out of Ole Miss. Even if he didn't actually have any money yet, SJ thought, Michael was sure to become really rich. And all he had gotten out of the deal was a single trip with Coach O through the Grove.

And so he had a question. He was in the back of a car one day, being chauffeured by his mother to one of his AAU basketball games, when he thought to ask it.

"Mom," he said, "can I ask you something about you and Dad's will?"

"Uh huh," she said, warily.

"Collins is going to marry Cannon and so she'll be a billionaire," he said.

"I wouldn't say that's a done deal."

"Michael is going to be a first-round draft choice in the NFL, so he'll be really rich."

"Uh huh," she said. "So?"

"So" asked Sean Junior, "why are they even *in* the will?"

"Because," said Leigh Anne. "That's just the way it's done."

THE TUOHY MOST directly responsible for the transformation of Michael Oher, Leigh Anne had the most trouble ignoring his implications. "Look at him," she would say, whenever Michael stood more than about ten feet away. "He has everything: integrity, ambition, and a future." Then she'd think a moment, with the critical detachment of a sculptor whose work was nearly, but not quite, finished. "The only thing he needs now is to learn to give."

Then she'd think again. Michael might be, very nearly, a finished product. He didn't need her time and attention—but that only raised an obvious question: who did? The inner city of Memphis alone teemed with kids whose athletic ability had market value. Very few ever reached their market. As Michael himself said, "If all the guys who could play got a chance to play, there would have to be two NFLs because one wouldn't be enough." Sports was the closest thing in America to pure meritocracy, the one avenue of ambition widely thought to be open to all. (Pity the kid inside Hurt Village who was born to play the piano, or manage people, or trade bonds.) And Michael Oher was in possession of what had to be among the more conspicuous athletic gifts. Apart from the seven foot tall basketball player, the six five, 350-pound kid who could fly had to be about the easiest future star to identify. And yet, without outside intervention even his talent would quite likely have been thrown away. Michael Oher would have become just another big fat man: Big Mike. If Michael Oher's talent could be missed—whose couldn't? Those poor black kids were like left tackles: people whose value was hidden in plain sight.

Leigh Anne thought about this, a lot. And one morning in early 2006 Sean was interrupted from lifting himself out of bed by his wife, who was brandishing the sports section of the morning paper. The Memphis *Commercial Appeal* had reported the story of a young man named Arthur Sallis. Sallis had been the star fullback on Memphis's East High team, which had been state champions in 1999 and runners-up in 2000. He'd averaged, incredibly, more than 10 yards a carry. "When I'm dreaming," he once told a reporter, "I'm suiting up and going on the field. It's like there's no stopping me. It's like I can't go down." Before Sallis's senior year, his high school coach Wayne Randall received phone calls from every head coach in the SEC. The Kentucky coach, Hal Mumme, told Randall that Sallis was one of the finest football players he had ever seen.

Sallis had been offered scholarships by the University of Kentucky and Ole Miss, but he never took them. High school proved to be the end of Arthur Sallis's football career. His grades were poor, and he was disqualified by NCAA rules. Prevented by the NCAA from going to college on a football scholarship Sallis had stayed home, in his old neighborhood, on the west side of Memphis.

In this Arthur Sallis was only typical. As it happened, East High—Sallis's public school—had been part of a study made of Memphis inner-city athletes. The study revealed that, for every six public school kids with the ability to play college sports, five failed to qualify academically. What was unusual about Arthur Sallis was the persistence of his desire to make something of his life, in spite of the odds against him. He never knew his father, and his mother was an alcoholic in and out of jail. "From the time he was a little boy Arthur lived by himself, out on the streets," said Coach Randall. In high school he'd gotten into all kinds of trouble, but most of it was driven by his need to get money to live. "I used to joke," said Randall, "that Arthur was the only football player I ever had who I had to keep a lawyer on retainer for."

But after high school, with his football coach's help, Arthur Sallis had gone straight. He eked out a living with his own carpet cleaning business. He'd fathered a baby girl, and was raising her by himself. "He was doing all the things a responsible person should be doing," said his former coach. Then, a few months after Arthur Sallis left high school, he caught two men stealing a car and tried to stop them. For his trouble he got himself shot, point-blank, once in the back and once in the chest. He very nearly died. When his old high school coach visited him in the hospital Sallis told him, "If God gets me out of this, Coach, I'm never going to be out on the street again."

He had been true to his word. The newspaper Leigh Anne dropped in Sean's lap told the story of what happened next. Arthur Sallis wasn't on the streets, but at home with his four-year-old daughter, when three men broke in. Sallis grabbed one, and another shot him three times in the head. Arthur Sallis could have been a teammate of Michael Oher's at Ole Miss. Instead, at the age of twenty-two, he was dead.

Sean was only just waking up, and yet his wife was pacing back and forth in front of him, angry and upset. She was crying but she was also pissed off, and that, in his experience, was a dangerous combination. "Do you realize that you could take this kid's name out and put Michael's name in and have the same story?" she said. "Why didn't *this* kid fall on our doorstep?"

Then and there Leigh Anne made a decision: she wasn't finished. "I want a *building*," she said. "We're going to open a foundation that's only going to help out kids with athletic ability who don't have the academics to go to college. Screw the NCAA. I don't care what people say. I don't care if they say we're only interested in them because they're good at sports. Sports is all we know about. And there are *hundreds* of kids in Memphis alone with this story."

Sean was now fully alert. *Hundreds* of kids. A *building*. His personal finances were always a bit more uncertain than he let on, even to his wife.

Sean's way of life depended on his ability to hide his fears and anxieties. Everything was always good and if it wasn't, he could fix it. He conveyed the impression so well that people naturally handed him things to fix; and people who were broken drifted to him, in hopes of being fixed. His own success and well-being were taken as given, but they weren't. Four years ago Taco Bell had been in a down cycle, and he'd teetered on the brink of bankruptcy. In the nick of time, Taco Bell made some changes in its menus and its sales had boomed. ("The quesadilla saved my ass," he explained.) But his fast-food stores were never a sure thing. "I'm not financially secure where I can sit back and do nothing," he said. "But I like my chances." On the other hand, if his wife was now going to attack single-handedly America's most intractable social problem, he liked his chances a bit less.

Leigh Anne must have seen him thinking because she left him to get himself up and dressed, found her phone, and called Michael Oher. "Michael, you better get off your ass and get to work," she said. "Because we got things we got to do with your money."

It wasn't clear to Michael what, if anything, he owed the world. He now received lots of phone calls from poor black friends and family, and all of them wanted money. His mother called him a lot more than she used to, and it bothered him enough that he often didn't return her calls. "People don't understand that I made the newspaper but nothing comes with that," he said. "I haven't made a dollar yet." Not long after college coaches informed him that he had a future in the NFL, Michael informed Leigh Anne that, if he indeed made it to the NFL, he intended to buy a house with thirteen bedrooms so that his mother and siblings would be guaranteed shelter. Now he wasn't so sure he wanted to do that. "They had the same chances I had," he said. "They need to get off their lazy asses and work. They need to start hearing 'no.' "

People are no better at seeing the various paths their lives might have taken than football fans are at seeing the many different things that might have happened on any single play. People note outcomes, and reason backward from them. Michael noted his outcome and concluded that his life was always going to work out. He refused to believe there was ever the faintest possibility that he was going to be anything other than a huge success. He had set out to become Michael Jordan and he was fulfilling that destiny, in his way. "I was always going to college," he said. "I guess I thought that if things didn't work out in the NBA, I'd have the NFL as my backup." If he didn't give a lot of credit to others for having changed his life—if he didn't feel that he owed much to many—it was, in part, because he didn't really believe he had changed. "I'm the same way I've always been," he said. "I'm exactly the same guy I was back in Hurt Village. The only thing that's changed for me is the environment."

The change in environment was no small thing, and it took the help of many people—Big Tony, the Briarcrest teachers, the families that had housed him—for him to function in the new environment. Still, when Michael thought about who he wanted to help, if he had the power to help, the only person he could think of was Craig.

In his first year and a half at the Briarcrest Christian School, Michael hadn't seen as much of Craig as he would have liked. Craig lived back on the west side of Memphis and that suddenly seemed a long way away. But the moment Michael had gotten his driver's license he knew what he wanted to do with it. When he and Leigh Anne arrived home from the DMV, Michael asked Leigh Anne if he could drive back to western Memphis and bring back an old friend. For nearly a year Leigh Anne had been pressing him to bring home his old friends, but he'd never done it. Off he drove and soon returned with this shy, quiet, sweet-natured boy whom Michael introduced as "Craig." This was the one friend Michael had told them about—his one close friend in the world—in whose existence Leigh Anne had ceased to believe. She had come to think of Craig, like Harvey the rabbit, as an imaginary friend. Now Harvey stood uncomfortably in her foyer. "I never been this far from home," Craig said.

Michael claimed that Craig was the one person in the world he fully trusted, and so Craig became a regular visitor to the Tuohy home. For his part Craig was perplexed: his friend leaves the 'hood to go to a new school and the next thing he knows he's not merely shacked up with these rich white people on the other side of Memphis but claiming they are his *family*.

"Big Mike call me one day and I ask him what he's doing," said Craig. "He say, 'I'm just driving to get something to eat with my brother.' I ask him, 'Which brother is that?' He say, 'My brother, Sean Junior.' I say, '*Who?*' "

Now Michael said, "If I ever make it to the NFL Craig *has* to come. We got so close 'cause he just like me. We the same people, just different size." Craig didn't have any more money than anyone else from his former life. And while Craig was his only real friend, Craig had never asked him for a thing. "I offer him something, he says, 'I'm good, I'm all right.' " That was one of the traits he admired most in Craig: he didn't go around acting like some victim. He had his pride.

At any rate he and Craig now spent more time together. One night Michael took him to see the Memphis Grizzlies play. They were making their way toward Sean's courtside seats when Craig noticed that a lot of people were staring at them and pointing. "They were all saying, 'That's Michael Oher! That's Michael Oher!' " Craig already knew that people in poor black Memphis assumed that Michael Oher was going to the league. "They all talk about him," he said. "Nobody call him Big Mike anymore. They just call him Michael Oher." Now he saw that Michael's fame had spread beyond poor black Memphis, to courtside at the Memphis Grizzlies game, and realized: "Everyone in Memphis know who Michael Oher is!"

As they found their seats, Craig asked Michael if he noticed the many people pointing and staring at him. Michael smiled and Craig could tell that he not only noticed but loved it. "What if you don't make it to the NFL?" was the question Craig wanted to ask next, but he didn't. Instead he asked, "When you think you be ready for the league?" At that Michael laughed and said, "I'm ready *now.*"

Craig laughed. The world might have changed, but his friend had not. "He's the same guy," Craig said. "Everyone say Michael got cocky. What they don't know is that he was *always* cocky. He just didn't show it."

Still, Craig thought Michael must be joking. He wasn't.

"I could take Dwight Freeney right now," said Michael, seriously.

Dwight Freeney played for the Indianapolis Colts. He was the most feared pass rushing defensive end in the NFL, and maybe the fastest the NFL had ever seen. He'd arrived in the NFL in 2002 with his 4.3 forty-yard dash and his wild spin moves, and quickly figured out where he needed to be: the blind side. Two seasons later he rocked the order of the football universe when he went by Jonathan Ogden and sacked the Ravens' quarterback not once but twice. No one went by Jonathan Ogden—but Freeney had.

Freeney understood he was a man working in a tradition. When he was eight years old he'd seen a highlight film of Lawrence Taylor and right then and there knew who he was going to be when he grew up. "If you ask me to list my favorite players, I'd tell you LT and there'd be nobody second," he said. "There'd just be LT." Freeney took it for granted his job was to defeat the superstar of the offensive line. Best on best. That was his great strength: finding ways to win the most important one-on-one contest on the football field. And so when he heard that there was this kid down in Memphis who thought he was on his way to the league and said he "could take Dwight Freeny right now," he just laughed and said, "That's the way he's got to be." But he was curious enough to ask, "Who is this kid?"

Dwight Freeney stood outside the Colts' locker room, sweating in his pads, helmet in his hand, and listened patiently to a summary of the brief career of Michael Oher. How Michael had been one of thirteen children born to a mother who couldn't care for them, and so had more or less raised himself on the streets of Memphis. How he hadn't reported to serious football practice until his junior year in high school—but by then was six five, 350 pounds, and had been timed running the forty-yard dash in 4.9 seconds. How his forty-yard dash time didn't really capture his speed: to appreciate his quickness you needed to watch him in short bursts. How he'd been one of the best basketball players in the state of Tennessee, and held his own on the court with high school All-Americans, and still secretly believed his natural position was shooting guard. How, on the brink of adulthood, with a measured IQ of 80, no formal education and no experience of white people, he had so insinuated himself into rich white Memphis that white people no longer noticed the color of his skin. How he was now six six and 325 pounds and the starting left tackle at Ole Miss, and a fair bet to be named to the All-SEC team at the end of next season. How, fast and strong as he had been at

350 pounds, he was faster and stronger now. How every day he felt a little bit less a lost boy and a little bit more a man with a mission.

Dwight Freeney understood the rules of his game. In the NFL, on the quarterback's blind side, you came and you went. You had your moment when you played so perfectly in the sun that you were mistaken for the sun—and then you were eclipsed. The summer before the start of the 2006 season was still his moment, and would remain his moment—until it wasn't. Until he lost a step. Or got hurt. Or until the next Jonathan Ogden showed up and was maybe a step quicker, or fractionally more gifted, than the original. As he listened to the biography of Michael Oher, Dwight Freeney's expression changed. He was no longer smiling.

"What's his name again?" he asked.

"Michael Oher."

"You tell Michael Oher I'll be waiting for him," he said, and walked into the locker room.

—

AUTHOR'S NOTE

I'M STILL SLIGHTLY EMBARRASSED BY HOW I CAME UPON THE STORY told by this book, and how slow I was to pick up on it. In the fall of 2003, while passing through Memphis, I called Sean Tuohy. Sean and I had been classmates for thirteen years at the Isidore Newman School in New Orleans, Louisiana. When very young we'd been good friends—there was a stretch between the first grade and the fourth during which I routinely followed him out of school to a dirt basketball court behind his house, to see how long it would take for him to score one hundred points against me. (Not long, usually.) But I hadn't seen or heard from him in twenty-five years when I called to tell him that I was writing a magazine article about our former high school baseball coach. That evening I heard about Michael Oher, who was quickly becoming a member of Sean's family—and paid almost no attention. I wrote the article about our coach for the *New York Times Magazine*, which became a book called *Coach* in which Sean appeared briefly, and moved on.

A few months later, kicking around the NFL for another magazine piece, I learned that the left tackle had become much more highly paid than other offensive linemen, and I wondered how that happened and what the left tackles themselves made of it. Then I learned from Sean that Michael was now being hounded by college football coaches who saw in him a future NFL left tackle. Now I was paying attention. Shortly thereafter Sean came to visit me. We went to dinner again, but this time my wife, Tabitha, came along. When we got around to the subject of Michael Oher it took Sean about ten minutes to get her laughing, twenty to get her crying, and thirty to ruin the meal. But it was worth it, because in the car on the way home she said, "I don't understand why you are writing about anything else." I had had the same thought but had dismissed it, as it seemed somehow unsporting, like hunting in a baited field, to turn to one's kindergarten classmate for literary material. It was one thing to include Sean as a foil in my memoir; it was another to ransack his life for a book. So now that it's time to slice up and distribute my gratitude, my wife deserves an extra big piece. If she hadn't pushed me to acknowledge my interest in Michael Oher, I'm not sure I'd have pursued it.

I must also thank Sean and Leigh Anne Tuohy. To them this book was a matter of some indifference. Actually, that's not quite right. Sean pretended to be indifferent but was actually a little bit amused; Leigh Anne pretended to be indifferent but was actually a tiny bit dubious. None of the Tuohys ever asked why I was spending so much time hanging around Memphis, or their living room. No one ever asked me what I planned to write; no one ever hinted at a desire to see the manuscript before it went to print. They gave me their time, and their points of view, and left it at that. I'll always be grateful for their openness and their generosity.

In learning about football I had a lot of help from people in college football and the NFL. Bill Walsh and Bill Parcells between them sat patiently through many sessions and countless hours of interrogation. Pat Hanlon and Ernie Accorsi of the New York Giants showed me the inside of an NFL front office several years ago, and both have continued to educate me. At the Indianapolis Colts, Craig Kelley and Bill Polian were more helpful than they know; at the San Francisco 49ers, Paraag Marathe was a steady source of knowledge and insight. Kevin Byrne of the Baltimore Ravens and Patrick Wixted of the Washington Redskins made my life a lot more fun than it should have been in their locker rooms. The Tennessee Titans' defensive coordinator, Jim Schwartz, has been kind enough over the last few years to serve as an occasional sounding board.

I also had help from many current and former NFL players. When I first set out to interview professional football players I was struck by how much easier they were to talk to than professional baseball players, who tend to treat questions as insults. I'd like to thank a few of them here for making an extra effort with me: Lawrence Taylor, Steve Wallace, Jonathan Ogden, Harry Carson, Tariq Glenn, Dwight Freeney, Anthony Muñoz, Tim Long, Joe Jacoby, Lindsay Knapp, Joe Theismann, Dan Audick, Randy Cross, and Will Wolford. To understand the market for football players I had the help of several agents: Tom Condon, Gary O'Hagan, Ralph Cindrich, and Don Yee. Yee's client, D'Brickashaw Ferguson, the new left tackle of the New York Jets, wound up on the cutting-room floor; but he, too, was generous with his time. Laurel Ayers, widow of John Ayers, offered a moving and indispensable view of her husband. Langston Rogers made it possible for me to interview essentially the entire Ole Miss football team, and made me feel welcome from the moment I first set foot on the Ole Miss campus back in the fall of 2004. Hugh Freeze was a constant source of football insight; if I were the Ole Miss athletic director I'd just hand Hugh the offense and let him run it. There can't be many coaches who know more about offensive line play than George DeLeone, who has left Ole Miss and now runs the offense at Temple University. I appreciate the many hours he spent trying to explain what he knows to me.

Saleem Choudhry opened his archives at the Pro Football Hall of Fame in Canton, Ohio, and helped me to dig through them. The editors of *Total Football II: The Official Encyclopedia of the National Football League* have my enduring gratitude for compiling such a fantastic resource. Kevin Lamb's essay on the evolution of football strategy, especially, was an inspiration. Rick Figueiredo made it possible for me to watch old 49er games. Tony Horwitz, Jacob Weisberg, and Eddie Epstein read the first draft of this book and offered me good conceptual advice. Rob Neyer went through it line by line and repaired a shockingly large quantity of my prose.

Inside W. W. Norton, which has published all but one of my books, I stressed out the production line even more than I usually do. Nancy Palmquist and Amanda Morrison did a wonderful job making sure that the misery I caused them wasn't in turn inflicted on readers. Don Rifkin was kind enough to triple-check everything. Debra Morton Hoyt created a lovely package.

On the streets of Memphis I also needed a lot of help. Wyatt Aiken proved to be the perfect tour guide of local spiritual life. Big Tony Henderson is one of those people who makes a lot of improbable things happen, and he worked his magic often on my behalf. Delvin Lane would count as my highest-ranking friend in the Gangster Disciples, if he hadn't relinquished his title as gang leader. When Delvin was Born Again, and decided to dedicate his life to Christ, he assumed he might be killed in the bargain. (The penalty for a senior figure quitting the Gangster Disciples was, typically, death.) So I'm grateful, I suppose, to the other Gangster Disciples for making an exception of Delvin, and permitting him to live, and to educate me. Without the help of Phyllis Betts at the University of Memphis, who spearheads the social science investigation of Hurt Village, this book would have been even less well informed than it is about life in the Memphis inner city. Debra Kirkwood shared her knowledge of the Tennessee foster care system; Pat Williams related his experience helping to found the Briarcrest Christian School; and Liz Marable offered insight into the Memphis public schools, and Michael's mind—acquired from the many hours she spent teaching basic math to him.

Michael was a funny subject because, at least at first, he had so little interest in talking about himself. He hoarded personal information the way he hoarded everything else. His memory might be a relative strength in his schoolwork, but it seemed to have neglected to record his own life experiences. When I asked Michael about his past, he claimed not to recall it and couldn't understand why I found it interesting. He wasn't happy to let people get to know him, and it didn't appear he was going to make an exception for me. After a year of pestering him, I felt doomed to learn about my main character exclusively from others. Then one day Michael phoned me out of the blue. "Are you the guy who keeps asking every other person in the world questions about me when you could just come and ask me?" he said. Our conversations soon became a lot more interesting. He remembered much about his past, often in vivid detail. One of the pleasures of working on this book has been those long conversations with Michael. I'll be cheering for him, I assume, for a long time to come.